THE *American Dream* OF
CAPTAIN JOHN SMITH

THE PORTRAICTUER OF CAPTAYNE JOHN SMITH / ADMIRALL OF NEW ENGLAND .

These are the Lines that shew thy Face; but those
That shew thy Grace and Glory, brighter bee :
Thy Faire-Discoueries and Fowle-Overthrowes
Of Salvages, much Civilliz'd by thee
Best shew thy Spirit; and to it Glory Wyn;
So, thou art Brasse without, but Golde within .

Captain John Smith, from his map of New England (1616)

THE *American Dream* OF
Captain John Smith

J. A. Leo Lemay

University Press of Virginia

Charlottesville and London

THE UNIVERSITY PRESS OF VIRGINIA
Copyright © 1991 by the Rector and Visitors
of the University of Virginia
First published 1991

Library of Congress Cataloging-in-Publication Data
Lemay, J. A. Leo (Joseph A. Leo), 1935–
   The American dream of Captain John Smith / J. A. Leo Lemay.
     p. cm.
   Includes bibliographical references and index.
   ISBN 0-8139-1321-7
   1. Smith, John, 1580–1631.   2. Governors—Virginia—Biography.
3. Explorers—America—Biography.   4. Explorers—England—
Biography.
5. Virginia—History—Colonial period, ca. 1600–1775.   I. Title.
F229.S7L46   1991
973.2′1′092—dc20
[B]   91–2285
                                            CIP

Printed in the United States of America

For Kate Clarke Lemay

CONTENTS

Illustrations

Acknowledgments

I reread the writings of Captain John Smith in 1983 after Professor Louis D. Rubin asked me to write the first chapter of *The History of Southern Literature*. That reading convinced me that I should write a book on Smith's American Dream. Rubin subsequently asked me to review the new edition of Smith's writings, edited by Philip L. Barbour. I happily agreed to do so, knowing that in my book I would want to cite Barbour's edition. So Louis D. Rubin is indirectly responsible for this book and directly responsible for the two articles on Smith that I have, in part, incorporated herein: "Captain John Smith" from *The History of Southern Literature*, edited by Louis D. Rubin et al. (Baton Rouge: Louisiana State University Press, 1985), and "The Voice of Captain John Smith," *Southern Literary Journal* 20, no. 1 (Fall 1987). The concluding section of the chapter on Smith and Powhatan, entitled "Subversive Naming: The Powhatan River," was delivered as the chairman's address to the American Literature Section of the Modern Language Association at the Cosmos Club in Washington, D.C., December 28, 1989, and will appear in the *Annual Report* of the American Literature Section in late 1990.

I am greatly indebted to my research assistants, Thomas J. Haslam and Darin Fields. In addition to performing numerous chores and research, they have each done me the favor of reading the manuscript. And I am indebted to my student Kevin J. Hayes, who compiled as his master's thesis a secondary bibliography of Captain John Smith, in the process supplying me with pertinent scholarship I might otherwise have overlooked. Kevin Hayes has also read the entire manuscript, giving me the benefit of his knowledge. I wish to thank the Huntington Library, San Marino, California, for permission to reproduce the illustrations from works by John Smith and Thomas Hariot in their collections.

THE *American Dream* OF
CAPTAIN JOHN SMITH

Introduction

Then seeing we are not borne for our selves, but each to helpe other, and our abilities are much alike at the houre of our birth, and the minute of our death: Seeing our good deedes, or our badde, by faith in Christs merits, is all we have to carrie our soules to heaven, or hell: Seeing honour is our lives ambition; and our ambition after death, to have an honourable memorie of our life: and seeing by noe meanes wee would bee abated of the dignities and glories of our Predecessors; let us imitate their vertues to bee worthily their successors.

—From the conclusion of Smith's
A Description of New England (1616; 1:361).[1]

From Smith's *True Travels* (1630), compartment 7 (lower left)

Bashaw

John Smith's American Dream

THE MAJOR mythic hero of the Middle Ages and Renaissance—and later, as numerous chapbooks, ballads, and Sir Walter Scott's novels testify—was the chivalric knight, whose heroic battles sometimes occurred in great arenas with the gentry and aristocracy looking on. America's indigenous heroes have been Indian fighters, frontiersmen, and gunfighters, such as John Mason, Thomas Church, Daniel Gookin, John Lovewell, Thomas Cresap, and Robert Rogers in the colonial period, and Daniel Boone, Davy Crockett, Kit Carson, Wild Bill Hickok, Wyatt Earp, and Buffalo Bill Cody from the Revolution to the end of the nineteenth century. Their confrontations usually occurred in isolated wilderness areas or small towns. Captain John Smith fulfilled the heroic roles of both the European Renaissance and the American frontiersman. His life documents and illustrates the changing nature of heroic action. Before sailing for Jamestown in 1607, Smith fought in two major theaters of European war, finally serving as captain of a Christian cavalry company in eastern Europe fighting against the "infidels." In early 1602 in Transylvania, now part of Hungary and Romania, Smith, as champion of the Christian army, jousted against and vanquished the Turkish champions in three separate tournaments.

Smith lived by his personal motto: *vincere est vivere*, "to conquer is to live." (His motto, a unique variation of the common *vincere vel more*, "to conquer or to die," is the earliest indication of his literary talents.) No Englishman among his contemporaries, certainly not the heralded chivalric figure of the age, Sir Philip Sidney (1554–1586), achieved the triumphs in deed or battle of the indomitable Captain John Smith. In 1603, at the epitome of his chivalric reputation, he resigned his sinecure in the Transylvanian court and returned to England to seek a different adventure—colonization in unknown America. There in 1607–9, he became transformed into a version of Nantaquoud, Powhatan's beloved Indian son. Smith became early Virginia's most famous and feared Indian fighter. Powhatan himself testified that "if a twig but breake, every one crie there comes Captaine Smith" (1:247). Severely wounded in battle at Rottenton, Transylvania, and presumed dead (1602), Smith was rescued by pillagers and eventually sold as a slave in Axiopolis and sent to Constantinople. Finding his treatment as a Turkish slave insufferable, he killed his master and made his way alone across northern Turkey and southern Russia, to emerge almost miraculously in Christian Europe (1603). In Virginia, in December 1607, after his companions had been slain by an overwhelmingly superior force, after he, attacked, had killed at least two Indians and wounded others, and after he gradually retreated into a swamp where the bog finally imprisoned him, Captain John Smith at first saved himself by a shamanistic display of a compass and an explanation of cosmology and cosmography and later was rescued by the intervention of Pocahontas, to emerge alive, again almost miraculously, at Jamestown. Smith's life seemed charmed—and his ideas proved indestructible.

Captain John Smith first fully formed an American Dream. Earlier British American proponents and explorers like Richard Hakluyt, Amadas Barlowe, and Thomas Harriot viewed America as an Eden,[2] as an outlet for England's supposed overpopulation,[3] as a place to get rich without labor,[4] and as the first stage in England's future overseas empire.[5] They celebrated colonization as a means to convert the Amerindians to Christianity.[6] They never, however, focused on the effects of the American experience upon the individual and certainly never thought of colonization as a transforming experience. Smith did. He was unique. Long after the Virginia settlement in 1607, writers about America and the American experience continued to view America in terms of England and the English. Though promotion writers often satirized what they considered to be the ills of English mercantile society,[7] they thought of America only as an escape from the old conditions rather than an alternative that promised new social structures based upon new customs, new laws, and new personal relationships. Later, the Plymouth (1620) and the Massachusetts Bay (1630) Puritans envisioned a new religious society, but as John Winthrop's "A Modell of Christian Charity" proves, they believed that the existing Renaissance postfeudal social hierarchy was the necessary foundation of social order.[8]

Though Smith's view of America and his public and private American Dream constantly developed, he realized as early as 1608, in the first book written from the earliest permanent English colony in America, that America provided the opportunity for an individual's standing in society to be determined by hard work and achievement rather than social position. Smith, however, lived in the sixteenth and early seventeenth centuries. He knew that his contemporaries believed in an inevitable social hierarchy. Unlike almost all of his contemporaries whose writings are extant, he argued that one's own achievement and merit, not one's inherited social position, should determine one's standing within the social order. He found the existing system corrupt and degenerate. A society consisting almost entirely of a few wealthy persons and a mass of extremely necessitous people was, he judged, inherently unstable. He wrote that the lower extremes of the social order should be abolished. (He knew that if he wrote that kings and nobles should be abolished, he would have become a public enemy and probably would have been executed.) No one, wrote Smith, should exist in a state of servitude and subjection.

The political and social ideals of Smith's day differed little from those of the fifteenth and sixteenth centuries, though a few intellectuals verbalized the possibilities of a new order. Avant-garde thinkers like Niccolò Machiavelli, Francis Bacon, and Michel de Montaigne occasionally expressed new and radical notions: they hinted that they believed in individualism, the self-worth of every person, and the achievements of the self- made man. Sixteenth and early seventeenth-century disciplines admitted and sometimes welcomed new blood. Within the intellectual, military, and mercantile worlds of Smith's time, talented individuals frequently emerged from humble origins to positions of great importance.[9] Smith's rise was hardly unique. Though the term was not created until the nineteenth century, Renaissance popular literature and oral tales were filled with stories of *self-made* men.[10] Smith's autobiography, *The True Travels, Adventvres, and Observations of Captaine John Smith* (1630), is the first American success story, describing the individual's rise from servitude and obscurity to fame and authority. Smith gradually became famous. William Strachey praised him. After his death, Smith was called by William Wood the "thrice memorable discoverer." A scholar wrote his biography in Latin.[11] Other contemporaries found his renown a suitable subject for a play and a satire.[12] His long epitaph was carved in the wall of St. Sepulchre's Church and printed in John Stow's *Survey of London* (3:390). Thomas Fuller included him in a mid-seventeenth-century biographical dictionary. Perhaps partly because of his yeoman background,[13] or his extraordinarily independent character, or his experiences—and dramatically changing fortunes (from champion to slave to hero) in the different cultures of Europe, the Near East, and Africa[14]—but certainly because of his American experiences, Smith said that inherited positions should not be as important to one's standing in society as the individual's achievement. Smith valued individuals for their hard work and personal achievements, not for their social standing. Indeed, he changed a few individuals' placement in the social hierarchy as he rewrote the Virginia tracts. He viewed America as the premier place for such personal transformation. In America former footmen and servants could rise to become soldiers, sailors, frontiersmen, and men of achievement. Thus his writings became the earliest major vision of the American Dream.

Controversy over Smith has concerned four issues. First, his adventures in Transylvania took place at such a distance, wrote Thomas Fuller in 1662, that "they are cheaper credited than confuted."[15] The eastern Europe exploits were generally accepted as being true until 1890, when Lewis L. Kropf, an amateur Hungarian historian, claimed in a series of notes that Smith obviously did not know the history or customs of Transylvania in 1602 and could not have been there.[16] Thereafter, Smith was widely regarded as a liar. Anyone who wrote about Smith between 1890 and 1953 had to begin by conceding that he had deceived his contemporaries about his eastern European adventures. Smith's biographer, Bradford Smith, however, had his doubts. When he began trying to investigate Smith's experiences in Transylvania, he realized he did not have the linguistic abilities to do the necessary research. So he enlisted the services of Laura Polanyi Striker, a Hungarian historian whose knowledge of Latin and eastern European languages enabled her to check Kropf's sources and to make her own original investigations. Her essay "Captain John Smith's Hungary and Transylvania" appeared as Appendix 1 in Bradford Smith's biography *Captain John Smith: His Life and Legend* (1953).

Striker demonstrated that Kropf had misrepresented and misinterpreted numerous sources and that he had overlooked others. Sixty-three years after Kropf's series of notes appeared, Striker completely discredited him. She proved that Smith knew details of the eastern European scene better than any other Westerner who wrote about eastern Europe in 1601–2. In a later essay, "The Hungarian Historian, Lewis L. Kropf, on Captain John Smith's *True Travels*," Striker surveyed Kropf's career as a writer, pointing out that he was consistently excessively opinionated and frequently had attempted muckraking. Reexamining Smith's writings, she concluded that Smith was, in fact, an excellent source for eastern European history in 1601–2. Striker's essays demolished the critics who said that Smith lied about his adventures in eastern Europe. At the same time, the earliest of several specialized essays by Philip L. Barbour, a self-trained but extraordinarily accomplished linguist fluent in Russian, Latin, and most European languages, added additional evidence to Striker's position: Smith had been in eastern Europe and the Middle East, and his account of those places is a valuable primary source.[17]

The second controversy—"The Great Debate" according to Bradford Smith (p. 12)—concerns the Smith/Pocahontas story. Was Powhatan about to have Smith executed? Did Pocahontas really take him into her arms and put her head down over his as the Indian executioners were about to beat out his brains?[18] In an argument that convinced many historians (George Bancroft was slow to change his mind—if he ever did), Henry Adams attacked Smith in the lead essay of the *North American Review* for January 1867.[19] Actually, Adams wrote the essay as Civil War propaganda in 1862 and commented in a private letter that "perhaps the thing is excusable, especially as it is in some sort a flank, or rather a rear attack, on the Virginia aristocracy, who will be utterly graveled by it if it is successful."[20] My own research has given me every reason to believe that the incident happened. Indeed, Adams seems to me to have been as malicious in his selectivity, in his omissions, and in his interpretations as Lewis L. Kropf. In my view, William Wirt Henry actually had the better arguments in his comparatively little-known 1875 rebuttal. Like others, however, I believe that Smith did not at the time understand the nature of the ceremony, for it seems probable that he was undergoing a ritualistic death and rebirth, with Pocahontas acting as his sponsor into Indian identity.[21]

The third area of controversy concerns Smith's dealings with the American Indians. Since the charge is a particularly modern one (reflecting not only a modern but also an ahistoric sensibility), it is not mentioned in Jarvis M. Morse's 1935 survey of the historiography of Captain John Smith.[22] Censures of Smith for his treatment of American Indians were anticipated by James Mooney's "The Powhatan Confederacy, Past and Present" in 1907, but it was not until the 1940s that several denunciations of Smith appeared within a decade. They reached a crescendo in the 1970s and flourish today.[23] Thus in 1988 Karen Ordahl Kupperman found "Smith at his most controversial" in his dealings with the Indians. In *The Invasion of America: Indians, Colonialism, and the Cant of Conquest* (1975), Francis Jennings claimed that John Smith and Samuel Purchas were responsible for a new view of the Indian after the massacre of 1622—the "Salvage" as beast. Gary B. Nash also found that the massacre of 1622 changed the whites' view of the Indian, though he conceded that Smith only agreed with the general change in perception and did not cause it. It is symptomatic that when Nash referred to the 1622 massacre, he put the word *massacre* in quotation marks, but when he referred to the retributions made by the whites, he used the word *genocidal*. J. Frederick Fausz argued that "white sensibility and Indian sensitivity to the Native-Americans' heritage" should preclude future use of the term *massacre* in reference to the 1622 uprising.[24] Like most other historians of the American Indian, Nash chose to focus upon passages where the whites found the Indians to be friendly and kind. Nash, followed by Peter Hulme, cited Gabriel Archer as one white who mistakenly suspected treachery when there was only friendship. Archer wrote that in the first exploration up the James River, the whites found that the Indians "are naturally given to trechery, howbeit we could not finde it in our travell up the river, but rather a most kind and loving people" (*JV* 103–4). Nash commented that the Indians "dined and wined" the whites, and he explained that these Powhatan Indians were enemies of the Chesapeake Indians who had initially attacked the whites at Cape Henry.[25]

Nash did not tell the reader that about one hundred Paspahegh Indians (a group subject to Powhatan) had attacked Jamestown on May 18 while Archer was there (*JV* 139) or that more than two hundred Paspaheghs, reinforced by other Powhatan Indians, attacked Jamestown on May 26, while Archer, Captain Christopher Newport, John Smith, and others were returning from their exploration up the James River. Nor did he say that Newport and his group suspected something was amiss at Jamestown because of the Indians' suspicious behavior as the whites returned. Only the ship's ordnance saved the Jamestown settlers from annihilation. Archer wrote his account after the attack. Contrary to Nash, Archer was not just imagining that the Indians were treacherous; he knew that Powhatan had commanded both the disarming displays of friendship and the ferocious attack.[26]

Reversing her earlier position,[27] Karen O. Kupperman agreed with Jennings, remarking that "after 1622 all the subtlety and sensitivity in his [Smith's] understanding of the Indian side of the equation are gone."[28] But Jennings (and all subsequent authors who agree with him) overlooked numerous English comparisons of the "barbarian" and "wildman" of the Middle Ages and Renaissance to animals, as well as numerous English comparisons of American Indians to beasts before 1622.[29]

Moreover, if all of Smith's subtlety and sensitivity toward the Indian disappeared in 1622, no new material sympathetic to the Indian should have surfaced in any of his later works, including, of course, *The Generall Historie* (1624). Chapter 6 below, devoted to Smith and the American Indian, will show that such is not the case.

H. C. Porter, whose *The Inconstant Savage: England and the North American Indian, 1500–1660* (1979) appeared several years after Jennings's work (but well before Kupperman's), traced the idea of the savage in Tudor literature, and he showed in his Hakluyt Society 1983 presidential address that such bestial images as Jennings and his followers imagined existed only after 1622 were typical of the ethnocentric Tudor English attitudes toward the Irish, the Amerindian, and others.[30] Even Alden Vaughan, who generally has appreciated the difficulties Smith faced in early Virginia, seems on occasion to be prejudiced against him. Vaughan has stated that, "Smith allowed no Indian recalcitrance," citing the time that Smith seized Opechancanough by the scalp lock and threatened him and the occasion when Smith grappled with the Paspahegh chief, "dragged him into a nearby river, and almost drowned him." Vaughan concluded: "Such tactics prevented open warfare. They did not promote cordiality or conversion."[31]

The reader who does not know these incidents well might be surprised to learn that in the first incident Opechancanough had betrayed Smith and his men, who had been invited to trade, and had surrounded the whites with several hundred warriors. Opechancanough intended to massacre them. Smith's action replied to Opechancanough's traitorous aggression and saved his own life and the lives of his men.[32] Likewise, an innocent reader might be surprised to learn that the Paspahegh chief, finding Smith alone and armed only with a short sword, "attempted to have shot him; but the President prevented his shot by grapling with him, and the Salvage as well prevented him from drawing his fauchion, and perforce bore him into the River to have drowned him" (1:261). In both cases, the Indian aggressors meant to kill Smith.

Time and again, historians such as Jennings, Nash, Fausz, and Kupperman imply that it was fine for the Indians to kill the whites, but that if the whites defended themselves, they were behaving in a cruel and heartless manner. These writers take pride in understanding and in identifying with the early seventeenth-century Indians but find the early seventeenth-century whites to have been absolute barbarians. Kupperman has written: "Because the European wars involved such scenes of revenge and destruction, the Virginia Company, while valuing Smith's experience and expertise, had good reason to try to force him and the colonists in general into a policy of good treatment and friendship toward the American Indians. The company did not want the brutal traditions of Europe to be carried thoughtlessly into the new relationship; their policy, which Smith scorned as weak and foolish, was founded on foresight and reflection."[33] Kupperman seems not to want to acknowledge that the Indians had their own brutal traditions, as the Chesapeakes and the Payankatanks could testify.[34]

Kupperman's belief that the Virginia Company leaders in London were ethically superior to their European and American contemporaries is without foundation. The Reverend Richard Hakluyt, the London Company's foremost expert on America, wrote in his "Epistle Dedicatory to the Council of Virginia" (1609) that the Indians were not to be trusted, "for they be the greatest traitors in the world," and that they were "as unconstant as the wether cock, and most readie to take all occasions of advantages." They were also brave and resolute—dangerous adversaries. He advised, "To handle them gently, while gentle courses may be found to serve, it will be without comparison the best: but if gentle polishing will not serve, then we shall not want hammerours and rough masons enow, I meane our old soldiours trained up in the Netherlands, to square and prepare them to our Preachers hands." Since Hakluyt's 1609 statements may have been influenced by Smith (he must have read Smith's *A True Relation* [1608] and perhaps read the draft of *A Map of Virginia* sent back to the Virginia Company with Captain Newport about December 1, 1608 [2:187–90]), I should note that

Hakluyt's opinion was the same in 1587.[35] Naturally, the London Company leaders and colonists appreciated that it was good common sense and policy to try to be friendly with the Indians. There was nothing new in this policy. Sir George Peckham had written in 1583 that all people "are rendred more tractable and easilier wunne for al assayes, by courtesie and myldnes, then by crueltie and roughnes." He gave detailed instruction on how to be friendly to the Indians. But if friendly measures failed, Peckham said that history, law, and religion all justified pursuing "revenge with force, and to doo whatsoever is necessary for the attayning of theyr safety: For it is allowable by all Lawes in such distresses, to resist violence with violence." Hakluyt and other company members well knew and echoed the policies advocated by Peckham in 1583.[36]

Even in today's courts, killing in self-defense, if absolutely necessary, is a valid defense for causing death. Consider, however, what Kupperman has said about John Smith's self-defense while fighting the Pamunkey Indians in December 1608. Several hundred Pamunkeys under Opechancanough accidentally discovered a barge with seven English soldiers safely anchored in the Chickahominy River. The Pamunkeys had some Indian women lure several whites ashore.[37] When Opechancanough's men attacked, all the English except George Casson escaped. While being tortured to death, Casson told the Indians that Smith had gone upstream with two whites and two Indians. The Pamunkeys followed, killed the two whites whom Smith had left with one Indian by the canoe, then went inland, located Smith, and attacked him. Smith defended himself by strapping his Indian guide to his left hand, until he had backed up into mud as high as his chest and could no longer fight.[38] Describing Smith's perilous situation, Kupperman made Smith seem like the aggressor: "Smith, having killed three Indians [we know that he managed to kill two], galled, or broke the spirit of the others with his gun, so that he was able to retreat toward his boat still behind his human shield."[39]

Smith knew that there must be some instances of warfare between the whites and the Indians, for the whites intended ultimately to settle on the land where the Indians hunted, farmed, and lived. Smith realized that in any absolute scale of values, the whites were wrong. Even animals, he said, would fight to protect their own dens. Smith lied to Powhatan about the intent of the whites, but he knew that "progress" was inexorable. The Indians were in a position similar to that of the Picts and early Britons when the Romans invaded England. Smith sympathized with the Indians, but he knew that they would kill him and the other whites if they could do so with impunity, and he fought them when necessary. But he treated them as fairly as possible. John Smith was, in fact, the best friend that the Indians ever had as governor in early Virginia.

The fourth criticism of Smith is that he was a braggart. Thomas Fuller voiced the criticism in 1662: "such his perils, preservations, dangers, deliverances, they seem to most men above belief, to some beyond truth." Fuller added that "it soundeth much to the diminution of his deeds, that he alone is the herald to publish and proclaim them." But since Fuller's day, numerous records of Smith's contemporaries have been published, and, insofar as they bear directly upon Smith, they confirm the truth of his accounts. A number of modern historians nevertheless persist in insulting Smith. Thus Kupperman has written: "Smith has often been the subject of ridicule because his work frequently sounds like the effusions of the barroom braggart. Not only did his writing center on himself and his exploits, but also his stories grew as they were told and retold in his later books, always in the direction of making his role more important and the stakes for which he was contending higher." Jarvis M. Morse, however, demonstrated in 1935 that in revising *The Proceedings* into *The Generall Historie*, "Smith made some changes which glorified himself, some which detracted from his renown, and many others which concerned his personal career not at all."[40] Yet the revisions concerning his personal prowess are minor in comparison to those expanding the roles of Anas Todkill and his Indian ally Mosco.[41] Obviously many commentators simply do not like Smith's self-assertive personality. Some of his contemporaries despised him—mainly because he was not obsequious to them as his superiors by birth and breeding.[42] The evidence, however, proves that Smith was no braggart.

My reading and interpretation of Smith have been mainly influenced by the works of Edward Arber, Bradford Smith, Laura Polanyi Striker, and especially by my late friend Philip L. Barbour. When Barbour's biography, *The Three Worlds of Captain John Smith* (1964) appeared, I read it with great admiration and appreciation. I believe, with T. S. Eliot, that the finest criticism supplies the necessary facts and historical contexts for understanding a writer.[43] But many contemporary scholars view Smith through a post-

Vietnam judgment of colonialism and a modern scrupulosity regarding human rights. They seem to forget that Smith lived in the Renaissance, when the society of the day generally valued only aristocrats and the "better sort," and ordinary persons were usually considered peasants or serfs, without equal rights.[44] I am an apologist for Smith—precisely because I do not think that he needs any apology. I admire him wholeheartedly. I am certain that without Smith the English colonization of Virginia would have failed. And without Smith, I do not believe that there would have been an English settlement in New England in 1620. (Instead, the Plymouth colonists might well have tried to settle in Guiana.) Further, I believe that Smith possessed an extraordinary vision of the possibilities of America and that he was, for his day, a radical social thinker. He believed in the right to life and to dignity of the ordinary person, including the ordinary Indian. But he, unlike some modern scholars, knew full well that he lived in the sixteenth and early seventeenth centuries and that he had to function within its structure of values and opinions.

The American Dream of Captain John Smith sets forth Smith's ideas and ideals and discusses his writings and character. My underlying assumption is that his ideals reflect his character, and though we have the evidence of a number of other writers concerning Smith's actions and motivations, none are so revealing as Smith's own writings. I use the writings of his contemporaries whenever they are appropriate, but the book is based primarily upon a rereading of all Smith's writings. Chapter 1, "Early and Late Dreams," traces his changing ideals and ambitions, from his youthful desire to be a sailor and soldier to his later commitment to the exploration and colonization of America. Smith first praised the idea of American identity and thoroughly identified with America. He portrayed himself as a self-made man, advocated the concept that an individual could create his own fortune, and saw himself as the most recent in a line of great explorers, beginning with Columbus. His final dream was to be the most important single founder of English colonization in America. I believe he achieved his greatest ambition.

The second chapter briefly characterizes each of Smith's ten pamphlets and books, comments on their sources, form, and contents, and traces Smith's development as a writer. The third chapter examines the two major components of travel literature in his writings, adventure and exoticism, finding him the greatest seven-teenth-century American master of both. Chapter 4, "The Promoter of America," discusses Smith's promotion literature. He was more realistic than any other promotional writer of his day, detailing the incredible difficulties awaiting the prospective colonist. Smith expected emigrants to come to America to better themselves—to acquire land and wealth. Unlike most writers of promotion literature, Smith said that the only way for the colonist to become wealthy was through hard work: "all you [can] expect from thence must be by labour" (2:330). Like all other early writers about America, he was tinged with a pastoral vision. He was the first American environmentalist, urging the planters to create their plantations with an eye toward the resulting landscape, which should include windbreaks and other tracts of virgin forests. By believing in the possibility of the betterment of ordinary individuals and by appealing to their desires, Smith wrote the greatest seventeenth-century promotion literature.

Though the entire book explores the character and ideals of Smith, chapter 5, "The Character of Smith," approaches the topic mainly by categorizing his appreciations of others. He respected courage and perseverance, fair-dealing and a kindly humanity, hard work, learning, and all skills, generosity and objectivity. He celebrated these qualities in numerous whites, some of whom emerge as versions of Smith. Even in his categorization of the colonists as gentlemen, soldiers, and artisans, one finds that Smith betrayed his radical views on the social order. He frequently displayed an ironic sense of humor and was not above making himself the butt of a joke. Chapter Six assesses Smith's attitudes toward the Indians. He liked individual Indians and appreciated Indian culture. He was a skilled diplomat and trader who treated the Indians fairly and with respect. He sympathized with their situation and appreciated their point of view. Like many later great Indian fighters, he was a thorough student of Indian culture. No one previously seems to have realized—and certainly no one has written—that Smith was the Indians' best friend in early Virginia. He even successfully reconciled various warring Indian tribes. Chapter 7, "Powhatan and Smith," describes and analyzes the relationship between Virginia's two great leaders in the epic period of Virginia's colonization, showing their mutual respect, their reciprocal hostility, and even their requited admiration.

Chapter 8, "Dissatisfaction with the Social Order," examines Smith's attitudes toward gentlemen and work, proving that he valued physical work of all kinds and held gentlemen, as such, in contempt. He scorned and ridiculed almost all the other members of the council—Virginia's official aristocracy. He repeatedly criticized the Virginia Company's attempt to set up a hierarchical system of offices in Virginia and proclaimed opinions that placed him securely within the radical traditions of his times. He believed that history proved that empires rose when young soldiers and adventurers were encouraged by their country—and that empires declined when rulers no longer rewarded the efforts of their youths.

The final chapter, "The New American Order," sets forth Smith's hopes for a new social system in America. The chapter examines Smith's influence upon New England, arguing that John Winthrop's "Modell of Christian Charity" attempted to reply to Smith's radical social vision for life in the New World. I also contend that Smith inspired the Massachusetts Bay colonists to take their charter to America. The chapter concludes by examining Smith's agrarian ideas for land distribution in America and by discussing his radical notions concerning the elimination of servitude.

A few previous students have briefly suggested that Smith envisioned a new kind of empire and social order in America, but no one has gathered so much evidence, and no one has perceived the depth of Smith's radical dream for the future America.[45] Smith was not only the greatest colonist and explorer of early America, he was also its greatest visionary.

1

Early and Late Dreams

I know I shall bee taxed for writing so much of my selfe,
but I care not much, because the judiciall know there are
few such Souldiers as are my examples, have writ their
owne actions, nor know I who will or can tell my intents
better than my selfe.

—Captain John Smith's apologia, in the fourth book of
The Generall Historie (1624; 2:317)

His three *fing.*
His Encounter *wit*

From *True Travels* (1630), compartment 4

Early Dreams

HEROIC chivalry dominated the Renaissance imagination. Heroic ideals pervade both elite literature (like Edmund Spenser's *The Faerie Queene* and Philip Sidney's *Arcadia*) and popular, inexpensive works, such as ballads, chapbooks, and even travel narratives.[1] Young John Smith gloried in tales of the Armada's heroes and wars abroad. When Smith (born 1580) was an adolescent in the early 1590s, the primary way one dramatically gained fame and fortune was by force of arms, i.e., by extraordinary service as a soldier or sailor. Those Elizabethan sea dogs who achieved success as privateers instantly became rich and famous. Ballads celebrated the famous pirates, soldiers, and adventurers, linking them to the traditional Seven Champions of Christendom and to the still popular mythical heroes of English romance like Sir Bevis of Hampton and Guy of Warwick (their exploits prefigure Smith's —both fought in eastern Europe, and Sir Bevis, like Smith, was sold into slavery in the Middle East).[2] A ballad published in the same year as two of Smith's Virginia tracts, "Saint George's Commendation" (1612), attests the spirit of the times:

> *Cumberland* and *Essex*
> > *Norris* and brave *Drake*
> I'th raigne of Queen *Elizabeth*
> > did many battles make.
> Aduentrous *Martin Frobisher*,
> > with *Hawkins* and some more,
> From sea did bring great riches
> > Vnto our English shore.[3]

As a boy, Smith dreamed of "brave adventures" at sea (3:154). He must have known all versions of the immensely popular ballad "Lord Willoughby." Peregrine Bertie, Baron Willoughby de Eresly, was Smith's local lord and his patron.[4] The song celebrated the 1587 victory won by Lord Willoughby in Flanders when Smith was seven years old. Released from apprenticeship by his father's death in 1596—and his mother's prompt remarriage, which left Smith his father's farm—Smith chose a military career. In his will, his father George Smith left to Lord Willoughby, "under whome I have many yeares lived as his poore tennant as a token of my dewtifull good

will the best of my two yeares old colts." More important, after a
bequest to his son John, he specified, "*John Smyth* my eldest sonne
whome I chardge and command to honoure and love my foresaide
good Lord *Willoughbie* during his lyfe" (3:377). As Smith reported
in *The True Travels*, his adventures began when "he found meanes
to attend Master Perigrine Barty into France, second sonne to the
Right Honourable Perigrine, that generous Lord Willoughby, and
famous Souldier" (3:154–55). In eastern Europe Smith achieved
the honors that the ballad accorded to Willoughby: "the bravest
man in battel / was brave lord Willoughbey . . . the foremost man in
a fight . . . nothing could the courage quell / of brave lord Willoughbey."[5]

By his extraordinary feats Smith rose to be major of a regiment
when but twenty-two years of age. Fighting in successive single
tournaments against three champions of the Turkish army, he became Christendom's most renowned warrior, knighted on the field
and rewarded with a major sinecure by the royal family of Hungary
and Poland. Such feats of individual heroism were the stuff of
Medieval and Renaissance popular legends. Sir Philip Sidney, who
lost his life in the same battle that made Smith's patron Lord Willoughby famous, became the most written-about soldier of the day
in England—because his aristocratic and wealthy family patron-
ized the poets who sang his fame.[6] In commendatory verses for
Smith's *Sea Grammar* (1627), John Hagthorpe commented on the
different treatment accorded the achievements of wealthy patrons
versus those of impecunious soldiers: "*If merit and desert were truly
weighed / In Justice Scales, not all by money swey'd*; / Smith *should not
want reward*" but "*poore mens words / Are wind, and aire: Great mens are
pickes, and swords*" (3:51). John Done (whom Barbour identifies as
"an obscure author and translator . . . not to be confused with John
Donne") similarly observed in his prefatory verses that "all goes
now by wealth" and that neither Smith's "wit, nor valour" would
gain the praise he deserved (2:49). Smith, who keenly appreciated
the ironies of life, fully understood his position: "Had I returned
rich, I could not have erred: Now having onely such fish as came to
my net, I must be taxed" (1:311). No money could be made by celebrating Smith—although there could be some profit in satirizing
him on stage as *The Hungarian Lion* or, at Smith's death, as the mock
hero *Captaine Iones*.[7]

No other Elizabethan or Jacobean soldier—not even the redoubtable commoner Richard Pike (who was celebrated in ballads, chapbooks, and plays for his heroism at Cadiz in 1625)—achieved the deeds of Captain John Smith.[8] In the spring of 1602, he won the lottery among the Christian cavalry captains to fight the Turkish challenger. In a large arena, "the Rampiers all beset with faire Dames, and men in Armes" (3:172), Smith and the Turkish champion strode out to a flourish of music, with pages leading their horses and bearing their lances, pistols, battle-axes, and swords. The rituals of knightly combat having been observed, the opponents fought to the death. Over the course of a week, Smith fought three times in individual combat—and thrice raised his dying opponent's helmet to cut off his head (3:172–74). Smith's personal motto epitomized the heraldic code of knightly chivalry—*vincere est vivere*, "to conquer is to live."

With these duels, Smith attained the epitome of Renaissance popular success. Other adventures followed. But fulfillment brought disillusionment. When the idealistic Smith thoroughly knew the devastation and pillage of the soldier and sailor, he found them disgusting (1:330–31, 3:223, 285). The realities of warfare belied the chivalric ideals that led Smith to his European adventures.[9] Fame gained by plunder and death became infamy. The twenty-four-year-old Smith had learned to despise the actuality of warfare. He abandoned his early dreams, gave up his sinecure of three hundred ducats a year at the Hungarian court, and turned his back on the glory bestowed on him as a famous Transylvanian army officer. Returning to England, he chose future adventures as a colonist (3:174–75, 178–79, 203).

Americans: Infamous or Glorious?

Colonization and an American Dream replaced Smith's boyhood vision of fame won by force of arms. That is the significance of the ostensibly puzzling last chapter—devoted to pirates—of Smith's *The True Travels* (1630). In his penultimate chapter, after writing, "Now to conclude the travels and adventures of Captaine Smith" (3:237), Smith recapitulated the story of his New World adventures. The last chapter, "The bad life, qualities and conditions of Pyrats; and how they taught the Turks and Moores to become men of warre," seems at first to be a postscript unrelated to what had gone before. Actually, it dramatizes Smith's belief that new kinds of heroes were superseding the old. Smith's own ambitions had changed, from an adventurous life as a sailor and soldier to a colonist—a planter of civilization in a new world. But pirates still were a major subject of common literature and the popular imagination. They continued to be heroes. Therefore Smith briefly discussed the best-known pirates of the last half century. He stressed the miserableness of their lives, emphasized their constant warring with each other, and pronounced the judgment: "any wise man would rather live amongst wilde beasts, than them" (3:240).

Smith claimed that the changing times made American colonists the new heroes. "Those titles of Sea-men and Souldiers, have beene most worthily honoured and esteemed" in times past "but now" were regarded "for most part, but as the scumme of the world." Soldiers and sailors should abandon their former occupations and endeavor rather to "adventure to those faire plantations of our English Nation." Opportunity awaited in America. Though colonists "in the beginning were scorned and contemned, yet now you see how many rich and gallant people come from thence, who went thither as poore as any Souldier or Sailer, and gets more in one yeare, than you by Piracie in seven" (3:240–41).

Really, though, Smith knew that American colonists, rather than soldiers and sailors, had the reputation as the "scumme of the world." Jacobean Englishmen identified Virginia with misery, starvation, and death; with mosquitoes, insects, wolves, and rattlesnakes; with prolonged cold and excessive heat; and with a harsh code of laws and hostile Indians. The Virginia Company hoped to create great baronies in America and therefore did not offer terms that would appeal to industrious farmers. Consequently by 1609 the company was dispatching vagabonds and convicted felons to Virginia. After Smith and others protested and after remigrants told of the miserable Virginia conditions, the London Company apologized in a broadside (1610) for sending over "unruly youths" of a "most lewd and bad condition."[10] Even the Virginia Company's promotion tract of 1612 conceded that earlier colonists had suffered "manifold difficulties, crosses, and disasters." The author testified that "the ignorant and simple-minded are much discouraged" and acknowledged that "the malicious and looser sort (being accompanied with the licentious vaine of stage Poets) have whet their tongues with scornfull laughs against the action it self, in so much as there is no common speech nor public name of any thing this day (except it be the name of God) which is more wildly depraved, traduced and derided by such unhallowed lips than the name of Virginia."[11] Reporting English colonization news to his Madrid superiors, the Spanish ambassador to England said in 1614 that Virginia "is in such bad repute that not a human being can be found to go there."[12]

But the London Company hypocritically continued to send over anyone it could get, privately "saying necessity would make them get victuals for themselves," and defended its actions with the argument that "good labourers . . . were more usefull here in England" (3:273). A group of persons sent to Bermuda about 1611 were described as "of such bad condition that it seemed they had picked the Males out of Newgate" and, Smith added, "the Females from Bridewell," both notorious London prisons (2:381). The company paid mariners six pounds apiece for emigrants—even if the passenger died (2:328). The mariners could sell qualified indentured servants in Virginia "for forty, fifty, or threescore pounds" (2:330). Since the ship captains made a considerable profit on all emigrants, they eagerly enticed people to America and employed agents (popularly called "spirits" to secure emigrants for them. Unscrupulous spirits even kidnapped children for service in Virginia (both this meaning of the word *spirit* and the word *kidnap* were created during the mid-seventeenth century to describe such practices).[13] Naturally the spirits and the captains who engaged in transporting emigrants became anathema. Before the mid-century, the cry of "A spirit! A spirit!" rallied city mobs to pelt the offender.[14] Defying the London Company, Smith protested against the "odious" practices of spirits and the sale of indentured servants (2:330). He satirically pointed out that "the honorable Company have bin humble suiters to his Maiestie to get vagabonds and condemned men to go thither; nay so much scorned was the name of Virginia, some did chuse to be hanged ere they would go thither" (1:433). Smith especially objected to transporting criminals. "Such delinquents as here cannot be ruled by all the lawes in England" must be even worse in Virginia (2:330).[15] Samuel Purchas agreed. In a prefatory poem for Smith's *Generall Historie* (1624), Purchas echoed a passage in Horace that said people who crossed the sea changed only their climates, not their natures (2:47): "caelum non animum mutant, qui trans mare currunt."[16]

By Smith's time, America had already developed two major (and opposing) images: one was a land of gold, and the other was a fool's paradise, fit only for beggars and convicts.[17] Early in the seventeenth century, even proponents of English plantations in America admitted that colonists were the outcasts and undesirables of society. Francis Bacon, in "Of Plantations" (1625), wrote: "It is a Shamefull and Unblessed Thing to take the Scumme of People, and Wicked Condemned Men, to be the People with whom you Plant; and not only so, but it spoileth the *Plantation*; For they will ever live like Rogues, and not fall to worke, but be Lazie, and doe Mischiefe, and spend Victuals, and be quickly weary, and then Certify over to their Country, to the Discredit of the *Plantation*." In 1630 John Winthrop called previous emigrants to America "unfit instruments, a multitude of rude and misgoverned persons—the very scum of the Land."[18] So too Philip Massinger, in his comedy *The City Madam* (acted in 1632), castigated Virginians as "Condemned wretches, forfeited to the Law . . . Strumpets and bawds, for the abomination of their life, spewed out of their own country."[19] Daniel Defoe's novels of transported criminals or kidnapped victims, like *Moll Flanders* (1722), and *Colonel Jack* (1722) summed up one popular notion of America.[20] Expressing the long-standing English opinion, Dr. Samuel Johnson labeled Americans "a race of convicts" who "ought to be thankful for anything we allow them short of hanging."[21]

But Captain John Smith, despite criticizing gentlemen, lazy colonists, and Virginia Company policies, refuted the aspersions on America and Americans (1:175–76, 218, 2:128, 247, 320, 323–26, 385, 391–92). Smith had special contempt for the third supply of colonists, partly because it brought back his old enemies John Ratcliffe, John Martin, and Gabriel Archer; partly because the colony's government had been altered in England and Lord De La Warr made governor; partly because, since the flagship was wrecked on a Bermuda reef, there was no clear line of authority; but mainly because there "were many unruly gallants packed thither by their friends to escape il destinies" (1:269). Smith nevertheless reminded his readers that "every thing of worth is found full of difficulties." He stated that "nothing" was as "difficult" as establishing "a common wealth so farre remote from men and meanes" and thereby implied that colonization was the greatest possible aspiration a person could undertake (1:211, 2:144). Numerous writers like Richard Hakluyt, Thomas Harriot, and John Brereton promoted American colonies before Smith, but he first celebrated the American. He disgustedly labeled those who attacked the colonists as "Spanolized

English" (3:284—that is, Englishmen who betrayed England's interest to the Spanish.[22]

Smith claimed the early colonists were heroes. His primary purpose in writing *The Generall Historie of Virginia, New-England, and the Summer Isles* (1624) was to eternalize "the memory of those that effected" the settlement of Virginia (2:136). He compared colonists to the greatest figures in history and in the Bible. As farmers, they followed the model of Adam and Eve, who first began "this innocent worke, To plant the earth to remaine to posteritie; but not without labour, trouble and industrie." As bringers of civilization, the colonists succeeded Noah and his family who "beganne againe the second plantation" and "planted new Countries" and whose progeny gradually brought "the world" to its present estate (1:360). Indeed, the first name for a colonist in the English language was a "planter," by which was meant someone who planted religion or culture in a new colony. Though the earliest usage of this meaning of *planter* in the *OED* is dated 1620, the exalted idea of a colonist and the word itself existed by 1602, well before the settlement of Jamestown.[23] As teachers of Christianity, the planters followed the model of Abraham, Christ, and the Apostles. Smith reminded his English readers that if such past evangelists had not "exposed themselves . . . to teach the Gospell . . . Even wee our selves, had at this present been as Salvage, and as miserable as the most barbarous Salvage yet uncivilized." Further, as the founders of a future empire, American colonists enacted the roles of "the greatest Princes of the earth" whose very best achievements were "planting of countries, and civilizing barbarous and inhumane Nations, to civilitie and humanitie." Just as those "eternall actions" of the greatest princes "fill our histories," so the deeds of the earliest Americans would fill future histories (1:360–61).[24] Smith's vision of American identity inverted the commonplace negative images of his time. No one before Smith celebrated American identity. No other founding colonist had as grand a secular view of what it meant to be an American. (Incidentally, Smith first expressed a special relationship between the American character and weapons, and he explained it with a frontier thesis: most colonists were well armed, the militia held drills on holidays, and the men frequently went "hunting and fowling." The result, Smith noted, was that "most part of them are most excellent marksmen" [3:217]).

The metamorphosis from Englishman to American would enable even gentlemen to transform themselves from discontented, useless drones into workers with fulfilling roles. Smith believed that England's social system prevented gentlemen from developing happy, useful lives. They were imprisoned by their own self-imposed limitations. What they could and could not do was decided by their awareness of traditional roles and by the shame that they would feel if others saw them engaged in physical work. Emigration to America, however, allowed them to cast off the traditional bonds of custom and the old limiting modes of behavior and freed them to taste the fulfillment of work. The new colony that Smith projected in *A Description of New England* (1616) would "so employ and encourage a great part of our idlers and others that want imployments fitting their qualities at home, where they shame to doe that they would doe abroad; that could they but once taste the sweet fruites of their owne labours, doubtless many thousands would be advised by good discipline, to take more pleasure in honest industrie, then in their humours of dissolute idlenesse" (1:338, 2:416).

Smith's attitudes were in advance of his time. Indeed, over a century and a half later, only a few avant-garde Americans like John Mercer, Joel Barlow, and Benjamin Franklin advocated such egalitarian ideals. Perhaps Franklin's expression is closest to Smith's. Franklin also realized that the different environment (and, in Franklin's day, relatively common attitudes) in America would allow (and, in his time, encourage) gentlemen to strive to achieve their goals even though their roles involved manual labor. In "Information to Those Who Would Remove to America" (1783), Franklin wrote: "Also, Persons of moderate Fortunes and Capitals, who, having a Number of Children to provide for, are desirous of bringing them up to Industry, and to secure Estates for their Posterity, have Opportunities of doing it in America, which Europe does not afford. There they may be taught & practice profitable mechanic Arts, without incurring Disgrace on that Account, but on the contrary acquiring Respect by such Abilities."[25]

Late Dreams—Discoveries

Smith's full formulation of a public American Dream should not be confused with his own personal dream. The two had common elements but also key differences. Smith appealed to the emigrant's desire to leave an estate for his family, but he never married and he left no family.[26] He repeatedly suggested a colonist could rise from the status of servant to master, but Smith had achieved gentry status before becoming a colonist by virtue of his feats as a soldier, a status reflected in his military rank, his personal coat of arms, and his being appointed to the council in Virginia by the Virginia Company. Smith also appealed to the emigrant's desire for land and wealth, but he had little desire for land and scorned riches. He often condemned the wealthy: "But rich men for the most part are growne to that dotage, through their pride in their wealth, as though there were no accident could end it, or their life . . . drawing by all manner of inventions, from the Prince and his honest subjects, even the vitall spirits of their powers and estates: as if their Bagges, or Bragges, were so powerfull a defence, the malicious could not assault them" (1:344–45; cf. 1:349–50, 357–58, 2:184–85, 462, 3:277–78). Thus Smith's public American Dream contained some elements he did not care about, some that he had long before achieved, and others that he privately abhorred. But its social ideals, its respect for an individual's hard work and achievement, and its vision of free men living in a better world—all these he believed in. They were part of his personal American Dream.

His personal American Dream also contained at least one key feature that was not part of the public dream. When he became a colonist, he committed his life to "knowledge of any discoveries for . . . future good" (2:405). He thought his discoveries (which he called his "inventions" [1:348]) were among the most significant in the world's history. Among his English contemporaries, only Smith appreciated and expressed the incredible westward extent of the North American continent. The Virginia Company officials accepted (was the wish father to the thought?) the myth of Verazzano's Sea. They thought the Pacific Ocean was just over Virginia's Blue Ridge Mountains (1:73, 166–67, 229, 234, 2:188, 222, 3:272, 285) and envisioned the Virginia colony as "a half-way house to China and the Spice Islands."[27] Misled by an Indian report in his first exploration of the Chesapeake, Smith in 1608 briefly indulged a similar expectation (1:229), but he soon realized that Virginia was part of a great continent.

He was the first person to hope and to believe that America would become a great empire. Defining Virginia in 1612, he wrote: "The bounds thereof on the East side are the great Ocean. On the South lyeth Florida: on the North nova Francia. As for the West thereof, the limits are unknowne" (1:143). When William Strachey copied the passage at the beginning of *Historie of Travell into Virginia Britania*, he added the old belief: "Only yt is supposed there may be found the Disent into the South-Sea," i.e., the Pacific Ocean.[28] Like most Englishmen of his day, Strachey wanted America to be an illusion. He hoped water passages would be found through it. The less land mass, the better. Smith, however, appreciated the size of America and wanted an alternative to the Old World. In *A Map of Virginia* (1612), Smith stressed how "small" "the proportion of ground . . . yet . . . discovered" was "in comparison of that yet unknowne" (1:160). Smith knew that the continent extended for an incredible distance. In 1616 he wrote that "Virginia is no Ile (as many doe imagine) but part of the Continent adjoyning to Florida" (1:325). Explorers thus far had only touched or seen "a little the edges of those large dominions, which doe stretch themselves into the Maine, God doth know how many thousand miles." He said, "We can yet no more judge" the interior of America, "then a stranger that saileth betwixt England and France can describe the Harbors and dangers by landing here or there in some River or Bay, tell thereby the goodnesse and substances of Spaine, Italy, Germany, Bohemia, Hungaria and the rest." No one, he affirmed, yet "understandeth or knowes what *Virginia* is" (1:326–27). Even Florida (which at that time was the name for most of Georgia as well as for the regions stretching westward to the Mississippi) was in Smith's opinion "A Country farre bigger then England, Scotland, France and Ireland" (1:325). No English colonist or theorist before Smith appreciated the sheer space occupied by the North American continent. And only Smith realized and wanted to believe that the landmass meant a future great empire.

Smith knew the importance of geography. He revised an expression by Samuel Purchas into a memorable aphorism: "For as Geography without History seemeth a carkasse without motion; so History without Geography, wandreth as a Vagrant without a certaine habitation" (2:338).[29] With great skill, Smith mapped the Chesapeake Bay area in 1607–9. It was "the most accurate and detailed map of any comparable area on the North Atlantic coast of America until the last quarter of the century."[30] In 1616, when Smith described the previous New England explorations, he carefully enumerated everyone "whose writings in this age is the best guide knowne to search those parts." He gave an excellent historical and bibliographical account of the former explorers and said that "posterity" was "bettered by the fruits of their labours." Smith knew that others "long before and since" those he named "have ranged" America, but their "descriptions are concealed, or never well observed, or died with their Authors: so that the Coast is yet still but even as a Coast unknowne and undiscovered" (1:325–26).[31]

Before he sailed to New England, Smith purchased half a dozen maps, "so unlike each to other, and most so differing from any true proportion, or resemblance of the Countrey, as they did mee no more good, then so much waste paper, though they cost me more." Smith drew a map "from Point to Point, Ile to Ile, and Harbour to Harbour, with the Soundings, Sands, Rocks, and Land-Marks as I passed close aboard the shore in a little Boat." He apologized for not exploring further, "for, being sent more to get present commodities, then knowledge by discoueries for any future good, I had not power to search as I would" (1:326, 2405). Nevertheless his chart remained the best guide to the New England coast for the next fifty years. Smith hoped to map the entire East Coast from Florida through New England. He stressed that between Florida and Canada, "more then halfe" the country "is yet unknowne to any purpose: no not so much as the borders of the Sea are yet certainly discovered" (1:326). Smith wanted to chart them and to explore and map America's unknown interior (2:306–7). In late 1616 he offered to join the Basque ships sailing to hunt whales "in the North" (i.e., Hudson's Bay) "for the purpose of surveying those parts" (3:323), but nothing came of the project.

Despite Smith's writings, the Virginia Company still, in 1622, claimed that the South Sea was just over the Blue Ridge Mountains. Edward Waterhouse, reporting *A Declaration of the State of . . . Virginia* after the massacre that year, appended a treatise "Written by that learned *Mathematician* Mr. Henry Briggs, of the Northwest passage to the South Sea through the Continent of Virginia."[32] When Smith proposed after the massacre to take one hundred soldiers to the colony as a "running Army" to fight the Indians, he also promised the Virginia company to "discover you more land unknowne then they all yet know" (2:306). He reminded the Company that he had already mapped parts of Virginia and New England. He now proposed to explore the areas "within the limits of those two Patents, and to bring them both in one Map, and the Countries betwixt them" (2:307). To the commissioners investigating the Virginia

Company and the state of the colony in 1624, he again proposed to "discover that yet unknowne" (2:326).

In 1631 he wrote that the distance across the North American continent from the Atlantic Ocean to the Pacific "is supposed by most Cosmographers at least more than two thousand miles" (3:286), and he referred, one last time, to his proposal to the Virginia Company and its successors to discover "them more land than they all yet know or have demonstrated" (3:293).

He did not achieve all that he had hoped. In some moods, as his fine poem "The Sea Marke" reveals (3:265), he felt that he had failed. But who, in his generation or even in his lifetime, attempted so much? He made more solid geographical contributions to knowledge of the North Atlantic East Coast than anyone else in the seventeenth century.[33] In my own opinion, Smith's attempts to gain knowledge by "discoveries for . . . future good" succeeded. Captain John Smith should be recognized as the greatest single founder of the American colonies.

Final Dreams—Genealogy, Identity, and Descendants

Smith chose to present himself as a "rude military man" (2:41), "a true Souldier" (3:14), whose writings were merely "the collections and observations of a plaine souldier" (1:422; cf. 1394).[34] When formal, he called himself and signed his name (as he has been known to posterity) "Captain John Smith." Though he had been promoted to major in 1602 and had received the title Admiral of New England in 1616,[35] the primary way he chose to portray himself was as an army captain—a rank low enough to be in the thick of the fight. The legend around his portrait in the map of *A Description of New England* (1616) says: "The Portraictuer of Captayne Iohn Smith / Admirall of New England" (1:320). Since the title could be interpreted as a ship captain, let me point out that he signed his commendatory verses for his friend Robert Norton in 1628 "Captaine *John Smith, Hungariensis*" (i.e., of the Hungarian [or Transylvanian] army [3:370]). He characteristically apologized that "it were more proper for mee, To be doing what I say, then writing what I knowe" (1:311).

Lurking under the persona of a plain, rude soldier who had fought—and commanded—on the frontiers of the Christian empire in Eurasia, Africa, and America lay the grand classical precedent of Julius Caesar. When Smith apologized for writing about his own achievements—"the judiciall know there are few such Souldiers as are my examples, have writ their owne actions" (2:317)—he expected the reader to recall that Caesar had also written his own experiences. He thought of himself as a lesser version of Caesar again when he wrote in the dedication of The True Travels: "Many of the most eminent Warriers, and others, what their swords did, their penns writ: Though I bee never so much their inferiour, yet I hold it no great errour, to follow good examples" (3:142). Twice he made the Caesar comparison explicit. In dedicating The Generall Historie, he asked: "Where shall we looke to finde a Julius Caesar, whose atchievments shine as cleare in his owne Commentaries, as they did in the field?" (2:41). Though the answer to that rhetorical question should be nowhere, Smith clearly suggested that he himself exampled Caesar's combination of soldier and writer. His friend Edward Worseley found the comparison apt; Worseley wrote, "Like Caesar now thou writ'st what thou hast done" (2:50). Smith again dared compare himself to Caesar in A Sea Grammar (1627): "Julius Caesar wrote his owne Commentaries, holding it no lesse honour to write, than fight" (3:47). Two more friends, Anthony Fereby and the librarian Richard James, used the Caesar comparison in commendatory verses for The True Travels (3:145, 147). But Caesar was not Smith's main model or his ideal. Caesar was an aristocrat.

Whatever else Captain John Smith may have been, he was and regarded himself as a self-made man. He alluded to an old proverb to make the point that he alone had accomplished whatever he had achieved: "my hands hath been my lands this fifteene yeares in Europ, Asia, Afric, or America" (1:133). No wealthy heir he—whatever Smith obtained had been by his own efforts. All those vignettes depicting Smith's Virginia adventures engraved in The Generall Historie (2:98–99) and those portraying his European adventures in The True Travels (3:242–43) show him as a man of action—and in all but two, he is a soldier, wearing armor. The two exceptions portray his adventures as a slave in the Near East: barefoot, dressed in a simple tunic, and wearing a slave's iron collar around his neck. One vignette captured him rebelling: "Capt. SMITH Killeth the BASHAW of Nalbrits and on his horse escapeth" (3:243, compartment nine).

Born the son of yeoman George Smith, Smith rose in the world.[36] His autobiography, *The True Travels, Adventures, and Observations of Captaine Iohn Smith* (1630), sets forth the course of his self-creation. The autobiography as a genre is synonymous with the rise of individualism; commenting on its modernity, William Dean Howells observed in 1905: "It seems to have risen from that nascent sense of the importance of each to all which the antique world apparently ignored."[37] Few English autobiographies existed before Captain John Smith wrote *The True Travels*. A recent student of seventeenth-century British autobiography noted that the author "usually placed his essential self in a social and subordinate relation to God, state and community. This habit of self-effacement has been typical of British autobiography up to the present century."[38] Nothing could be less true of Captain John Smith's assertive persona. He was especially extraordinary in his own day.

The idea of the self-made man was anathema to the social order of Smith's time. Most writers of the period put expressions of radical individualism into the mouths of notorious rebels like the English Jack Cade[39] or the Roman Cassius. In Shakespeare's *Julius Caesar*, Cassius says, "The fault, dear Brutus, is not in our stars, / But in ourselves, that we are underlings" (1:2.138–39). The audience knew that such a philosophy would turn all to chaos. John Donne spoke for the age when he condemned individualism and egalitarianism:

> 'Tis all in peeces, all cohaerence gone;
> All just supply, and all Relation:
> Prince, Subject, Father, Sonne, are things forgot,
> For every man alone thinkes he hath got
> To be a Phoenix, and that there can bee
> None of that kinde, of which he is, but hee.[40]

Times, however, were changing. The most popular English fable about the transformation of a poor obscure country boy into a rich, powerful, and honored individual appeared about 1600. References to Richard Whittington's rise from poverty and obscurity to fame and fortune appeared in *Eastward Hoe!* (1605) and in Thomas Heywood's play *If You Know Not Me* (1605). On February 8 1604/5, Thomas Pavyer obtained a license for a play entitled *The History of Richard Whittington, of His Lowe Birthe and Great Fortune*.

On July 16, 1605, a song entitled "A Ballad, Called 'The Vertuous Lyfe and Memorable Death of Sir Richard Whittington,'" was licensed to John Wright. In 1612 Richard Johnson's "A Song of Sir Richard Whittington" appeared in *The Crown Garland of Goulden Roses*.[41] The story of Richard Whittington became the archetypal success story. The fact that the rise was not true of the real Richard Whittington, the lord mayor of London who died in 1423,[42] only emphasizes the growing appeal of the self-made man idea and the mythic power of the rise-from-rags-to-riches legend.[43]

Avant-garde intellectuals, too, expressed a philosophy of individualism, with its accompanying belief that an individual could influence—if not create—his own destiny. Francis Bacon frequently articulated the belief in his essays and other writings, as did Cervantes in *Don Quixote*, Michel de Montaigne in his essays, and—on occasion—Niccolò Machiavelli.[44] As Samuel Pepys recognized a half century later, such a philosophy justified the rise of entrepreneurial and administrative geniuses like himself.[45] Intellectuals found support for the belief in several classical touchstones. Perhaps most famous was Sallust's expression in a letter to Caesar: "Sed res docuit id verum esse, quod in carminibus Appius ait, fabrum esse suae quemque fortunae" ("But experience has shown that to be true which Appius says in his verses, that every man is the architect of his own fortune"). Only slightly less well known was Plautus's assertion in his play *Trinummus*: "Nam sapiens quidem pol ipsus fingit fortunam sibi: eo non multa quae nevolt eveniunt nisi fictor malust" ("For I tell you, a man, a wise man, molds his own destiny: so not much happens to him that he does not want, unless he be a poor molder"). Livy similarly characterized Cato the Elder: "In hoc viro tanta vis animi ingeniique fuit ut quocumque loco natus esset, fortunam sibi ipse facturus fuisse videretur" ("In this man there was such force of mind and character that in whatever station he had been born it seemed he would have made his fortune for himself").[46]

The supposedly anachronistic underlying morals of Smith's autobiography—the rise of the individual, a philosophy of individualism, and the celebration of the self-made man—were not lost on his contemporaries. Christopher Potter, writing commendatory verse for *The True Travels*, echoed the classic expression of the self-made man doctrine in a Latin couplet: "Quisque suae sortis* [*Appius] Faber: an Faber exstitit unquam / Te (Smithe) fortunae verior usque suae? ("Appius says every person is the maker of his own destiny: has any smith ever more truly forged his own fortune than you, Smith?" [3:150]). If a good Puritan had risen to Smith's stature, he would have said that he had merely been an instrument of God. Smith, however, generally left God out of the equation. Smith believed that the individual creates himself. Moreover, Smith liked to think that his own models—his ideal genealogy—were themselves self-made men.

His ideal forebears were those persons who had "advanced Themselves from poore Souldiers to great Captaines" (1:328, 3:301)—not the "great Captaines" of war (though some, like Smith, achieved success in war as well) but of exploration and discovery. Describing the unknown extent of Florida, he waxed eloquent over "the wonderful endevours of Ferdinando de Soto a valiant Spaniard: whose writings in this age is the best guide knowne to search those parts" (1:325). Smith saw himself as the latest in an international line of explorers. His platonic genealogy appears repeatedly in his writings. Christopher Columbus, Hernando Cortés, Francisco Pizarro, Hernando de Soto, and Ferdinand Magellan had blazed the trail (1:327, 360, 2406, 3:301). These great explorers, "to the wonder of all ages," succeeded, "when many hundreds of others farre above them in the worlds opinion . . . came to shame and confusion in actions of small moment" (1:327; cf. 3301).

Smith's contemporaries thought the comparison natural. Thomas Abbay, a former Virginia companion, likened Smith to Columbus as early as 1612(1:135). The first prefatory poem, anonymous, in *The Generall Historie* compared Smith to Columbus, the Cabots, Martin Frobisher, Humphrey Gilbert, Philip Amadas, Sir Walter Ralegh, Richard Grenville, Sir Francis Drake, Bartholomew Gosnold, and Martin Pring: "*Though these be gone, and left behinde a name, / Yet Smith is here to Anvile out a peece / To after Ages, and eternall Fame*" (2:45). Smith hoped to achieve for England what Cortés, Pizarro, Soto, Magellan, and others had achieved for Spain. A large volume would be required, said Smith, "to recite the adventures of the Spanyards, and Portugals, their affronts and defeats, their dangers and miseries; which with such incomparable honor and constant resolution so farre beyond beleefe, they have attempted and indured in their discoveries and plantations." Those former captains of exploration and empire suffered similar crosses to the ones Smith bore. "Yet the Authors of those new inventions, were held as ridiculous, for a long time, as now are others, that doe but seek to imitate their unparalleled vertues" (1:348). The discoveries of former explorers, however, had led the way to wealth and empire.

"Why," asked Smith, "should the brave Spanish Souldiers brag. The Sunne never sets in the Spanish dominions, but ever shineth on one part or other we have conquered for our King." He reminded his readers that Spain, "within these few hundred of yeares, was one of the least of . . . his neighbours." The Spanish boast should animate "every English man . . . to doe the like for" our king, "who is in no way his inferior" (3:299). By the nineteenth century, the motto was common in English—"The sun never sets on England." In some ways, Smith had a less glamorous role than his predecessors, but the challenge of the unknown lands still existed. Just as "all the Romanes were not Scipioes: nor all the Geneweses, Columbuses: nor all the Spanyards, Corteses" (1:360)—so he knew that not all the English were Captain John Smiths. He grieved "that the actions of an Englishman" did not surpass the adventures or the triumphs of the Spanish in accruing empire: "I meane not as a Tyrant to torment all Christendome, but to suppresse her disturbers, and conquer her enemies" (2:318).

The success of England's American colonization was Smith's greatest and final dream. He committed himself to it in 1605 at the age of twenty-five, and for the next twenty-six years he devoted his life to exploring, mapping, reading, thinking, and writing about America. By 1612 the celebrated veteran of European wars believed that the most important and valuable contribution he had made was in America. The fighting he endured in the Lowlands from 1598 to 1600 (when his captain, Joseph Duxbury, was killed in the decisive battle of Nieuport, June 22, 1600), the later ordeals he suffered in eastern European wars between armies of tens of thousands of troops (in which Smith won incomparable fame)— these trials were all insignificant in comparison to the colonization of Virginia. By 1612 he knew "it is the best service I ever did to serve so good a worke" (1:133). He told the commissioners investigating the London Company in 1624 that in neither Virginia nor New England did he own "one foot of Land, nor the very house I builded, nor the ground I digged with my owne hands," but he did not care. "Yet that doth not so much trouble me, as to heare and see those contentions and divisions which will hazard if not ruine the prosperitie of Virginia" (2:326).

Disappointed that he had not achieved more, Smith nevertheless claimed in 1622 that all existing English colonies in America
were "but pigs of my owne sowe" (1:435). In 1624 he called them
his "children, for they haue bin my wife, my hawks, my hounds, my
cards, my dice, and in totall my best content, as indifferent to my
heart as my left hand to my right" (1:434; cf. 3:223). In 1626 he
claimed that "most of those faire plantations [Virginia, New England, and the Summer Isles] did spring from the fruites of my
adventers and discoveries" (3:13). In 1630 he repeated that they
were "his children that never had mother," remarking that "few fathers ever payed dearer for so little content" (3:223). And in 1631,
the year of his death, he again proclaimed that he was "ready to live
and dye" in America and called the colonies in Virginia and New
England his posterity, his "heires, executors, administrators and as-
signes" (3:300). Smith's personal American Dream was to play the
key role in discovering, exploring, mapping, and settling North
America's East Coast and in founding a new civilization where a
common man could achieve success through his own personal efforts. In my judgment, he succeeded.

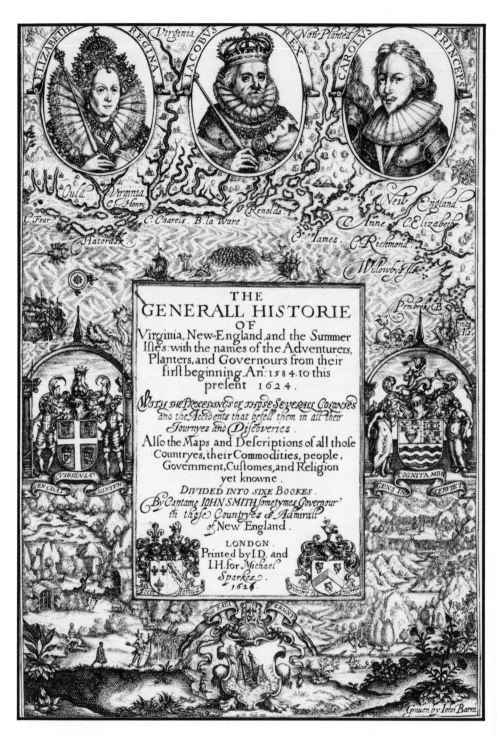

Engraved title page of *The Generall Historie* (1624)

2

The Writings of Captain John Smith

The Sea Marke.

Aloofe, aloofe, and come no neare,
    the dangers doe appeare;
Which if my ruine had not beene
    you had not seene:
I onely lie upon this shelfe
    to be a marke to all
    which on the same might fall,
That none may perish but my selfe.

—The first stanza of Smith's poetic epitaph upon
himself, from his last work, *Advertisements* (1631; 3:265)

CAPTAIN John Smith's American experiences made him a writer. He began with a long letter about Virginia, *A True Relation of Such Occurrences and Accidents of Noate as Hath Hapned in Virginia* (1608). The Stationers' registers recorded the forty-page quarto pamphlet on August 13, 1608. The earliest publication from the first permanent English colony in America, *A True Relation* was written as a report to an English friend. Such "letters" (it probably took up more than eighty manuscript pages) were commonly copied and widely circulated. Perhaps he also thought that Richard Hakluyt (1552–1616), the great compiler and editor of travel literature, might use the account in a future edition of *The Principal Navigations* (first edition, 1589; second edition, revised and enlarged, 1598–1600). But Smith knew that the London Company wanted to control the information and publicity concerning Virginia. It had decreed that all writings from Virginia must be directed to the company (which it could use as it wished). No one was "to write any Letter of any thing that may Discourage others" (*JV* 53–54). Smith violated the policy.

Copies of Smith's letter circulated widely. When *A True Relation* first appeared, the author was unknown. An early transcriber was only interested in the contents. The printed title page attributed the pamphlet to "Thomas Watson." Completely unknown to early Virginia history, Watson may have been the London friend to whom Smith sent the letter, or he may have been a copyist of the letter or the person who gave it to John Healey who, in turn, gave it to the printer. The publisher was soon informed that Watson was not the author, so he changed the title page to read "Written by a Gentleman of the said Collony." John Healey then wrote a preface for the pamphlet (the addition expanded the pamphlet from forty to forty-four pages), explaining that he had come across the manuscript "at the second or third hand" and had sent it to the printer before identifying the author. Now he had learned that it was "written by Captaine Smith, who is one of the Counsell there in Virginia" (1:24). The printer, no doubt happy to learn that the author was a person of rank in the colony, changed the title page for the third time, now attributing the pamphlet to "Captain Smith, Coronell of the said Collony." The title "Coronell" (which could be a variant of *colonel* but suggested the coronet or crowned head of a colony) was evidently the printer's exaggeration. Quickly questioned about the title by irritated London Company officials, the printer inked out "Cor" and "ll" in the word "Coronell" in the copies he had already printed and reset the title page for the fourth time, finally identifying Smith modestly as "One of the said Collony."[1]

A *True Relation* tells of the colony's (and especially Smith's) history from mid-December 1606, when the colonists sailed from Blackwall (just east of London) until June 2, 1608, the date Smith delivered the manuscript of A *True Relation* to Francis Nelson, captain of the *Phoenix*, then off Cape Henry on his return to England (1:97, 224). Smith chronicled the main events in Virginia, including Indian attacks and the bickering of the various council members, but the tract's editor, John Healey, cut the manuscript: "somewhat more was by him written, which being as I thought (fit to be private) I would not adventure to make it publicke" (1:24). Judging by a comparison with Smith's *Generall Historie* (1624), it seems likely that the editor of A *True Relation* cut out some references to the Indians' hostility, to bickering among the leaders of the Virginia Company, and to the early supposed mutiny of Captain John Smith on the voyage to Virginia[2]—although information about these topics (all bad publicity for the Virginia Company) nevertheless appears in the published tract.

Despite Healey's cuts and Smith's rapid composition of the letter—perhaps without notes or earlier drafts—A *True Relation* contains much fascinating information about the earliest Virginia explorations and Indian customs. With the letter Smith sent a rough map of the lower portion of the Chesapeake Bay, including a dotted line tracing his captivity trail.[3] Smith skimmed over the first starving time during the summer of 1607, when "the living were scarce able to bury the dead" (1:33), but he included many homely, graphic descriptions of Jamestown and early Virgina: "As yet we had no houses to cover us, our Tents were rotten, and our Cabbins worse than nought: Our best commoditie [for trading with the Indians] was Yron which we made into little chissels" (1:35).

A *True Relation* narrates his capture in December 1607. Taken before Opechancanough, Smith "presented him with a compasse diall, describing by my best meanes the use therof, whereat he so amazedly admired, as he suffered me to proceed in a discourse of the roundnes of the earth, the course of the sunne, moone, starres and plannets" (1:47). When Smith reached Opechancanough's permanent camp, Smith asked to send a message to Paspahegh

(Jamestown) "by which they should understand, how kindly they used me, and that I was well, least they should revenge my death" (1:49). Retelling his early Virginia adventures in *The Generall Historie* (1624, Smith added that when the Indians deposited his note outside Jamestown, "seeing men sally out as he had told them they would, they fled; yet in the night they came againe to the same place where he had told them they should receive an answer, and such things as he had promised them, which they found accordingly, and with which they returned with no small expedition, to the wonder of them all that heard it, that he could either divine, or the paper could speake" (2:149).

A notable addition to travel literature, *A True Relation* contains passages of high adventure, detailed observations of exotic customs, and precise descriptions of hitherto unknown geographical areas. One only wishes that Smith had kept a daily journal and supplied more dates and that in this first account of his captivity, he had mentioned Pocahontas's saving him. But he omitted numerous death-defying escapades during his captivity and in the exploring expeditions. It is a compliment to Smith that a reader wants more—more details concerning the adventures, more descriptions of Indian customs and ceremonies, more appreciations (and denigrations!) of his companions, and more information on the geography of the strange new Indian land. That he told so much in one hurriedly written letter to an English friend is nevertheless amazing.

Smith wrote his second pamphlet, *A Map of Virginia* (1612), a fifty-page quarto,[4] to accompany the great map he drew of the Chesapeake Bay area. The first explorers feared when they penetrated into the unknown that they might never be able to find their way back to their tiny outposts. Indeed, they dreaded that Jamestown and the other places they knew might (like the Roanoke colonists' camp) disappear from the English consciousness. Smith had few such fears, but he understood that the best way to master the unknown wilderness was to map it. Maps tamed the unknown, reduced it to civilization, and harnessed it for Western consciousness. What was Smith doing when he was captured by Indians in December 1607? He had left the small barge behind in the James River; he had left two companions and an Indian who accompanied him farther up the river behind to guard the canoe when he went on with an Indian guide. Though we only pick up the information in bits and pieces, we learn that Smith was carrying a compass, a tablet, and writing materials (as well as, of course, a snapchance pistol, a sword, and a musket). Clearly, he was mapping the area. Exploring the local streams and landmarks with an Indian guide, he encountered a large hunting party and was captured. As all who have read Smith's writings know, in the summer of 1608 he explored— in two trips filled with incredible dangers and hardships—the Chesapeake Bay and all its major rivers. Why? To bring a geographical blank to knowledge.

A Map of Virginia (1612) presumably expanded and revised the "Mappe of the Bay and Rivers, with an annexed Relation of the Counties and Nattions that inhabit them" (2:187–90) that Smith sent back with Captain Christopher Newport about December 1, 1608. To accompany the 1612 pamphlet, Smith made an excellent map of the Chesapeake Bay area.[5] He drafted details and overviews of the Chesapeake Bay for William Hole who engraved the map on a copper plate. The map itself appeared before August 7, 1612 (when Samuel Purchas entered *Purchas His Pilgrimage* in the Stationers' registers), but the pamphlet entitled *A Map* was printed slightly later that year.[6] The Maltese crosses that mark the limits of Smith's own exploration are an extraordinary feature. The legend in the map's upper right explains: "To the crosses hath bin discouerd / what beyond is by relation." (The same information appears in the pamphlet [1:150–51].) In his map, Smith characteristically discriminated reality from myth. The map is a masterpiece, amazingly accurate for the areas that he actually explored.

Neurotic naysayers of the late nineteenth and early twentieth centuries claimed that Smith could not have been responsible for the map because he never formally studied cartography—which is like saying Shakespeare could not have written his plays because (of all the inane reasons!) he did not go to college.[7] Anyone who has read Smith carefully knows that he not only had an excellent education but that he studied (and trained physically) independently to make himself a master of his chosen fields of expertise. He was capable of immense discipline. It would have been out of character for him not to have learned mapmaking as well as navigation— skills essential to his early professions as a soldier and sailor and to his later occupations as an explorer and colonist.

Unlike *A True Relation*, *A Map* is divided into chapters. Ideally, the organization should have been presented in a table of contents, but chapter divisions occur, without announcement or numbering, as one reads the pamphlet. After the general geographical description, the first three divisions are entitled: "Of such things which are naturall in Virginia and how they use them" (1:151); "Of their Planted fruits in Virginia and how they use them" (in effect, a chapter on Indian agriculture [1:156]); and "The commodities in Virginia or that may be had by industrie" (1:159—a brief two paragraphs on the possibilities of Virginia as a place for pasturage and shipbuilding. Among the many passages in Smith's writings (and in colonial American literature) that the modern reader appreciates with both a feeling of superiority and with sympathy for the greenhorn is Smith's description of a third kind of plum (the persimmon): "The fruit is like a medler; it is first greene, then yellow, and red when it is ripe: if it be not ripe it will drawe a mans mouth awrie, with much torment; but when it is ripe, it is as delicious as an Apricock" (1:152).

Over half of *A Map* concerns Smith's observations of the Virginia Indians (1:160–77), devoting special attention to their religion and government. Smith's commentary in *A Map* is full of geographical information. He recorded Indian names, Indian tribes, locations of Indian villages, information from Indians, and information about specific Indians. Smith added his observations upon Indian customs, manners, religion, mores, and government. No other seventeenth-century observer gave so many acute ethnological details—except, possibly, Roger Williams. In structure, *A Map* was modeled upon Thomas Harriot's *A Briefe and True Report of the New Found Land of Virginia* (1588), but just as Smith's pamphlet contains a much more detailed and accurate map, so too its information about the geography, the flora and fauna, the raising of corn and other crops, and the Indian culture in general is all much fuller than Harriot's. We must regret, though, that Smith, unlike Harriot, had no artist with him comparable to John White. Consequently, no set of engravings like those that adorned Harriot's folio edition (1590) of *A Briefe and True Report* are found in *A Map*.

Smith's third Virginia pamphlet, *The Proceedings of the English Colonie in Virginia* (1612),[8] a 116-page quarto appended to *A Map*, narrates the Virginia colony's history from December 1606 to the summer of 1610. Since Smith left Virginia in October 1609, the latter part of *The Proceedings* was based upon others' reports. Indeed, Smith claimed merely to compile *The Proceedings* from the writings of others: especially Thomas Studley (the first cape merchant, who died August 28, 1607), Anas Todkill (a servant of Captain John Martin), Dr. Walter Russell, Nathaniel Powell (d. 1622), Richard Wiffin and William Fettiplace (who later collaborated on a commendatory poem for Smith's *Description of New England*), and Richard Pots (a 1608 colonist and clerk of the council in Virginia). Smith evidently took their various writings,[9] revised and expanded them, and made them into a connected story of early Virginia history. Then he turned the manuscript over to the Reverend William Symonds for further editing. Howard Mumford Jones hypothesized convincingly that Symonds provided the book's excellent structure (the division into twelve chapters), but contrary to Jones, I cannot believe that Symonds wrote the eighteen set speeches. They are based upon actual speeches, and Smith wrote rhetorical pieces in his earlier tract, *A True Relation*, and certainly wrote later speeches.[10] Perhaps Jones only meant, however, that Symonds was responsible for distinguishing the speeches rhetorically. They are more deliberately set off in *The Proceedings* than they were in *A True Relation*—and Philip Barbour's edition deliberately differentiates them even more by typography. Both the rhetorical and the typographical emphases increase their dramatic effect. Though many persons contributed to *The Proceedings*, the pamphlet was primarily Smith's.

The Proceedings (1612) lacks many adventures and personal touches of *A True Relation* (1608), but it gives more details concerning the voyage to Virginia, and it imposes a better structure upon the early years. The events that Smith rather breathlessly and confusingly told earlier are now divided into four chapters. Chapter 1 describes the voyage, the first exploration, the settlement at Jamestown, and the exploration up the James River, ending with Captain Newport's departure for England on June 15 (a mistake for June 22), 1607, and a list of the "first planters" (1:207–9). Chapter 2, "What happened till the first supply," chronicles the sickly time during the summer of 1607 when 50 of the 105 colonists died, the building of Jamestown, Smith's early trading expeditions, his captivity, and the attempts by some colonists to flee from Virginia. Chapter 3, "The arrival of the first supply with their proceedings and returne," tells of Newport's effort to trade with Powhatan, the burning of Jamestown, the foolish loading of Newport's ship with supposed gold, and the sailing of Newport with Edward Maria

Wingfield and Gabriel Archer for England on April 10, 1608. And chapter 4, "The arivall of the Phoenix, her returne, and other accidents," chronicles the rebuilding of Jamestown, the arrival of Captain Francis Nelson in the *Phoenix*, continuing troubles with the Indians, a sarcastic account of "The adventures of Captaine Martin" (who returned with Nelson to England), and the names of those in the first supply who came with Newport and with Nelson in 1608.

The following eight chapters cover events not in *A True Relation*, beginning with two chapters briefly describing Smith's exploring expeditions up the Chesapeake Bay. Happily, the realistic, homely details that characterize Smith's personal vision and writings frequently appear herein. After encountering a second summer storm (the first was "an extreame gust of wind, raine, thunder, and lightning"; and the second blew overboard "our fore-mast," filled the barge with water, and nearly sunk it), Smith's company, in the following calm, repaired "our fore saile with our shirts" and "set saile for the maine" (1:225–26). Chapters 7 through 11 tell the story of Smith's presidency, including the danger-filled expedition in January 1608/9 to Powhatan at Werowocomoco and on to Opechancanough at Pamunkey.

The twelfth and final chapter tells of the dissensions and troubles brought by the third supply and of Smith's terrible accident returning back down the James River from present-day Richmond: "Sleeping in his boat . . . accidentallie, one fired his powder bag, which tore his flesh from his bodie and thighes, 9, or 10. inches square in a most pittifull manner" (1:272). After Smith left Virginia for medical help, the chapter quickly brings the events down to the arrival of Sir Thomas Dale on May 10, 1611. *The Proceedings* concludes with the Reverend William Symonds's note upon returning the revised manuscript ("the fruit of my labours") to Smith (1:278).

Smith's three Virginia tracts constitute our primary source for Virginia's earliest years. He gave more detailed and exact information than any other early writer; his writings are more exciting than others (though William Strachey's later "True Reportory of the Wreck and Redemption of Sir Thomas Gates, Knight" is a classic shipwreck narrative—and inspired Shakespeare's *Tempest*);[11] and his plain style is more readable than his contemporaries' ornate and fulsome prose. The three pamphlets, however, are primarily reportorial, with only occasional glimpses into his dissatisfaction with the existing social order and without the clearly stated radical vision that America should and would be the scene of a new social order. Anticipations of these attitudes occur, but they are comparatively muted.

Smith devoted his next two pamphlets to New England. The first, *A Description of New England* (an eighty-two-page quarto[12] entered for publication in the Stationers' registers on June 3, 1616) reveals that he had become an excellent writer of travel and promotion literature and that an American Dream had come to obsess him. Like *A Map of Virginia*, his *Description of New England* was written to accompany a map, the New England coast from Cape Cod to Penobscot Bay and Castine, Maine. Just as his Chesapeake Bay map excelled all others to the last quarter of the seventeenth century, so too his New England map was the best for a half century. Happily, the New England map contains in the upper left an engraving of Smith, the only good source for his physical appearance. Smith drafted *A Description* in the late summer or early fall of 1615, while a prisoner on a French pirate ship commanded by Captain Poyrune, sailing "about the Iles of the Assores, where to keepe my perplexed thoughts from too much meditation of my miserable estate, I writ this Discourse, thinking to have sent it to you of his Majesties Councell by some ship or other" (2:432). He revised and expanded the book in spring 1616 and the printers finished it on June 18, 1616 (1:361).

A Description chronicles Smith's voyage to New England in 1614, describes New England's location, notices the area's Indian tribes and its natural resources, cites various successful fishing expeditions to Cape Cod and the Maine coast, and makes a notable appeal for colonization. In perhaps his most brilliant neologism, Smith named the area "New England"; Smith's projected New England colony was of the utmost importance in the history of American colonization. Smith also narrated his unsuccessful 1615 attempt to sail to New England and his adventures among the French pirates who captured him. Throughout the tract, he emphasized America's continental size, its economic possibilities, and its opportunities for adventurous, hardworking individuals. In New England, "there is victuall to feede us, wood of all sorts, to build Boats, Ships, or Barkes; the fish at our doores, pitch, tarre, masts, yards, and most of other necessaries onely for making" (1:332).

More imposing as a publication than his earlier writings, *A Description of New England* shows that by 1616 Smith was a knowledgeable author. Books stood a better chance of being thought important if they had testimonials. In the seventeenth century, literary expertise was as highly respected as economic success. Smith solicited commendatory verses from three litterateurs. To judge by the authors of the poems for this and his later books, Smith associated more with London's men of letters and intellectuals than with its courtiers or businessmen. He asked three litterateurs to contribute verses: the poet and essayist John Davies (1565?–1618), the playwright and theater manager Richard Gunnell (c. 1585–1634), and the young poet (and later Puritan) George Wither (1588–1667). He solicited poems from five former comrades-in-arms in Virginia: John Codrington, Rawley Crashaw, Michael Fettiplace, William Fettiplace, and Richard Wiffin. Perhaps most surprising, he asked two of his former soldiers in eastern Europe for testimonial verses— Sergeant Edward Robinson and Ensign Thomas Carlton. Smith also had several special presentation copies printed with unique dedications: two survive, one dedicated to Lord Ellesmere, the lord chancellor and the other to Sir Edward Coke.[13] Despite all attempts to play the literary patronage game, Smith failed to gain supporters—no doubt partially because his independent personality contradicted the courtier's role.

Smith's second New England pamphlet, a brief twenty pages, was entered at Stationers' Hall on December 11, 1620. *New Englands Trials* (1620)[14] was actually a slightly revised version of a letter Smith had written to Francis Bacon (who had on July 12, 1618, been raised to the peerage as Baron Verulam). Though the letter to Bacon failed to enlist his financial support for the New England project, it evidently inspired Bacon to write his essay "Of Plantations." As E. G. R. Taylor has noted, Bacon reflected Smith's writings throughout the essay. Bacon's specific opinion that the "establishment of subsistence farming should be the colonists' first care" and his list of the kinds of occupations especially needed at the founding of a colony were direct borrowings.[15] Interestingly, Sir Edward Coke, the great lawyer, judge, and major creator of England's rights of the people, was the only person to whom Smith dedicated two of his works, with special cancels honoring Coke bound in both *A Description of New England* (1616) and *New Englands Trials* (1620).[16]

Smith's New England tracts solicited backers for colonization. In both the letter to Bacon and *New Englands Trials*, he recapitulated his former description and exploration of New England before giving economic details concerning the financial success that could be realized by fishing off the New England coast. His "proofs" enumerated the ships that had productively sailed to that coast since his 1614 voyage. In the Bacon letter he brought the record of New England voyages down to 1618, then, in *New Englands Trials*, to "this yeare," 1620, adding a note on the ships preparing to sail in 1621. He estimated the chances of setting up a New England colony and concluded with a peroration. In the letter to Bacon, he asked for that noble's support; and in *New Englands Trials*, he requested the backing of the nobility, the merchant companies, and others to "inhabit as good a countrey as any in the world." He promised that he would commit "my life, and what I have . . . if God please, and you permit" (1:405).

No one has remarked that the Bacon letter and its two expansions are structured upon the commonest seventeenth-century prose genre, the sermon. They all begin with a "text," in this case not a biblical quotation but a thesis—wealth was to be gained in New England. Smith followed with a series of amplifications: quotations or allusions from authorities like John Dee, Tobias Gentleman, John Keymor, and others. Then a series of "Proofes" (labeled as such in the margins) occupy the body of the tract, just as they do in the common sermon of the day. A refutation of possible objections follows (1:400–402). In the only change from the normal Anglican, and especially Puritan, formal sermon structure,[17] Smith supplied a list of the economic charges for a voyage (1:402–3). Concluding the pamphlet, Smith wrote an appeal and peroration (1:404–6).

In 1622, after news of the Virginia massacre reached England, Smith issued a revised version of *New Englands Trials*, expanding it from twenty to thirty-two pages.[18] He added an account of the founding of the Plymouth colony (1:429–32), an interesting letter from "New Plimmoth in New England" by William Hilton,[19] a report of how he controlled the Indians when he was in Virginia (1:432–33), a reference to his captivity and to being saved by Pocahontas, and additional propaganda for colonization. His allusion to the *Paragon*'s sailing "this 16 of October" to supply the Plymouth colonists (1:434) fixes the pamphlet's composition as during October 1622.

Smith's next work was his magnum opus. His earlier publica-

tions—the three Virginia tracts and the two New England ones—
had all been pamphlets. Only *A Description of New England* had presented itself as a high-style publication, with the usual trappings of
literary importance. But *The Generall Historie of Virginia, New-
England, and the Summer Isles* (entered in the Stationers' registers on
July 12, 1624)[20] was a full-dress folio (all the earlier works had been
quartos)—a large imposing book of 254 pages, complete with a
beautifully engraved title page,[21] revised versions of Smith's maps
of Virginia and New England, an engraving of Frances Stuart,
duchess of Richmond and Lennox, to whom the folio was dedicated (she no doubt subsidized its publication), a map of Bermuda
and the Summer Isles, and, happily, a "Map of Ould Virginia" depicting Smith's Virginia adventures. Smith solicited new commendatory verses by friends like Samuel Purchas and reprinted those
that had appeared earlier in his *Description of New England*. As the
internal date of September 23, 1622, indicates (2:88),[22] Smith evidently set at work on *The Generall Historie* before he paused to com-
pose the revised version of *New Englands Trials*.

The *Generall Historie* first comprehensively treated America's
English colonization and remained the only overview of the English American colonies until John Ogilby's 1671 *America*.[23] Smith
incorporated and expanded his earlier publications into *The Generall Historie*, though he used the well-organized *Proceedings* (1612) as
his primary Virginia source rather than the breathless, jumbled *A
True Relation* of 1608, thereby omitting some materials unique to
the earlier pamphlet. But Smith retold his Virginia and New England explorations and exploits with as much additional detail as
he could remember—and with as many additional sources as were
available. The most adventure-filled story of early American discovery and exploration, *The Generall Historie* is also the best single
source for Chesapeake Bay area Indian ethnology.

Smith divided *The Generall Historie* into six books. Book 1, based
primarily upon materials published in Hakluyt's *Principal Navigations* and Purchas's *Purchas His Pilgrimage* (1613; rev. ed., 1614; rev.
ed., 1617), takes the story of the English explorations and settlements of America from the mythical Middle Ages accounts to 1605
(2:62–96). Book 2 revised and reprinted Smith's *Map of Virginia*
(2:100–132). Book 3 revised, greatly expanded, and reprinted *The
Proceedings* (2:136–227). Book 4 tells the Virginia story from

Smith's departure in 1609 to 1624 (2:231–334). The fifth book, devoted to the history of Bermuda from 1593 to 1624, relied upon manuscripts and printed materials by others, with occasional observations and asides by Smith. And Book 6, on New England (2:397–475), revised and enlarged his earlier works, the *Description of New England* and *New Englands Trials*, adding materials from manuscripts, oral sources, and the second Plymouth colony promotion tract, *A Relation or Journal of the Beginning and Proceedings of the English Plantation Setted at Plimoth in New England* (1622), by William Bradford, Edward Winslow, and others.[24]

Book 4, the action-packed story of Smith's adventures in Virginia, gives the story of his captivity in greater detail, with several additional episodes told for the first time, though two incidents found in *A True Relation* were omitted. The most famous addition, of course, is the episode wherein Pocahontas saved Smith. His writing here is at its worst, the story occupying one long, convoluted, rambling sentence (perhaps revealing, even in 1624, his reluctance to show himself helpless and saved by a girl):

> The Queene of Appamatuck was appointed to bring him water to wash his hands, another brought him a bunch of feathers, in stead of a Towell to dry them: having feasted him after their best barbarous manner they could, a long consultation was held, but the conclusion was, two great stones were brought before Powhatan: then as many as could layd hands on him, dragged him to them, and thereon laid his head, and being ready with their clubs, to beate out his braines, Pocahontas the Kings dearest daughter, when no intreaty could prevaile, got his head in her armes, and laid her owne upon his to save him from death: whereat the Emperour was contented he should live to make him hatchets, and her bells, beads, and copper; for they thought him as well of all occupations as themselves. [2:151]

No one in Smith's day ever expressed doubt about the episode, and many persons who must have known the truth—including John Rolfe, Pocahontas, her sister, and brother-in-law—were in London in 1616 when Smith publicized the story in a letter to the queen (2:258–60).[25] As for the exact nature of the event, it seems probable that Smith was being ritualistically killed. Reborn, he was adopted into the tribe, with Pocahontas as his sponsor. But Smith, of course, did not realize the nature of the initiation ceremony.

Retelling in *The Generall Historie* the story of his encounter in December 1607 with Opechancanough, Smith added details and an episode that he earlier omitted. Trapped in the swamp, he had just surrendered.

> Then according to their composition they drew him forth and led him to the fire, where his men were slaine. Diligently they chafed his benummed limbs. He demanding for their Captaine, they shewed him Opechankanough, King of Pamaunkee, to whom he gave a round Ivory double compass Dyall. Much they marvailed at the playing of the Fly and Needle, which they could see so plainely, and yet not touch it, because of the glasse that covered them. But when he demonstrated by that Globe-like Jewell, the roundnesse of the earth, and skies, the spheare of the Sunne, Moone, and Starrs, and how the Sunne did chase the night round about the world continually; the greatnesse of the Land and Sea, the diversitie of Nations, varietie of complexions, and how we were to them Antipodes, and many other such like matters, they all stood as amazed with admiration. Notwithstanding, within an houre after they tyed him to a tree, and as many as could stand about him prepared to shoot him, but the King holding up the Compass in his hand, they all laid downe their Bowes and Arrowes, and in a triumphant manner led him to Orapaks, where he was after their manner kindly feasted, and well used. [2:147]

The expanded version makes the scene more dramatic and makes Smith's explanations more realistic. The incident of tying Smith to a tree and preparing to shoot him was omitted from *A True Relation* (1608); the captivity is barely mentioned in *The Proceedings* (1612).

But the longest additions to *The Generall Historie* do not concern his captivity. They describe more details in the two expeditions up the Chesapeake Bay (present only in abbreviated form in *The Proceedings*). Another significant addition to *The Generall Historie* is the letter that Smith sent to "the Treasurer and Councell of Virginia" about December 1, 1608. It abruptly began:

I Received your Letter, wherein you write, that our minds are so set upon faction, and idle conceits in dividing the Country without your consents, and that we feed You but with ifs and ands, hopes, and some few proofes; as if we would keepe the mystery of the business to our selves: and that we must expresly follow your instructions sent by Captain Newport: the charge of whose voyage amounts to neare two thousand pounds, the which if we cannot defray by the Ships returne, we are like to remain as banished men. To these particulars I humbly intreat your Pardons if I offend you with my rude Answer. [2:187–88]

Smith sarcastically told the London gentlemen of the council that they had been repeatedly duped by Newport and the sailors, that they knew nothing of the actual conditions in Virginia, and that they should leave decisions to those in Virginia: "Though I be no scholer, I am past a schooleboy; and I desire but to know, what either you, and these here doe know, but that I have learned to tell you by the continuall hazard of my life" (2:188). To the statement that the charge of Captain Newport's voyage "amounts to neare two thousand pounds," Smith replied that the colonists "have not received the value of an hundred pounds" of goods and not food worth "twenty pounds" (2:188, 189). Smith claimed that Newport, the sailors, and the company's officers siphoned off both goods and food: "The Souldiers say many of your officers maintaine their families out of that you send us: and that Newport hath an hundred pounds a yeare for carrying newes." He referred contemptuously to Newport's explorations and added: "Now that you should know, I have made you as great a discovery as he, for lesse charge then he spendeth you every meale; I have sent you this Mappe of the Bay and Rivers, with an annexed Relation of the Countries and Nations that inhabit them, as you may see at large" (2:189). He presumably referred to drafts of both the map of Virginia and the pamphlet later entitled *A Map of Virginia* (1612). He concluded by insulting the council with instructions on keeping accounts: "And I humbly intreat you hereafter, let us know what we should receive, and not stand to the Saylers courtesie to leave us what they please, els you may charge us with what you will, but we not you with any thing" (2:190).

Moses Coit Tyler pronounced the letter "a most vigorous, tren-

chant, and characteristic piece of writing, a transcript of the intense spirit of the man who wrote it, all ablaze with the light it casts into that primal hot-bed of wrangling, indolence, and misery, the village of Jamestown." "Hotspur rhetoric," Tyler called it, "jerking with impatience, truculence, and noble wrath."[26] Appropriately, the first reply from the New World to English assumptions of superiority announced that the English were fooling themselves and that the colonists would talk back.

In his New England writings and in *The Generall Historie*, Smith changed from a writer of personal adventures and discoveries to a promoter of colonization and a visionary propagandist for a different kind of civilization and social order in the New World. He still in great part wrote about his personal experiences, but the philosophy underlying his experiences and the theses pervading the pamphlets and book became increasingly his most important message.

After publication of *The Generall Historie*, Smith no doubt thought of himself as a writer as well as an expert soldier, sailor, explorer, and colonist. In 1626 war with Spain threatened England. A new navy had to be raised. Smith, an old sea dog, saw a need and an opportunity. No good guide to seamanship existed. Urged by Sir Samuel Saltonstall (3:142), he wrote one: *An Accidence [i.e., the basics], or The Path-way to Experience. Necessary for All Young Sea-men, or Those That Are Desirous to Goe to Sea* (entered in the Stationers' registers on October 23, 1626).[27] The title page proclaims his achievements and expertise: "Written by Captaine Iohn Smith sometimes Governour of *Virginia*, and Admirall of New England." The historian of navigation D. W. Waters has commented, "In 1626 there probably was no man of forty-five in England so well qualified to instruct the 'many young Gentlemen and Valiant spirits of all sorts' desirous, now that war had broken out again . . . 'to Trye their Fortunes at Sea.'"[28]

A forty-six-page pamphlet, *An Accidence* begins by listing the names and duties of the sailors aboard a ship. Smith described the specialized vocabulary used for all a ship's parts, for the sea's variable conditions, and for armament. Smith also advised commanders how to behave and what provisions to take. The list of provisions concludes with relatively expensive delicacies like "the best wines, the best Waters, the juyce of Lemons for the Scurvey," and more. Smith knew such items would seem extravagant to some

landlubbers and unnecessary to some old sea dogs—and to most
beginning captains—so he explained:

> Some it may bee will say, I would have men rather to feast
> then fight. But I say the want of those necessaries, occa-
> sions the losse of more men, then in any English fleet hath
> bin slaine in any fight since 88. for when a man is ill sicke,
> or at the poynt of death, I would know whether a dish of
> buttered Rice, with a little Cinamon and Sugar, a little
> minced meate, or roast beefe, a few stewed Prunes, a race
> of greene ginger, a flap-Jacke, a Can of fresh water brued
> with a little Cinamon, Ginger and Sugar, be not better then
> a little poore John, or salt fish, with oyle and mustard, or
> bisket, butter, cheese or oatemeale pottage on fish dayes,
> salt beefe, porke and pease and sixe shillings beere, this is
> your ordinary ships allowance, and good for them are well,
> if well conditioned, which is not alwayes, as sea-men can
> too well witnesse. [3:29]

The most interesting part of *An Accidence* is not, however, the
beginning or the ending (where the above apology occurs)—Smith
broke into dramatic narrative when he began to consider, as the
marginal heading proclaims, "The Termes of Warre." War fired his
imagination. He abandoned the dry, dictionary-like listing of terms
that otherwise fill the book. He shifted into an account of a sea
fight. Not an actual one but a combination of all the fights at sea he
had lived through and was now reliving. Nothing like it occurs in
the book that may have inspired Smith's title, Gervase Markham's
The Souldier's Accidence (1625).[29] Indeed, nothing approaches
Smith's lively imaginative passage in any dictionary I know. The
long description of a sea fight, rendered in short, breathless verbal
clauses, is a wonderful example of Smith's literary ability and imagination. Here is an excerpt (about a quarter of the whole) from the
narrative:

> Give him a chase peece, A broad side, and runne a head,
> make ready to tacke about, give him your sterne peeces, be
> yare at helme, hale him with a noyse of Trumpets. We are
> shot through and through, and betweene winde and water,
> trye the pumpe. Maister let us breathe and refresh a little,
> sling a man overboord to stop the leake, done, done, is all

ready againe, Yea, yea: beare up close with him, with all your great and small shot charge him; Boord him on his wether quarter, lash fast your graplins and sheare off, then runne stemlins the mid ships. Boord and boord, or thwart the hawse; we are foule on each other: The ships on fire; Cut any thing to get cleere, and smother the fire with wet clothes, We are cleere, and the fire is out, God be thanked. The day is spent, let us consult. [3:22]

Smith proceeded to take up the topic of relationships between fleets. Concluding the pamphlet, Smith asked that his "brief Discourse, and my selfe" be left to the "friendly construction and good opinion" of those who actually ventured to sea (3:29).

He signed *An Accidence*, "John Smith Writ this with his owne Hand." Within the year, a manuscript copy of Henry Mainwaring's "Seaman's Dictionary" came to Smith's attention. Mainwaring defined many terms that Smith used in his *Accidence* and numerous others. So Smith revised and enlarged his book on seamanship, added all of Mainwaring's additions, organized it into fifteen chapters, and published it as *A Sea Grammar, with the Plaine Exposition of Smiths Accidence for Young Sea-men, Enlarged* (1627).[30] A substantial quarto of eighty-eight pages, *A Sea Grammar* "is usually considered the first work on seamanship in the English language" (3:42). Smith knew that he was making a new contribution and said: "much hath bin writ concerning the art of war by land, yet nothing concerning the same at Sea" (3:47). Smith gave the book full-dress treatment and solicited commendatory poems from his good friends Sir Samuel Saltonstall and Sir Samuel's son Wye; from Edward Jorden, who had evidently been in Virginia; and from the minor litterateurs Edward Ingham and George Buck. Filled with information, *A Sea Grammar* is distinguished by occasional bits of personal information and experience. Smith's definitions of various kinds of storms conclude with "A Hericano": "A Hericano is so violent in the West Indies, it will continue three, foure, or five weekes, but they have it not past once in five, six, or seven yeeres; but then it is with such extremity that the Sea flies like raine, and the waves so high, they over flow the low grounds by the Sea, in so much, that ships have been driven over tops of high trees there growing, many leagues into the land, and there left, as was Captaine Francis Nelson an Englishman, and an excellent Sea man for one" (3:92).

Smith revised his fine imaginative passages on a fight at sea and the terrible conditions of ordinary sailors. He also revised the bibliographical references to books about gunnery and navigation. The references enumerate all the best treatises available on the two subjects. Smith, however, ever practical, added at the end of his list of books on gunnery, "But to bee a good Gunner you must learne it by practise" (3:108), and concluded his advice on navigation with, "get some of these bookes, but practice is the best" (3:111). The approach typifies Smith's usual procedure—study the theory and then practice and practice. D. W. Waters wrote: "*The Sea Grammar* in fact did for ships and seamanship what had already been done by other writers for navigation and gunnery; it collected, collated, codified, defined, and explained the ordinary workaday knowledge of seamen and their ships; how they built, rigged, manned, victualled, armed, handled, fought, and sailed a ship at sea."[31]

An Accidence and *A Sea Grammar* mark a hiatus in Smith's development as a writer. They demonstrate that he had become a professional author and could, if he desired, turn out an expert book for a particular purpose. They added both to his already well-established patriotism and to his well-known abilities as a sailor. But for his all-important intellectual and literary careers, they are essentially static statements, advancing our knowledge of his thought and abilities little.

In 1630 Smith published his autobiography, *The True Travels, Adventvres, and Observations of Captaine Iohn Smith* (entered in the Stationers' registers on August 29, 1629).[32] The title page features his most extraordinary adventures, "his three single combats betwixt the Christian Armie and the Turkes . . . how he was taken prisoner by the Turks, sold for a Slave . . . how he slew the Bashaw of Nalbrits in Cambia, and escaped from the Turkes and Tartars." Smith did not retell any of his American adventures, for *The True Travels* was printed as a folio of seventy-two pages so that it could be considered a supplement to *The Generall Historie*—as the long title announced, *Together with a Continuation of His Generall History of Virginia, Summer-Isles, New England, and Their Proceedings, since 1624. to This Present 1629.*

The ambiguous relationship between Smith's autobiography and *The Generall Historie* is remarkable. On the one hand, Smith could be said to have been modest in *The True Travels* by not reprinting all those passages in *The Generall Historie* that describe his adventures and explorations; but on the other, Smith could be said to have been encompassing the entire history of the English explorations within his own autobiography, making them coterminous with himself. No doubt it simply made good sense to omit his American adventures from *The True Travels*; but there is a symbolic truth, from Smith's point of view, in regarding the entire English colonization of North American as an aspect of his own life.

The True Travels is a classic autobiography of initiation and adventure. Smith's story of being hoodwinked and cheated at age twenty by "foure French Gallants well attended, faining to him the one to be a great Lord" (3:157), has archetypal reverberations of the innocent youth. The book (through chapter 20) is filled with high adventure. Smith's appreciation of the French pirate Captain Merham is striking. Driven by a storm from Safi, Morocco, to the Canary Islands, Merham encountered two Spanish men-of-war. They pretended to be "but two poore distressed Biskiners" and told Merham "to come aboord them, and take what he would" (3:212). But Merham was not fooled. "The old fox, seeing himself in the lions pawes, sprung his loufe," wrote Smith zestfully. Merham fought the Spanish men-of-war for two days. The Spanish boarded him twice and both times were repulsed. Finally, during the second night, the Spanish "either lost them, or left them" (3:213). Merham lost twenty-seven men and had sixteen wounded. After examining the ship, Merham found "they had received 140. great shot." Smith never mentioned himself or what role he played in the fight—but we can be sure that he was in the thick of the action.

The highlight of *The True Travels* is Smith's three duels in single combat against the champions of the Turkish army. Each tournament took place in a large arena, "the Rampiers all beset with faire Dames, and men in Arms," the champions striding out to a flourish of music, their pages leading their horses and bearing their lances, pistols, battle-axes, and swords. Smith described the first Turkish champion in detail: "Turbashaw with a noise of Howboyes entred the field well mounted and armed; on his shoulders were fixed a paire of great wings, compacted of Eagles feathers within a ridge of silver, richly garnished with gold and precious stones, a Janizary before him, bearing his Lance, on each side another leading his horse" (3:172). The ritualistic pageantry ended in a grisly finale, with the survivor raising the helmet of his dead opponent and cutting off his head. The victor then put the head on the top of his lance and presented it to his commander. Acceptance of the head marked the commander's pleasure with the course of the combat.

Smith's last publication was a forty-eight-page quarto pamphlet, *Advertisements for the Unexperienced Planters of New-England, or Any Where* (1631).[33] Though it was not entered in the Stationers' registers, interior evidence reveals that it was written in October 1630 (3:293). As George Watson Cole, Howard Mumford Jones, and Everett Emerson have all said, from a literary point of view it is Smith's best single publication.[34] He evidently wrote rapidly, and in all his other works the prose is occasionally jumbled and confusing. But it is consistently clear and excellent in *Advertisements*. Howard Mumford Jones pointed out that a tone of "sardonic humor everywhere" distinguishes the work.[35] Well-organized into fifteen chapters, *Advertisements* encompasses more general information than any of Smith's earlier writings. Though it does not rise to the pitch of exhortation achieved by *A Description of New England*, immerse the reader in the exotic ethnology of *A Map of Virginia*, relate the numerous adventures of *The Generall Historie*'s Virginia books, or tell such incredible feats as *The True Travels*, it contains more solid general information about colonization than any previous English book. With a thorough knowledge of all past English successes and failures, Smith assessed the present and future prospects for England's colonies.

Smith's *Advertisements* contains his fine poem entitled "The Sea Marke." Because the poem is very good, some scholars have doubted that he wrote it. After all, he was not certainly known to have written any other poetry. My discovery in the early 1960s, however, that Smith had written commendatory poems for two books by friends proved that he could be, on occasion, a competent poet (3:369–70). In his third and last poem, Smith portrayed himself as a buoy or sea mark—a sign to warn sailors of the danger of a treacherous place. From the beginning "Aloofe, aloofe, and come no neare" (Aluff, i.e., luff your helm, keep clear) to the off/eye rhyme "Dome" (doom) in the final word, the poem effectively portrays Smith as a trailblazer who had expended his own life marking the way for others to follow.

Smith's last two publications, *The True Travels* and *Advertisements*, present retrospective and prospective visions of life in the Old World and in the New. They reveal more bitter dissatisfactions with the remains of the feudal system than any of his previous writings and at the same time express greater hopes for the future, particularly for future Americans, than he had dared voice in his earlier publications. As he grew older, his radicalism grew more obvious;

his discontents grew greater (foreshadowing, perhaps, the numerous radical expressions of the 1640s and 1650s); his achievements grew, in retrospect, more awesome; and he grew more famous. The last book, *Advertisements for the Unexperienced Planters*, expresses all these strains simultaneously, within an authorial voice that ironically surveys the totality of his life and accomplishments.

Even with the publication of *Advertisements*, the fifty-one-year-old Smith hoped that his writing was not over. He was composing another great work—in scope larger than *The Generall Historie of Virginia*—a "history of the Sea." At the end of his life, Smith saw himself as a successor to Hakluyt and Purchas. He evidently planned to trace the history of exploration of the world from the ancients to the present, featuring the development of seamanship technology (the compass and quadrant made the exploration of the world possible) and the history of mapping and mapmakers. He had been collecting accounts of exploration and adding his own "observations"—"if God be pleased I live to finish it" (3:290)—but he died on June 21, 1631, age fifty-two, too weak to sign his will.[36]

3

Smith as Travel Writer

This river is a musket shot broad, each side being should
[shallow] bayes, a narrow channell, but three fadom, his
course for eighteene miles, almost directly South, and by
West, where beginneth the first inhabitants; for a mile it
turneth directly East, towards the West, a great bay and a
white chaukie Iland, convenient for a Fort: his next
course South, where within a quarter of a mile, the river
divideth in two, the neck a plaine high Corne field, the
wester bought a high plaine likewise, the Northeast
answerable in all respects: in these plaines are planted
aboundance of houses and people. They may containe
1000. Acres of most excellent fertill ground, so sweete, so
pleasant, so beautifull, and so strong a prospect, for an
invincible strong Citty, with so many commodities, that I
know as yet I have not seene: This is within one daies
journey of Chawwonocke. The river falleth into the
Kings river, within twelve miles of Cape Henrie.

—Smith's description of the Nansemond River (tributary of the
lower James, which he here called "the Kings river") in *A True
Relation* (1608; 1:81)

C.Smith taketh the King of Pamavnkee priſoner 1608

From Smith's map of "Ould Virginia" (1624), top right compartment

THOREAU wrote: "We may say there have been but so many men as there are surnames, and of all the John-Smiths there has been but one true John Smith, and he of course is dead."[1] Captain John Smith, for Thoreau, dominated all other persons ever named John Smith because his style constantly affirmed his unique personality and place in American literature. He was the one early seventeenth-century American[2] writer whom Douglas Bush selected to discuss in the Oxford history of English literature. Smith's vigorous personality, sturdy eloquence, devotion to America, and perseverance are the qualities that Bush admired.[3] In this brief chapter, I intend to assess only two qualities of Smith's writings characteristic of travel literature. Of course, the traveler himself is the most interesting single subject of travel literature, but the analysis of Smith's character is a major subject of this entire book.

Adventure

The best travel literature has the appeal of adventure and/or the exotic. Captain John Smith's writings have both. His life was full of high adventure: fighting in great massed battles as one of thousands of soldiers, dueling as champion in single combat, serving as a slave in the Middle East, rebelling and killing his master and making his way back through Russia to Europe, being abducted by pirates and fighting in various ship battles throughout the Mediterranean world, exploring in America, defending himself and other whites from numerous Indian attacks, being captured by Indians and saved from execution by Pocahontas . . . the exploits go on and on. Further, Smith explored more unknown areas in America and reported in detail more unknown Indian tribes and exotic rituals than any contemporary.

His most famous single deliverance was being saved by Pocahontas, but that episode is celebrated more for its romantic and mythic overtones than for action. More dramatic—and more typical of Smith's great adventures—was the time when he and his men were surrounded by Opechancanough's tribe at Pamunkey in mid-January 1608/9. Invited by Powhatan, Smith had gone to Werowocomoco and then to Pamunkey to trade for corn. While Smith and fourteen men were in the longhouse bargaining with Opechancanough and a few other Indians, John Russell, left outside as a sentry, burst in and announced "that we were all betrayed: for at least seven hundred Salvages well armed, had invironed the house, and beset the fields" (2:200).

Since the company was "dismaied with the thought of such a multitude," Smith exhorted them with a speech:

Worthy Countrey-men, were the mischiefes of my seeming friends no more then the danger of these enemies, I little cared were they as many more: if you dare doe, but as I. But this is my torment, that if I escape them, our malicious Councell with their open mouthed Minions, will make me such a peace breaker (in their opinions in England) as will breake my necke. I could wish those here, that make these seeme Saints, and me an oppressor. But this is the worst of all, wherein I pray you aid mee with you opinions. Should wee beginne with them and surprise the King, we cannot keepe him and defend well our selves. If wee should each kill our man, and so proceed with all in the house; the rest will all fly: then shall wee get no more than the bodies that are slaine, and so starve for victuall. As for their fury it is the least danger; for well you know, being alone assaulted with two or three hundred of them, I made them by the helpe of God compound to save my life. And wee are six-teene, and they but seaven hundred at the most; and as-sure your selves, God will so assist us, that if you dare stand but to discharge your pieces, the very smoake will be suffi-cient to affright them. Yet howsoever, let us fight like men, and not die like sheepe: for by that meanes you know God hath oft delivered mee, and so I trust will now. But first, I will deale with them, to bring it to passe wee may fight for something, and draw them to it by conditions. If you like this motion, promise me you will be valiant. [2:201]

Smith ironically noted that since there was no time for any ar-guments, the men all "vowed to execute whatever hee attempted, or die." Smith first turned to Opechancanough and proposed to fight him man-to-man, winner take all: "I see Opecacanough your plot to murder me, but I feare it not. As yet your men and mine have done no harme, but by our direction. Take therefore your Armes, you see mine, my body shall bee as naked as yours: the Isle in your river is a fit place, if you be contented: and the conquerour (of us two) shall be Lord and Master over all our men. If you have not enough, take time to fetch more, and bring what number you will; so every one bring a basket of corne, against all which I will stake the value in copper, you see I have but fifteene, and our game shall be, the Conquerour take all" (2:201).

Opechancanough, however, tried to placate Smith, saying that the whites had nothing to fear, and asked him to receive a "great present" that waited outside the door of the longhouse. Smith commanded one of his men "to go see what kind of deceit this was, and to receive the present." But the man, afraid, "refused to doe it." With the refusal, wrath overcame Smith. Nearly blind with fury "at that Coward," Smith "commanded Lieutenant Percie, Master West, and the rest to make good the house," ordered Henry Powell and Robert Beheathland to guard the door, and then: "in such a rage snatched the King by his long locke in the middest of his men, with his Pistoll readie bent against his brest. Thus he led the trembling King, neare dead with feare amongst all his people: who delivering the Captaine his Vambrace, Bow, and Arrowes, all his men were easily intreated to cast downe their Armes, little dreaming any durst in that manner have used their King" (2:202).

Standing before hundreds of encircled Indians and holding his snapchance pistol against Opechancanough, Smith offered war or peace. He claimed he promised his God to attempt to maintain friendly relations with the Indians and suggested the supernatural was his ally: "I see (you Pamaunkees) the great desire you have to kill me, and my long suffering your injuries hath imboldened you to this presumption. The cause I have forborne your insolencies, is the promise I made you (before the God I serve) to be your friend, till you give me just cause to be your enemy. If I keepe this vow, my God will keepe me, you cannot hurt me, if I breake it, he will destroy me."

Smith added that he did not depend entirely upon God. He vowed personal revenge upon the Pamunkeys if they attacked his men: "But if you shoot but one Arrow to shed one drop of bloud of any of my men, or steale the least of these Beads, or Copper, I spurne here before you with my foot; you shall see I will not cease revenge (if once I begin) so long as I can heare where to finde one of your Nation that will not deny the name of Pamaunk."

And what if they attacked Smith himself? The warrior Smith challenged them: "But if I be the marke you ayme at, here I stand, shoot he that dare. You promised to fraught my Ship ere I departed, and so you shall, or I meane to load her with your dead carcasses, yet if as friends you will come and trade, I once more promise not to trouble you, except you give me the first occasion, and your King shall be free and be my friend, for I am not come to hurt him or any of you" (2:202). War or peace. Pistol in one hand, Opechancanough's scalp lock in the other, Smith demanded an answer.

The upshot was that "away went their Bowes and Arrowes," and the Indians brought in their corn to trade. But Smith's troubles were hardly over. When the exhausted commander returned to the longhouse, lay down, and fell asleep, some Indians "perceiving him fast asleepe, and the guard somewhat carelesly dispersed, fortie or fiftie of their choise men each with a club, or an English sword in his hand began to enter the house with two or three hundred other, that pressed to second them." Their noise awakened Smith who "being halfe amazed with this suddaine sight, betooke him strait to his sword and target; Master Crashaw and some others charged in like manner; whereat they quickly thronged faster backe then before foreward." And so Opechancanough made a long oration to excuse the intrusion (2:202–3).

As they made their way back down the James River to Jamestown, the Indians tried to ambush them and managed to poison Smith, Francis West, and a few others, but the poison only made them sick and vomit. Smith beat Wecuttanow, the man who brought the poisoned food, and "spurned him like a dogge, as scorning to doe him any worse mischiefe" (2:205). And so they finally arrived back in Jamestown, without losing any men or killing any Indians.

Smith had more adventures than any other colonial writer. Not until Daniel Boone (or perhaps Thomas Cresap or Robert Rogers) did a comparable figure appear in American literature. And what person among the later heroes had as many hairbreadth escapes from dangers and from death? Unlike most later heroes, however, Smith was the primary chronicler of his own exploits. And he told his adventures in a brusque, dramatic, forceful, and lean prose style that differs greatly from his euphuistic contemporaries. His style perfectly matched the man and the adventures.

The Exotic

Smith also featured that other great quality of travel literature— the exotic. The opossum, sea horse, and stingray were among the strange American fauna that he minutely described. Of course, the various Indian individuals, tribes, and ceremonies were all wondrous subjects to the English reader. Smith also told technical details of woodcraft (how to camp comfortably in the bitter cold when the frozen ground was covered with snow [2:191]) that were to become a staple of American writing for the English (William Byrd's *History of the Dividing Line*, Cadwallader Colden's *History of the Five Nations*, and William Bartram's *Travels* later featured such materials). Smith's two exploring expeditions up the Chesapeake Bay combined adventure and the exotic. The exploration of unknown rivers, the discovery of new Indian tribes, and the numerous Indian attacks make these chapters (especially as revised and expanded in *The Generall Historie* [1624]) highpoints of Smith's travel writing. There even occurs one passage of the mysterious exotic. Smith reported that the werowance of Accomack "told us of a straunge accident": "Two dead children by the extreame passions of their parents, or some dreaming visions, phantasie, or affection moved them againe to revisit their dead carkases, whose benummed bodies reflected to the eies of the beholders such pleasant delightfull countenances, as they had regained their vital spirits. This as a miracle drew many to behold them, all which, (being a great part of his people) not long after died, and not any one escaped" (1:225). The strange exotic is also well used in Smith's description of his first opponent in the duels he fought in Transylvania.

In rewriting his earlier accounts of Indian ceremonies for *The Generall Historie*, Smith not only gave greater detail but also attempted to explain the significance of rituals. In *A True Relation* Smith described an elaborate ceremony that took place "three or foure dayes after" he was taken prisoner (1:59). According to the early account, "seven of them in the house where I lay, each with a rattle began at ten a clocke in the morning to sing about the fire, which they invironed with a Circle of meale, and after, a foote or two from that, at the end of each song, layde downe two or three graines of wheate, continuing this order till they have included six or seven hundred in a halfe Circle, and after that two or three more Circles in like maner, a hand bredth from other. That done, at each song, they put betwixt everie three, two or five graines, a little sticke, so counting as an old woman her Pater noster." Though fascinating and detailed, the account is not very dramatic, nor did Smith here discriminate between the different medicine men.

The account in *The Generall Historie* is much fuller. Smith recapitulated being led from Pamunkey to several different Indian tribes on the Rappahannock and Potomac rivers, then back to Pamunkey, "where they entertained him with most strange and fearfull Conjurations" (2:149).

> Not long after, early in a morning a great fire was made in a long house, and a mat spread on the one side, as on the other, on the one they caused him to sit, and all the guard went out of the house, and presently came skipping in a great grim fellow, all painted over with coale, mingled with oyle; and many Snakes and Wesels skins stuffed with mosse, and all their tayles tyed together, so as they met on the crowne of his head in a tassell; and round about the tassell was a Coronet of feathers, the skins hanging round about his head, backe, and shoulders, and in a manner covered his face; with a hellish voyce and a rattle in his hand. [2:149]

In the earlier account, one could not tell that there was a chief medicine man or that he came alone into the longhouse just after the guards left. Smith did, however, include a description of one medicine man's dress in *A True Relation* (a comparison makes it clear that he was the chief medicine man described in *The Generall Historie*), together with details of the sacrifice he made: "One disguised with a great Skinne, his head hung round with little Skinnes of Weasels, and other vermine, with a Crownet of feathers on his head, painted as ugly as the divell, at the end of each song will make many signes and demonstrations, with strange and vegement actions; great cakes of Deere suet, Deare, and Tobacco he casteth in the fire. Till sixe a clocke in the Eneving, their howling would continue ere they would depart (1: 59). That concludes the description of the ritual in *A True Relation*. Smith evidently had forgotten about the sacrifices by the time he wrote *The Generall Historie*, for it is the one detail of this ceremony not in the latter account.

The Generall Historie makes it clear that the other medicine men were subordinates and joined the ritual later than the chief. It also describes the quite different appearance of the other six assistants. The Indians' dress, postures, and relative positions are all carefully particularized in the revision.

> With most strange gestures and passions he began his invocation, and environed the fire with a circle of meale;

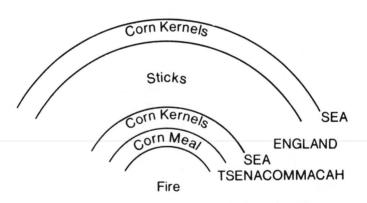

Corn Kernels

Sticks

Corn Kernels

Corn Meal

Fire

SEA

ENGLAND

SEA

TSENACOMMACAH

The Powhatan world view. Reprinted by permission of the Smithsonian Institution Press from *Cultures in Contact: The European Impact on Native Cultural Institutions in Eastern North America, A.D. 100–1800.* © Smithsonian Institution: Washington, D.C., 1985, p. 240, fig. 4.

which done, three more such like devils came rushing in
with the like antique tricks, painted halfe blacke, halfe red:
but all their eyes were painted white, and some red
stroakes like Mutchato's, along their cheekes: round about
him those fiends daunced a pretty while, and then came in
three more as ugly as the rest; with red eyes, and white
stroakes over their blacke faces, at last they all sat downe
right against him; three of them on the one hand of the
chiefe Priest, and three on the other. Then all with their
rattles began a song, which ended, the chiefe Priest layd
downe five wheat cornes: then strayning his armes and
hands with such violence that he sweat, and his veynes
swelled, he began a short Oration: at the conclusion they
all gave a short groane; and then layd down three graines
more. After that, began their song againe, and then another Oration, ever laying downe so many cornes as before, till they had twice incirculed the fire; that done, they
tooke a bunch of little stickes prepared for that purpose,
continuing still their devotion, and at the end of every
song and Oration, they layd downe a sticke betwixt the divisions of Corne.

The duration of the ceremony, the fasting of the medicine men
during the day, and the symbolic significance of the meal, corn, and
sticks are all valuable additions to the clearer and more dramatic
description: "Till night, neither he nor they did either eate or
drinke, and then they feasted merrily, with the best provisions they
could make. Three dayes they used this Ceremony; the meaning
whereof they told him, was to know if he intended them well or no.
The circle of meale signified their Country, the circles of corne the
bounds of the Sea, and the stickes his Country. They imagined the
world to be flat and round, like a trencher, and they in the middest"
(2:149–50).
Though the description of the ceremony in A True Relation was
valuable and contained one bit of information not in the later version, The General Historie account is more graphic, contains much
fuller and more detailed data, and concludes with its significance,
transforming it from a description of a brief, inexplicable ritual to
a fascinating and sympathetic, yet exotic, attempt to make sense of
events.[4]

For Smith, however, as for so many writers, the touchstone of the exotic was sensualism; and Smith's most memorable exotic description concerned Indian maidens. Smith stated that guests among the Indians were well treated, "and at night where his lodging is appointed, they set a woman fresh painted red with *Pocones* and oyle, to be his bedfellow" (2:121). Smith never told whether he had such a bedfellow. The most sensual exotic event narrated in seventeenth-century American literature took place in October 1608, when Smith with four companions went to Werowocomoco to prepare for Powhatan's coronation. Since Powhatan was away, Pocahontas and her maiden friends entertained Smith with a "Virginia Maske." The ceremony's beginning so startled Smith and his four men that they feared they were being attacked and prepared to fight: "In a fayre plaine field they made a fire, before which, he sitting upon a mat, suddainly amongst the woods was heard such a hydeous noise and shreeking, that the English betooke themselves to their armes, and seized on two or three old men by them, supposing Powhatan with all his power was come to surprise them" (2:182, 1:235). Seeing the Englishmen's alarm, Pocahontas immediately came to their camp, saying they could kill her if they thought any "hurt were intended." When Smith realized that the group with her consisted mainly of women and children, he was reassured. The ceremony proceeded.

> Then presently they were presented with this anticke; thirtie young women came naked out of the woods, onely covered behind and before with a few greene leaves, their bodies all painted, some of one colour, some of another, but all differing, their leader had a fayre payre of Bucks hornes on her head, and an Otters skinne at her girdle, and another at her arme, a quiver of arrowes at her backe, a bow and arrowes in her hand; the next had in her hand a sword, another a club, another a pot-sticke; all horned alike: the rest every one with their severall devises. These fiends with most hellish shouts and cryes, rushing from among the trees, cast themselves in a ring about the fire, singing and dauncing with most excellent ill varietie, oft falling into their infernall passions, and solemnly againe to sing and daunce; having spent near an houre in this Mascarado, as they entered in like manner they departed.
> [2:183; cf. 1:235–36]

The ceremony, however, was not over yet. A feast and a partner for the night were yet to come: "Having reaccommadated themselves, they solemnly invited him to their lodgings, where he was no sooner within the house, but all these Nymphes more tormented him then ever, with crowding, pressing, and hanging about him, most tediously crying, Love you not me? love you not me? This salutation ended, the feast was set, consisting of all the Salvage dainties they could devise: some attending, others singing and dauncing about them; which mirth being ended, with fire-brands in stead of Torches they conducted him to his lodging" (2:183, 1:236).[5]

John Lawson reported a similar entertainment by dancing Indian maidens in early eighteenth-century North Carolina and concluded by telling what happened after the dance: "every Youth that was so disposed, catch'd hold of the Girl he liked best, and took her that Night for his Bed-Fellow, making as short Courtship and expeditious Weddings, as the Foot-Guards us'd to do with the *Trulls* in *Salisbury Court*."[6] Despite Lawson's additional note about the aftermath of the dance, his description is not as sensual as Smith's—tantalization, not consummation, characterizing the best sexual exoticism. Indeed, not until William Bartram described Georgia Indian maidens picking strawberries in the late eighteenth century did American literature attain a description of comparable exotic sensuality.[7] If Smith ever slept with Pocahontas (and within Indian custom, lovemaking following the ritual would have been normal), this was the only logical occasion for it. However young (thirteen? fourteen?) Pocahontas may have been, her arranging and partaking in the "Virginia Maske" (Smith implied that she led the ceremony) proved that she was considered, within the Algonquian culture, mature enough to play a woman's role in an orgiastic tribal fertility rite.[8]

As Smith became more familiar with the Powhatan Indians, other tribes seemed more exotic. The Susquehannocks greatly impressed him. He had heard from Powhatan and others about them. In his second exploring trip up the Chesapeake Bay, in the late summer of 1608, Smith and twelve other men came to the head of the bay, learned that the Susquehannocks were only two days' journey upriver, and persuaded a local Indian to go and invite them down. Four days later, sixty Susquehannocks, including several who were over six feet tall, showed up: "Such great and well proportioned men, are seldome seene, for they seemed like Giants to the English, yea and to the neighbours, yet seemed of an honest and simple disposition, with much adoe restrained from adoring the discoverers as Gods" (1:149).

The awe, however, was mutual. The Susquehannocks saw that Smith and his men possessed the shields and arrows of the Massawomekes, and Smith probably pretended that he had fought and routed them. The Susquehannocks certainly knew that these hairy, short, white men were mighty warriors. On the other hand, the whites had rarely seen such big men as the corn-fed Susquehannocks. Their language, an Iroquois dialect, was entirely different from the Algonquian dialects that Smith had previously encountered:

> Those are the most strange people of all those Countries, both in language and attire; for their language it may well beseeme their proportions, sounding from them, as it were a great voice in a vault, or cave, as an Eccho. Their attire is the skinnes of Beares, and Woolves, some have Cassacks made of Beares heades and skinnes that a mans necke goes through the skins neck, and the eares of the beare fastned to his shoulders behind, the nose and teeth hanging downe his breast, and at the end of the nose hung a Beares Pawe, the halfe sleeves comming to the elbowes were the neckes of Beares and the armes through the mouth with pawes hanging at their noses. One had the head of a Woolfe hanging in a chaine for a Jewell, his Tobacco pipe 3 quarters of a yard long, prettily carved with a Bird, a Beare, a Deare, or some such devise at the great end, sufficient to beat out the braines of a man, with bowes, and arrowes, and clubs, sutable to their greatnesse and conditions.

Having given a detailed description of the Indian warriors' exotic dress, Smith assessed their military possibilities before portraying the largest and most impressive Susquehannock warrior:

> These are scarse knowne to Powhatan. They can make neere 600 able and mighty men and are pallisadoed in their Townes to defend them from the Massawomekes their mortall enemies. 5 of their chiefe Werowances came aboard the discoverers and crossed the Bay in their Barge.

The picture of the greatest of them is signified in the
Mappe.[9] The calfe of whose leg was 3 quarters of a yard
about, and all the rest of his limbes so answerable to that
proportion, that he seemed the goodliest man that ever we
beheld. His haire, the one side was long, the other shore
close with a ridge over his crown like a cocks combe. His
arrowes were five quarters long, headed with flints or
splinters of stones, in forme like a heart, an inch broad,
and an inch and a halfe or more long. These hee wore in a
woolves skinne at his backe for his quiver, his bow in the
one hand and his clubbe in the other, as is described.
[1:149–50]

The Susquehannocks fascinated Smith. His detailed description of
them has, in turn, captivated his contemporaries and generations
of readers since.

Another Indian tribe that Smith heard stories about before
meeting them was the Massawomekes (evidently the Powhatan Indians' name for the Iroquois), who often came down to raid the
Indians living near the Chesapeake Bay. According to Smith's Indian informants, the Massawomekes were a very populous people
who lived "upon a great salt water." Smith theorized that the water
was "either some part of Cannada, some great lake, or some inlet
of some sea that falleth into the South sea" (2:119). When Smith
met the Massawomekes, he made astute observations about their
degree of culture and way of life: "Seaven boats full of these Massawomekes wee encountred at the head of the Bay; whose Targets,
Baskets, Swords, Tobacco pipes, Platters, Bowes, and Arrowes, and
every thing shewed, they much exceeded them of our parts, and
their dexteritie in their small boats, made of the barkes of trees,
sowed with barke and well luted with gumme, argueth that they are
seated upon some great water" (2:119). In this description and
throughout his writings on the Indians, Smith not only keenly observed and shrewdly appreciated different Indian customs, he also
revealed that he had a vision of the comparative method and stage
theory of civilization. The Massawomekes made more complex and
more serviceable objects than the Algonquian Indians. He later described in detail their targets or shields, explaining why they were
superior (2:174).[10] Smith gave more specific information concerning Indians, their dwellings, agriculture, hunting, customs, dress,

religion, and social structure than any other seventeenth-century observer. In an age before anthropology, Smith was the best ethnologist of his time. Just as no other American of his day had more adventures than Smith, so too no other American gave so many, or such detailed, exotic descriptions of Indian life and culture.

But Smith's main appeal in his writings (except for the two tracts on seamanship) was to prospective American emigrants. The characteristics of the man and the writing that made him the seventeenth century's greatest promotion writer are presented in the following chapter.

4

The Promoter of America

And of all the foure parts of the world that I have yet
seene not inhabited, could I have but meanes to
transport a Colonie, I would rather live here [in New
England] then any where: and if it did not maintaine it
selfe, were wee but once indifferently well fitted,
let us starve.

—From Smith's *A Description of New England* (1616; 1:330)

A TRVE RE-
latiͻn of ſuch occur-
rences and accidents of noate as
ha:h hapned in Virginia ſince the firſt
planting of that Collony, which is now
reſident in the South part thereof, till
the laſt returne from
thence.

Written by Captaine Smith *one of the ſaid Collony, to a*
worſhipfull friend of his in England.

LONDON
Printed for *Iohn Tappe*, and are to bee ſolde at the Grey=
hound in Paules-Church·yard, by *W.W.*
1608

Title page of *A True Relation* (1608)

Realism

SMITH'S American Dream made him the most effective seventeenth-century promotion writer. Some scholars have actually thought that Smith wrote demotional rather than promotional literature.[1] Typically, other promotion writers claimed that colonization could be "attained without any great danger or difficulty."[2] Such pie-in-the-sky exaggerations had become stereotypes long before the Virginia colony was founded in 1607. George Chapman, Ben Jonson, and John Marston, echoing Thomas More's *Utopia* and Harriot's *Virginia*, lampooned the promotional propaganda in *Eastward Hoe!* (1605):

> *Seagull.* I tell thee, Golde is more plentifull there then Copper is with vs: and for as much redde Copper as I can bring, Ile haue thrice the waight in Golde. Why man all their dripping Pans, and their Chamber pottes are pure Gold; and all the Chaines, with which they chaine vp their streetes, are massie Golde; all the Prisoners they take, are fetterd in Gould: and for Rubies and Diamonds, they goe forth on holydayes and gather 'hem by the Sea-shore, to hang on their childrens Coates, and stick in their Cappes, as commonly as our children weare Saffron guilt Brooches, and graotes with hoales in 'hem.[3]

Smith, a realist, knew the dangers of colonization and the popular English scoffing at the promotion literature. He proclaimed that emigrants must "hazard" their lives (1:343). Colonization was dangerous. But it offered phenomenal possibilities. Courage could substitute for capital; risk, for riches; and hard work, for a wealthy family. The reward was land. Pioneering remained precarious for the next three centuries. Everyone who actually thought of committing himself to America knew its perils. Most emigrants died. Virginia seemed cursed. All but 38 of the earliest 105 immigrants to Virginia died in the first six months (2:227–28, 259, 323, 3:237). The "first supply" added 120 persons to the 38 left alive, but 28 more died before the early fall of 1608 (1:234, 2:181). With Smith as president, the colonists suffered only seven or eight deaths during the winter of 1608–9 (1:265), but the greatest mortality was yet to come. Five hundred colonists remained in Virginia when Smith sailed for England in October 1609. But after that winter of 1609–10, "the starving time," only a few "more then 60. most miserable and poore creatures" still lived (1:276). Even if one accepts a recent historian's revisionist figures (100 people left alive from 250), three-fifths of the colonists died that winter.[4] We are not concerned here with the precise numbers, but rather with what the early seventeenth-century English people believed to be the reality. Virginia was death. The situation did not soon improve. A 1613 observer reported that every year more than half the Virginia colonists died. In fact, nearly 75 percent of the colonists who were sent over between 1619 and 1623 died.[5]

Other promotion writers ignored or glossed over the ghastly reality. No one with any sense believed the blind optimists. Smith confronted the charges and the rumors. The reputation of Virginia was hurt "by the vulgar rumor" that foolishly charged the air there to be unwholesome and the country barren—"as though all England were naught, because the Fens and Marshes are unhealthy; or barren, because some will lie under windowes and starve in Cheap-side, rot in Goales, die in the street, high-waies, or any where, and use a thousand devices to maintaine themselves in those miseries, rather than take any paines, to live as they may by honest labour." A great part of "the Planters of Virginia" were like such Englishmen and were partly responsible for "those defailements" (2:320). Smith explained that exposure and a poor diet—or simply starvation—caused most deaths: "For the mortality of the people accuse not the place, for of the old Planters and the families scarce one of twenty miscarries, onely the want of necessaries are the occasions of those diseases" (2:287).

Smith gave the facts, explained how so many people could perish, emphasized that colonization necessarily entailed risks, and told what kind of people would live and succeed in America—hard workers. Most promotion writers refused to acknowledge that eastern North America had no great flourishing Indian cities filled with gold and silver and no great mines comparable to those in Mexico and South America. "There is no Country to pillage as the Romans found: all you expect from thence must be by labour" (2:330). To Smith's disgust, the colonists filled the first two ships to return from Virginia to England with worthless dirt, which captains John Martin and Christopher Newport and others believed to be gold. "There was no talke, no hope, no worke, but dig gold, wash gold,

refine gold, load gold, such a brute of gold, as one mad fellow desired to bee buried in the sandes, least they should by their art make
gold of his bones" (1:218, 2:157; cf. *JV* 76).

In the early seventeenth century, only Smith emphasized that
hard manual labor was necessary for survival and success in America. Prospective emigrants knew the anti-American ballads and satires and America's unsavory reputation.[6] They knew that ships
from Virginia came back filled with worthless dirt. They wanted to
learn the truth. Those scholars who do not appreciate Smith's tal-
ent as a promotion writer ignore both his audience and human nature. Like the second-rate promotion writers, the scholars who de-
nigrate Smith must believe that most prospective emigrants were
persevering fools, not only unaware of the deaths in Virginia but
also ignorant of the satires upon America and the common opinion
that Virginia was death.

Early explorers of the Maine coast praised it extravagantly.
George Popham, a founder of the short-lived Sagadahoc colony in
Maine, wrote James I on December 13, 1607, that the Indians had
told him of a great sea only seven days' journey to the west. Popham thought he knew what the sea's identity must be: "This can
be none other than the Southern [i.e., the Pacific] Ocean, stretching towards the land of China which doubtless cannot be far away
from this region." Despite being on the spot ("Fort St. George, Sagadahoc, Virginia") in a freezing winter, Popham saw the Maine
coast in terms of the old dream of the New World as the Orient,
complete with Asian spices: "As regards commercial resources, all
the native inhabitants repeatedly assert that there are nutmegs,
mace and cinnamon in these parts, besides bitumen, Brazilwood,
cochineal and ambergris, along with many other important and
valuable things, and all very plentiful at that."[7]

Other early New England explorers like John Brereton, Martin
Pring, and James Rosier were not blinded by the Oriental image of
America, but they all exaggerated the fertility of New England's
soil, the commodiousness of its rivers, abundance of fish, greatness
of the trees, pleasantness of the climate, friendliness of the natives,
and security of the natural harbors.[8] Smith, however, saw what was
before him. His view of the Maine coast was realistic:

But all this Coast to Pennobscot, and as farre I could see
Eastward of it is nothing but such high craggy Cliffy Rocks

and stony Iles that I wondered such great trees could
growe upon so hard foundations. It is a Countrie rather to
affright, then delight one. And how to describe a more
plaine spectacle of desolation or more barren I knowe not.
Yet the Sea there is the strangest fishpond I ever saw; and
those barren Iles so furnished with good woods, springs,
fruits, fish, and foule, that it makes mee thinke though the
Coast be rockie, and thus affrightable; the Vallies, Plaines,
and interior parts, may well (notwithstanding) be verie fertile. But there is no kingdome so fertile hath not some part
barren: and New England is great enough, to make many
Kingdomes and Countries, were it all inhabited. [1:339,
2:416–17]

Finally an enthusiast for even the Maine coast, Smith misled no one
(unlike numerous other promotion writers) with exaggerated images of America that made it a Garden of Eden.[9]

When John Brereton described Cape Cod, Martha's Vineyard,
and the surrounding area in 1602, he portrayed the "fat and lustie"
soil, the "abundance of Strawberies" and numerous other foods,
the "great store of Deere," diverse "fowles, in great plenty," and the
incredible supply of fish, concluding with the following vision of
fertility:

But not to cloy you with particular rehearsall of such
things as God & Nature hath bestowed on these places, in
comparison whereof, the most fertil part of al England is
(of it selfe) but barren; we went in our light-horsman from
this Island to the maine, right against this Island some two
leagues off, where comming ashore, we stood a while like
men rauished at the beautie and delicacie of this sweet
soile; for besides diuers cleere Lakes of fresh water
(whereof we saw no end) Medowes very large and full of
greene grasse; euen the most woody places (I speake onely
of such as I saw) doe grow so distinct and apart, one tree
from another, vpon greene grassie ground somewhat
higher than the Plaines, as if Nature would shew her selfe
aboue her power, artificall.[10]

In contrast, Smith found Cape Cod "onely a headland of high hils
of sand, overgrowne with shrubbie pines, hurts, and such trash"

(1:340). He could hardly foresee that it would become a favorite vacation spot over three centuries later for those seeking to escape inland North America's summer heat. Though Smith recapitulated Brereton's early explorations in *The Generall Historie*, he could not bring himself to perpetuate Brereton's ecstatic praise. When Smith came to the passage quoted above, he cited only the first clause before breaking off: "but not to cloy you with particulars, what God and nature hath bestowed on those places, I refer you to the Authors owne writing at large" (2:90).

The American Way to Wealth

Smith combined practicality with visionary ideals. Though he appealed to honor, virtue, fame, and magnanimity, and though he envisioned a better social world in America, he tempered these ideals with common sense and brusque practicality, saying in *A Description of New England* that he had learned by his Virginia experience that only the hope of wealth would make most people become colonists, not "Religion, Charity, and the Common good." "I am not so simple, to thinke, that ever any other motive then wealth, will ever erect there a Commonweale; or draw companie from their ease and humours at home, to stay in New England to effect my purposes" (1:346, 2:423). Everett Emerson wrote that this passage revealed Smith to be "fundamentally materialist and bourgeois."[11] Actually, however, it showed that Smith realistically judged most people's desires and motives. He said that only the lure of wealth, not "my purposes," would bring them to America. His "purposes" were obviously different. He was not himself greatly interested in wealth, and he scorned the London Company's dream of gold in America (1:234, 2:181, 188, 222, 300, 387, 3:272, 285).

Since Smith was writing about the prospective settlement of New England, one might agree with Samuel Eliot Morison, Allen French, and Philip L. Barbour (1:415) that Smith was wrong and that religion was indeed responsible for the settlement of the Plymouth colony (1620), Massachusetts Bay (1630), Connecticut (1636), and Rhode Island (1636).[12] Everyone will acknowledge that such leaders as William Bradford, John Winthrop, Thomas Hooker, Thomas Shepherd, and Roger Williams were primarily inspired by religious reasons for their emigration. But other motives entered into consideration even for them.[13] And not everyone came for religious reasons. Some came purely for material reasons. As one Massachusetts Bay colonist said, "I will be tenant to no man."[14] Some early Massachusetts Bay leaders even mocked religion.[15] Maryland, too, one might argue, was settled for religious reasons (in this case by Catholics), but everyone admits that the majority of Maryland colonists were Protestants, not Catholics. Southern colonists in general came to improve their fortunes, not their souls.[16]

Really, however, the whole question is moot. Everyone who understands Smith rightly will grant his point. What Smith and all writers before him meant by a religious reason for emigrating was conversion of the Indians[17]—not the creation of a Puritan, Catholic, or some other religious colony of whites. As Smith knew, the Virginia Company pretended that it was concerned with religious motivation and repeatedly paid London ministers to preach sermons on Virginia.[18] Smith elaborated the point a few pages later: "Religion, above all things, should move us (especially the clergie) if wee were religious, to shewe our faith by our works; in converting those poore salvages, to the knowledge of God" (1:350, 2:427). The entire paragraph expands and glosses Smith's earlier statement. Even in his last publication, Smith disgustedly wrote that the merchants who ran the company made "religion their colour, when all their aime was nothing but present profit" (3:272). Good scholars have misunderstood Smith because they have taken his words out of context and because they have applied anachronistic judgments to his statement.

Smith thought that labor was the real source of wealth. While admiring the courage and achievements of the great Spanish and Portuguese explorers and soldiers, he had only contempt for the "golden" basis of their empires. In 1605 Smith himself planned to go to Guiana with Captain Charles Leigh, but his experiences in America later made him scorn the "search for gold" by Leigh and Sir Walter Ralegh (3:224–25; cf. 1:406, 2:474). Holland was his favorite model of a contemporary empire, for the Dutch became a great and wealthy nation "chiefly by fishing at a great charge and labour in all weathers in the open Sea." Never, said Smith, "could the Spaniard with all his Mynes of golde and Silver pay his debts, his friends, and army, halfe so truly, as the Hollanders stil have done by this contemptible trade of fish." Smith knew that most soldiers—certainly those who had fought in Europe in the Lowlands and been paid by Holland—regarded fishing with contempt.

Gentlemen, even gentlemen soldiers, also regarded fishing with contempt. But Smith here reminded them that their Dutch pay came from fishing and trade. "This contemptible trade of fish" paid for the wars in Flanders where most soldiers of Smith's time gained their experience and fame. Hard work and commerce were the bases of Holland's wealth—and would be the bases of America's. By hard work, Holland had become "so mighty, strong and rich, as no state but Venice, of twice their magnitude, is so well furnished with so many faire Cities, goodly Townes, strong Fortresses, and that aboundance of shipping and all sorts of marchandize, as well of Golde, Silver, Pearles, Diamonds, Pretious stones, Silkes, Velvets, and Cloth of golde." Fishing, Smith claimed, was "their Myne; and the Sea the source of those silvered streames of all their vertue; which hath made them now the very miracle of industrie, the pattern of perfection for these affaires; and the benefit of fishing is that Primum mobile that turnes all their Spheres to this height of plentie, strength, honour, and admiration. Herring, Cod, and Ling, is that triplicitie, that makes their wealth and shippings multiplicitie" (1:330–31).[19]

Smith's vision of the American colonies was extraordinary in his time. Only one previous colony—the "Lost Colony" of Roanoke—had been intended as a settlement of farmers and families. The other early English colonies were all, like the Virginia Company, based on military models. They consisted of men (no women or small children) who hoped and expected to enslave the Indian societies, as Spain had done in Mexico and South America. Smith stressed that such expectations were foolish for the eastern coast of North America. It did not contain "mines of gold and silver, nor such rare commodities as the Portugals and Spaniards found in the East and West Indies" (1:257). Virginia was "a lande, even as God made it." There "we found only an idle, improvident, scattered people; ignorant of the knowledge of gold, or silver, or any commodities; and carelesse of any thing but from hand to mouth, but for bables of no worth; nothing to encourage us, but what accidentally wee found nature afforded" (1:257). What English North America offered, said Smith, was a place where a farmer, a fisherman, or any hard worker could live a good life and become wealthy through his own labor. "And who is he hath judgement, courage, and any industrie or qualitie with understanding, will leave his Countrie, his hopes at home, his certaine estate, his friends, pleasures, libertie, and the preferment sweete England doth afford to all degrees, were it not to advance his fortunes by injoying his deserts?" (1:349). The New World promised that the ordinary man deserved the fruit of his labors, and in America, ordinary citizens who worked hard would "quicklie growe rich" (1:348).

Smith's vision of America as a land where hard work was the road to success became the dominant American Dream, celebrated by such later seventeenth-century promoters as Edward Winslow and Edward Johnson in New England and John Hammond and George Alsop in the South.[20] It continued to be the most important image of America, only strengthening as time passed. In their poem on "The Rising Glory of America" (1771), the Princeton classmates Philip Freneau and Hugh Henry Brackenridge showed that the Revolutionary generation had learned the lesson first taught by Captain John Smith:

> More blest are we, with whose unenvied soil
> Nature decreed no mingling gold to shine,
> No flaming diamond, precious emerald,
> No blushing sapphire, ruby, chrysolite,
> Or jasper red—more noble riches flow
> From agriculture, and the industrious swain.[21]

Benjamin Franklin wrote the greatest promotion tract of the eighteenth century, "Information to Those Who Would Remove to America" (1782). He explained American values to Europeans. He said that in America, "People do not inquire concerning a Stranger, *What IS he?* but, *What can he DO?*" Franklin affirmed both Smith's contempt for the mere gentleman and Smith's praise of work and respect for the person who achieves and contributes:

> If he has any useful Art, he is welcome; and if he exercises
> it and behaves well, he will be respected by all that know
> him; but a mere Man of Quality, who on that Account
> wants to live upon the Public, by some Office or Salary, will
> be despis'd and disregarded. The Husbandman is in honor
> there, & even the Mechanic, because their Employments
> are useful. The People have a Saying, that God Almighty is
> himself a Mechanic, the greatest in the Universe; and he is
> respected and admired more for the Variety, Ingenuity,
> and Utility of his Handiworks, than for the Antiquity of his

Family. They are pleas'd with the Observation of a Negro,
and frequently mention it, that *Boccarorra* (meaning the
Whiteman) make de Blackman workee, make de Horse
workee, make de Ox workee, make ebery ting workee; only
de Hog. He de Hog, no workee; he eat, he drink, he walk
about, he go to sleep when he please, *he libb like a Gentleman*. According to these Opinions of the Americans, one
of them would think himself more oblig'd to a Genealogist,
who could prove for him that his Ancestors & Relations for
ten Generations had been Ploughmen, Smiths, Carpenters, Turners, Weavers, Tanners, or even Shoemakers, &
consequently that they were useful Members of Society;
than if he could only prove that they were Gentlemen,
doing nothing of Value, but living idly on the Labour of
others, mere *fruges consumere nati*,[22] and otherwise *good* for
nothing, till by their Death, their Estates like the Carcase of
the Negro's Gentleman-Hog, come to be *cut up*.[23]

Like Smith, Franklin was ahead of his time. He probably created
the "Saying" he attributed to "the People" and rewrote the anecdote about the "Observation of a Negro."[24] Smith's attitudes concerning labor and the worth of the individual anticipate later
American values, including Franklin's radical egalitarian notions.[25]

America as Garden

In addition to his typical realistic common sense, Smith could be a
visionary. His American Dream (as the epigraph for this chapter
proves) sometimes contained elements of the traditional pastoral.
Like all European observers, Smith celebrated the abundance of
nature in America. Writing of Virginia, he said that "no place affordeth more plentie of Sturgeon" in summer than the James River,
"nor in winter more abundance of fowle" (1:146–47). Cedar Isle on
the James supplied Smith and his men with such an abundance of
oysters that they lived on them for ten weeks (1:146). He recommended keeping "hogs, horse & cattell, conies or poultry" on the
islands off the New England coast, where they would be "secure for
little or nothing, and to command when you list, onely having a
care of provision for some extraordinary cold winter" (3:288). As
Smith predicted, the islands became successful breeding grounds

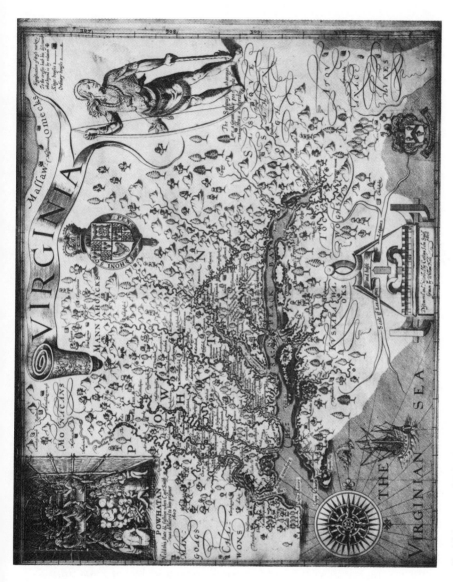

Smith's map of Virginia (1612)

for domestic animals. Perhaps the earliest large-scale increase of sheep occurred on Aquidneck Island, Rhode Island, where, after all the wolves were killed (by 1642), the sheep doubled yearly.[26] The islands not used for livestock could, Smith said, become "nurseries for fruits and plants" (3:288).

Showing the sensitivity of a landscape gardener, Smith suggested a scheme for making much of America a preserve. The colonists should carefully plan the landscape's later appearance and use. They should not thoughtlessly cut down all the trees.[27] Smith turned the common complaint about America being all woods[28] into a celebration of its possibilities as a great, natural garden. Occasional stands of virgin forest could serve as windbreaks, as borders of property, as ornaments for the tops of hills, as a natural preserve for the way nature was before the white man came, and simply as decorations for the terrain: "you may shape your Orchards, Vineyards, Pastures, Gardens, Walkes, Parkes, and Corne fields out of the whole peece as you please into such plots, one adjoyning to another, leaving every one of them invironed with two, three, foure, or six, or so many rowes of well growne trees as you will, ready growne to your hands, to defend them from ill weather, which in a champion [open land] you could not in so many ages" (3:289). By the time of his last publication, *Advertisements* (1631), Smith realized with abhorrence that the colonists were despoiling the wilderness and that the result would be like the worst sections of England, but he had hoped in *The Generall Historie* (1624) to preserve at least part of the original state of North America's East Coast: "her treasures having yet never beene opened, nor her originals wasted, consumed, nor abused" (2:411).

In 1631 Smith still thought that with proper planning, the American countryside could be brought to resemble the most beautiful gardenlike areas of England: "and this at first you may doe with as much facility, as carelesly or ignorantly cut downe all before you, and then after better consideration make ditches, pales, plant young trees with an excessive charge and labour." In Smith's vision, America could—and should—become almost instantly a countryside similar to but more fruitful and beautiful than the parklike areas surrounding a friend's English estate. America should keep stands of its great trees, "like unto the high grove or tuft of trees, upon the high hill by the house of that worthy Knight Sir Humphrey Mildmay, so remarkable in Essex in the Parish of

Danbury, where I writ this discourse, but much taller and greater."
Even in appreciating the lovely surroundings around Humphrey
Mildmay's house, Smith praised America, though adumbrating the
later foolish and jingoistic bragging that American nature was bigger and better.[29] He was the keenest early observer of geography
and realized that the size and character of the trees and the foliage
enable one to tell the fertility of the soil: "The best is ever knowne
by the greatnesse of the trees and the vesture it beareth" (3:289).[30]
Engineers using satellites and modern technology know the truth
of Smith's observations about the relationship between the vegetation and the soil.

Smith predicted the greatest premodern industries of New England—fishing (1:330–32), farming (1:334), trapping and trading
for furs (though he warned that "the furs Northward are much
better, and in more plentie, then Southward" [1:336, 341]), and
shipbuilding (1:229–30, 337–38). New England's trees were especially "proper for shipping," and all the "chiefe materials" necessary for building ships could be found in New England "within a
square of twenty leagues" (3:289). The process of earning a living
in America offered "sweet content," whereas in England the laborer
found "charges and losse" (1:347). A note of primitivism occurs in
his listing of England's ills—faults absent in an undeveloped society: "And here are no hard Landlords to racke us with high rents,
or extorted fines to consume us, no tedious pleas in law to consume
us with their many years disputations for Justice: no multitudes to
occasion such impediments to good orders, as in popular States"
(1:332).

Though he was more realistic than his contemporaries,[31]
Smith's vision of the American way of life was tinged with the pastoral ideal. On one occasion he portrayed the life of the colonists in
idyllic terms, stressing in his imaginary portrait the colonists' ownership of land and their own boats, their freedom of personal
choice, and the family's loving sharing of work and play. The portrait conveys satisfaction, pleasure, and wealth. It is a beautifully
written idyll, and the finest celebration of fishing before Isaac
Walton:

> What pleasure can be more, then (being tired with any oc-
> casion a-shore) in planting Vines, Fruits, or Hearbs, in con-
> triving their owne Grounds, to the pleasure of their owne

mindes, their Fields, Gardens, Orchards, Buildings, Ships,
and other works, etc. to recreate themselves before their
owne doores, in their owne boates upon the Sea, where
man woman and childe, with a small hooke and line, by angling, may take diverse sorts of excellent fish, at their pleasures? And is it not pretty sport, to pull up two pence, six
pence, and twelve pence, as fast as you can hale and veare
a line? . . . If a man worke but three dayes in seaven, he
may get more then hee can spend, unlesse he will be excessive. Now that Carpenter, Mason, Gardiner, Taylor, Smith,
Sailer, Forgers, or what other, may they not make this a
pretty recreation though they fish but an houre in a day, to
take more then they eate in a weeke: or if they will not eate
it, because there is so much better choise; yet sell it, or
change it, with the fisher men, or marchants, for any thing
they want. And what sport doth yeeld a more pleasing content, and lesse hurt or charge then angling with a hooke,
and crossing the sweete ayre from Ile to Ile, over the silent
streames of a calme Sea? [1:347]

Nor was Smith entirely free from the usual comparison of the
New World to Paradise. In his Virginia writings, he made occasional promotional exaggerations. A *True Relation* finds the Nansemond River area especially appealing. It had plains that "may containe 1000. Acres of most excellent fertill ground, so sweete, so
pleasant, so beautifull, and so strong a prospect, for an invincible
strong Citty, with so many commodities, that I know as yet I have
not seene [its match]" (1:81). A *Map of Virginia* thus characterizes
the entire Chesapeake Bay area:

Within [the opening of the Chesapeake] is a country
that may have the prerogative over the most pleasant
places of Europe, Asia, Africa, or America, for large and
pleasant navigable rivers, heaven and earth never agreed
better to frame a place for mans habitation being of our
constitutions, were it fully manured and inhabited by industrious people. Here are mountaines, hils, plaines, val-
leyes, rivers and brookes, all running most pleasantly into a
faire Bay compassed but for the mouth with fruitfull and
delightsome land. [1:144, 2:101]

He had other passages celebrating Virginia (e.g., 2:113–14), but his most extravagant words of praise were reserved for Massachusetts, "which is the Paradise of all those parts: for, heere are many Iles all planted with corne; groves, mulberries, salvage gardens, and good harbors" (1:340).

The Characteristic Voice

Besides being a resourceful and incredibly lucky adventurer, Smith became the greatest American propagandist of the seventeenth century. The reason for his extraordinary appeal is the philosophy underlying his writings. It is present almost constantly in Smith's voice—an extraordinary voice in the seventeenth century. In an age of patronage and social hierarchy, the voice of the commoner and yeoman's son breaks through the conventions of servility and courtliness with its distinctive barbaric yawp. "I know I shall be taxed for writing so much of myselfe, but I care not much" (2:317). The characteristic voice of Smith is always proud, assertive, independent, and challenging; sometimes commonsensical, blunt, honest, and gruff; and not infrequently impatient and irritated. His half-length portrait, engraved in his map of New England, projects and affirms these qualities. Smith's hair style is full and bushy, just covering the ears, and slightly longer in the back. His beard is full and rounded, with a long, bristling mustache. His whisk (or standing collar) is of plain starched linen, though almost all whisks were made of lace.[32] His doublet (which might be of chain mail—one could be certain in a painting but not in this engraving) is unusually plain, though the long sleeves do conclude in turned-up starched cuffs. The cuffs, like his whisk, are of plain linen, not the usual lace or ruffles. Altogether the portrait conveys deliberate plainness. He wears no cloak, no hat, no gloves, no ruffles, and no laces—all common and even expected features of early seventeenth-century gentlemen's dress.[33]

Except for a few features, one would judge Smith's portrait to be of a wealthy merchant who wanted to present himself as a very plain individual and who deliberately avoided any suggestion of superfluity. But three details of the portrait are quite striking. The full, round beard was uncommon in the day. As Alden Vaughan has noted, it is not in the common aristocratic Vandyke style.[34] In fact, it is individualistic. Second, Smith's left hand grasps the cup-like hilt of the sword he is wearing. To judge by the hilt, it is probably a rapier—a long, slender, two-edged sword. In portraiture, a sword is, of course, an icon of an officer and/or a gentleman. Third, Smith wears a chain-mail gorget, a collar that would have constituted part of his armor.[35] The combination of gorget and sword identifies Smith as a military man and an officer.[36] Altogether, the portrait presents Smith as a no-nonsense military officer, one who reasonably conforms to the usual standards of fashion (the whisk and matching cuffs) but who deliberately prizes plainness and his own individuality. Only imagine how a lovelock (a common feature of men's hair style at the time) would clash with the figure presented. Smith's direct gaze and the posture (right hand on the hip and left on the sword) almost seem to challenge the viewer, though the pose was common.[37]

Smith's writings constantly assert the nascent values of individualism and pragmatism—values, of course, that came to be especially associated with America. (It is significant that the most appropriate words for Smith's values did not exist in his own day.) He considered himself to be a self-made man (a third anachronism) and celebrated his own achievements. Smith's publications assert his attitudes, beliefs, and values with a resonance that captures more fully and accurately the aspirations of the Renaissance and seventeenth-century common people than all the theological reasonings of the New England Puritans. The dominant meaning of America—even in the early seventeenth century—was the possibility of a rise in this world, not a sainthood in the next. Smith's characteristic voice constantly affirmed the possibility of the individual's extraordinary achievement. Not until Benjamin Franklin wrote the following passage in his *Autobiography* do we have a greater statement of belief in the individual: "And I was not discourag'd by the seeming Magnitude of the Undertaking, as I have always thought that one Man of tolerable Abilities may work great Changes, and accomplish great Affairs among Mankind, if he first forms a good Plan, and, cutting off all Amusements or other Employments that would divert his Attention, makes the Execution of that same Plan his sole Study and Business."[38] The marginal heading in Smith's *A Description of New England* (1616) beside the most famous promotional passage in seventeenth-century American literature reads: "A note for men that have great spirits, and smal meanes" (1:343).

Here Smith advocated his belief that ordinary people were generally discontented with their lot under the existing English hierarchical system, that they really possessed "great spirits," that they
desired to transform and transcend their inherited and expected,
limiting roles, and that America promised them the opportunity to
achieve all their possible desires. Smith not only pointed out the
way that an ordinary person could change his status, he clearly believed the ordinary person could, would, and should do so.

Smith was the seventeenth century's greatest promotion writer
because he best understood the aspirations of ordinary persons
and because he wholeheartedly believed in an American Dream.
Smith saw America as possibility. He appealed to a sense of adventure. He knew that the common people wanted to better themselves. He believed that ordinary people were capable of extraordinary determination and hard work. He inspired his readers with a
belief in the importance of colonization and in their possibly heroic
contribution to it. Smith grandly appealed to the imagination and
ideals of the common person. Though his classic expression of the
American Dream repeated a number of the hackneyed motifs of
promotion literature (such as the conversion of the Indians and the
winning of lebensraum for England's supposed overpopulation),
Smith's personal voice distinguished his version of the American
Dream.

Who does not want to think of himself as possessing "great spirits"? The marginal heading alone, with its contrast of *great* and
small, makes those people with "small means" discontented. Emigration was the answer. Smith, an extraordinary leader who inspired fierce loyalty,[39] asserted that "great spirits" exist in common
men. And, of course, the belief itself created and inspired the reality. Here is his pitch:

Who can desire more content, that hath small meanes; or
but only his merit to advance his fortune, then to tread,
and plant that ground hee hath purchased by the hazard
of his life? If he have but the taste of virtue, and magna-
minitie, what to such a minde can bee more pleasant, then
planting and building a foundation for his Posteritie, gotte
from the rude earth, by Gods blessing and his owne industrie, without prejudice to any? If hee have any graine of
faith or zeale in Religion, what can hee doe lesse hurtfull

to any; or more agreeable to God, then to seeke to convert those poore Salvages to know Christ, and humanitie, whose labors with discretion will triple requite thy charge and paines? What so truely sutes with honour and honestie, as the discovering things unknowne? erecting Townes, peopling Countries, informing the ignorant, reforming things unjust, teaching virtue; and gaine to our Native mother-countrie a kingdom to attend her; finde imployment for those that are idle, because they know not what to doe: so farre from wronging any, as to cause Posteritie to remember thee; and remembering thee, ever honour that remembrance with praise? [1:343–44, 2:420–21]

That classic passage appeared in *A Description of New England* and was repeated in *The Generall Historie*. In Smith's series of rhetorical questions, the major appeal is land. Smith here combined realism and idealism, a touch of the idyllic and a summons to adventure. His commonsensical and fundamental appeal realized that the common people were discontented with the servitude and lack of possibility for advancement that existed in the Old World. Come to America and transform yourself! Here in America you will have the opportunity to achieve material success, honor, self-respect, and fame!

5

The Character of Smith

What shall I say? but thus we lost him, that in all his proceedings, made Justice his first guid, and experience his second; ever hating basenesse, sloth, pride, and indignitie, more then any dangers; that never allowed more for himselfe, then his souldiers with him; that upon no danger would send them where he would not lead them himselfe; that would never see us want what he either had, or could by any meanes get us; that would rather want then borrow, or starve then not pay; that loved actions more then wordes, and hated falshood and cousnage worse then death: whose adventures were our lives, and whose losse our deathes.

—One of Smith's men (perhaps William Fettiplace), who remained in Virginia after Smith, "blowne up with powder," returned to England in October 1610. *The Proceedings* (1612; 1:273).

Arms of Smith, from *True Travels* (1630)

FROM the seventeenth cenury to the present, some scholars have called Smith a braggart. A *braggart* is "one given to loud, empty boasting; a bragger." [1] Smith was certainly assertive, but he did not brag. Only if he frequently exaggerated his personal achievements could one reasonably call him a braggart. There is little evidence that he did so. The opposite is true. Edward Arber pointed out in 1884 that "in regard to all personal matters, he systematically understates rather than exaggerates anything he did" (*AB* xxiv; cf. xxii). Almost all students of Smith agree that he was energetic, disciplined, assertive, brave, independent, brusque, and, on occasion, impatient. I show here that he was practical yet idealistic, studious and learned as well as a man of action, a social visionary as well as a pragmatist, and a kindly humanitarian as well as a disciplined soldier and forceful leader. Other aspects of his character—and further confirmation of the above qualities—are disclosed by examining his appreciations of others.

Changing Social Status

One of Smith's admirable characteristics as a leader and as a human being was his recognition of the good qualities of his companions. At the same time, the qualities Smith praised reveal not only those virtues he especially prized but those that he thought requisite for a colonist. Indeed, a few contemporaries, like Anas Todkill, Nathaniel Causey, Edward Waters, and Thomas Nuce, seem almost to become versions of Smith. When he enlarged the account of his Virginia adventures, Smith celebrated the courage and abilities of Anas Todkill. Naturally Smith reflected the social realities of his own times. He arranged the various lists of colonists according to the pervasive social hierarchy, though the lists, carefully analyzed, reveal Smith's underlying values. In naming the "first planters" (1:207–9), Smith placed first the six members of the council, then the minister, and then twenty-nine gentlemen, for a total of forty-two gentry. Then he listed four carpenters, two persons without any identifying category, eight artisans, twelve laborers, a surgeon, and four boys, for a total of thirty-one persons below the gentry. Everyone has commented on the high proportion of gentlemen (eleven more gentlemen than commoners listed). There is, however, another remarkable feature in the list—the lack of any identifying rank or occupation for two persons, Anas Todkill and John

Capper. Smith grouped them with the craftsmen (although they were evidently not craftsmen) and above the laborers. We know quite a lot about the extraordinary qualities of these two anomalous persons. Capper was an exact man of honest principles who would not be swayed by the ruling party of aristocrats (*JV* 224), and Todkill emerged in *The Generall Historie* as the second most heroic and accomplished frontiersman (behind only Smith himself) among the earliest colonists.

Todkill was the only colonist who accompanied Smith on all his major explorations. In addition, he searched alone in Virginia's interior for the lost Roanoke colonists (2:215), volunteered for exchange as an Indian hostage, and on one occasion saved Smith and the exploring party by sounding an alarm that should have resulted in his own death. But he escaped "all bloudy by some of them who were shot by us that held him, but as God pleased he had no hurt" (2:174). Todkill was one of the men whom Smith trained as a sailor (1:149, 2:106), as a soldier (1:85, 218–19, 2:180–81, 310–11, 3:277), and, evidently, as a lumberman (1:238–39, 2:185–86). Indeed, in the later lists of those who explored the Chesapeake Bay with Smith, Todkill has been transformed. Smith categorized him as a soldier in *The Proceedings* (1:224, 230 [giving him priority by listing him first]) and finally as a gentleman in *The Generall Historie* (2:155; cf. 1:216).

But we know from Todkill's own account that he emigrated as a servant (a footman?) to Captain John Martin (1:221) and soon became disgusted with his master. Todkill sarcastically wrote that though Martin remained a year in Virginia, he never left Jamestown except for going "twice by water to *Paspahegh*, a place neere 7. miles from *James* towne, but lest the dew should distemper him, was ever forced to returne before night" (1:221). Todkill evidently adopted Smith as his model. No wonder Smith did not group him with the other twelve "Labourers." In a listing that could only reflect the early seventeenth-century social hierarchy, Todkill should not have been classified among the gentlemen, and he was not a craftsman, but Smith refused to categorize him simply as a laborer. In Smith's opinion, Todkill was obviously more worthy than the "sillie" John Ratcliffe or than Todkill's ostensible master, timorous John Martin. Smith's portrayal of Anas Todkill's transformation from English servant into a redoubtable American frontiersman is among the glories of *The Generall Historie*.

The several lists of colonists disclose two other persons whose status Smith seems to have changed. Four uncategorized persons in the "first supply" were evidently overlooked at first—and so their names were appended (probably during the printing of *The Proceedings*) at the bottom of the logical page without any classification (1:223, but Smith ranked them in the revised list published in *The Generall Historie* (2:160–62), with Richard Fetherstone among the gentry, the others with the laborers. Though Francis Perkins appears in *The Proceedings* as a laborer (1:223), in 1624 he is listed as a gentleman (2:161). Since Perkins wrote to an English patron asking his friend to have him appointed to the council (*JV* 158–64), Smith may simply have made a mistake in initially identifying Perkins as a laborer.[2] More interesting is William Spence. In *A Map of Virginia* (1612), Smith categorized William Spence (who came over with the "first supply" in 1608) as a laborer (1:223). Then in *The Generall Historie of Virginia* (1624), Smith placed Spence not with the laborers but with the gentlemen (2:161). Smith's reason for installing Spence among the gentry emerged when he wrote about "the benefit of giving" men the possibility of working for themselves and of farming their own land. Smith celebrated Spence as Virginia's first good farmer. John Rolfe had mentioned that "Ensigne William Spencer, and Thomas Barret a Sergeant, with some others of the ancient Planters being set free [i.e., allowed to work for themselves rather than the company], were the first farmers that went forth; and have chosen places to their content, so that now knowing their owne land, they strive who should exceed in building and planting" (2:268. Smith added his own evaluation of Spence: he was "an honest, valiant, and an industrious man, and hath continued [to be] from 1607. to this present [1624]" (2:247). Evidently these qualities, sustained over time, made Spence—in Smith's opinion—a gentleman.[3] Hard work, skill (in this case, in farming), honesty, and courage were the qualities that Smith admired in Spence.[4]

The Qualities of a Soldier

As one expects of a soldier, Smith repeatedly praised the military virtues of courage, boldness, and resolution. Despite George Percy's aristocratic scorn for Smith, Smith judged Percy and John Codrington to be "two Gentlemen of as bold resolute spirits as could possibly be found" (2:216). Captain Richard Waldo, "whom he knew to be sure in time of need" (1:242, 2:192), accompanied Smith on dangerous expeditions (2:182, 192). Smith also celebrated James Watkins, who, like Todkill, volunteered to be held as a hostage (1:227–28). In warfare, both industry and dispatch are essential. Smith noted the contrary qualities with disgust when captain Peter Winne lost the opportunity for timely action by "trifling away the night" (1:261). Smith praised captains William Norton and Thomas Dermer for their industry (2:304, 1:427) and commended Matthew Scrivener and Dermer for their understanding (2:154, 1:427).

Smith complimented Michael Sicklemore as "a very honest, valiant, and painefull souldier" (1:244). Typical of the details that Smith added in revising his earlier accounts of the Virginia adventures was his memorial tribute to George Forest: "Here I cannot omit the courage of George Forrest, that had seaventeene Arrowes sticking in him, and one shot through him, yet lived six or seaven dayes, as if he had small hurt, then for want of Chirurgery dyed" (2:221). Edward Rowcroft, alias Stallings, who served with Smith in Virginia and later in New England, was memorialized as "a valiant souldier" (1:427). Courage alone was not sufficient for survival: Smith condemned Captain Nathaniel Powell, who had accompanied Smith on his second exploring expedition up the Chesapeake Bay and who had searched alone among the Indians for the Roanoke colonists. Powell became too trusting and secure and made the mistake of thinking the Indians simple: "Powell one of the first Planters, a valiant Souldier, and not any in the Countrey better knowne amongst them [the Indians]; yet such was the error of an over-conceited power and prosperitie, and their simplicities, they not onely slew him and his family, but butcher-like hagled their bodies, and cut off his head" (2:295).

Nothing appealed to Smith more than accounts of people who endured hardships and defeats but who, by persevering, went on to later triumphs. He praised Matthew Morton as "a Gentleman that was shot and mortally supposed wounded to death [at the first landing on Cape Henry, April 26, 1607], with me in Virginia, yet since hath beene twice with command in the East Indies" (3:225). Although Nathaniel Causey was "cruelly wounded" in the 1622 massacre and the Indians were all about him, he nevertheless managed to "cleave one of their heads" with an ax "whereby the rest fled and he escaped" (2:295). Edward Waters and his wife were captured by the Indians but managed to escape, causing Smith to comment: "Thus you may see how many desperate dangers some men escape, when others die that have all things at their pleasure" (2:309). Captain Francis Nelson was another survivor, "an honest man, and an expert Marriner." Such, however, "was the lewardnesse of his Ship (that though he was within the sight of Cape Henry)," he was forced "by stormy contrary winds" out to sea. But "so well he had managed his ill hap" that he saved all his men, managed to make his way to the West Indies "for the repaire of his Masts, and a reliefe of wood and water," and returned to Virginia with abundant supplies (2:158 154).

The mutual responsibility of comrades in hardship often appears as a theme in Smith. He applauded those individuals who fulfilled the ideal. Michael Fuller went ashore with a group of settlers, was trapped with his friends on the mainland, and was surrounded by hostile Indians. Despite the Chesapeake Bay's freezing February waters, he managed to sit astride a piece of wood and, "by padling with his hands and feet in the water, beyond all expectation God so guided him three or foure houres upon this boord, he arrived at their ship." Though he was nearly frozen, "such was his courage and care of his distressed friends, he returned that night" to rescue them (2:319).

Smith remembered his former companions in arms and celebrated those who suffered hardships with him. He wrote *The Generall Historie* in part to memorialize those who died in planting Virginia. Dedicating *The True Travels*, he wrote: "To speake only of my selfe were intolerable ingratitude; because, having had so many copartners with me; I cannot make a Monument for my selfe, and leave them unburied in the fields, whose lives begot me the title of a Souldier; for as they were companions with me in my dangers, so shall they be partakers with me in this Tombe" (3:141–42). He recalled Nathaniel Causey, wounded in the 1622 massacre, as one "of the old company of Captaine Smith" (2:295). Samuel Collier, who came to Virginia as a boy in 1607 and accompanied Smith with three men to Werowocomoco in October 1608 (when Pocahontas performed her "Virginia Maske" [1:235]), had become proficient in Indian languages and customs and risen to be head of a town. Smith lamented his accidental death in 1623: "after the Watch was set, Samuel Collyer one of the most ancientest Planters, and very well acquainted with their [the Indians'] language and habitation, humors and conditions, and Governor of a Towne, when the Watch was set going the round, unfortunately by a Centinell that discharged his peece, was slaine" (2:315). Smith evidently valued Collier's achievements.

Smith's consideration for the reputation of others is notable. Typically, Smith did not reveal the name of the trigger-happy sentinel who accidentally killed Collier. That would have publicly branded him with shame forever. Smith likewise suppressed the name of the "coward" at Pamunkey who fearfully refused to leave the longhouse to see what new treachery waited outside (2:202). Neither did Smith reveal the name of the bumbler who accidentally fired Smith's own powder bag, mutilating and nearly killing him. The man ruined Smith's life, but it was an accident, and so Smith refrained from naming and shaming him (2:223).

Smith generously praised his former companions. After describing the great defeat at Rottenton in the late spring of 1602, Smith celebrated the memory of his comrades-in-arms who perished there: "Give mee leave to remember the names of our owne Country-men with him in those exploits, that as resolutely as the best in the defence of Christ and his Gospell, ended their dayes, as Baskerfield, Hardwicke, Thomas Milemer, Robert Mullineux, Thomas Bishop, Francis Compton, George Davison, Nicholas Williams, and one John a Scot, did what men could doe, and when they could doe no more, left there their bodies in testimonie of their mindes" (3:186).

Other Respected Attributes

The kindly humanity of others always appealed to Smith. Chronicling the death of Captain William Norton, Smith recorded that he was "a valiant industrious Gentleman, adorned with many good qualities, besides Physicke and Chirurgery, which for the publike good he freely imparted to all gratis, but most bountifully to the poore" (2:304). Captain Thomas Nuce was another who behaved "fatherly and kindly" (2:310), looked out for his dependents, and shared his food during shortages. Smith gathered and printed reports about Nuce:

So long as Captaine Nuse had any thing we had part . . .
some small quantity of Milke and Rice the Captaine had of
his owne, and that he would distribute gratis as he saw occasion; I say gratis, for I know no place else, but it was sold
for ready paiment. . . . This I protest before God is true
that I have related, not to flatter Nuse, nor condemne any,
but all the time I have lived in Virginia, I have not seene
nor heard that any Commander hath taken such continuall paines for the publike, or done so little good for himselfe, and his vertuous wife was no lesse charitable and
compassionate according to her power. [2:311–12]

Summarizing Bermuda's history, Smith reported the island's
depressed condition due to the current low price of tobacco and
then commented (no doubt with the pun in mind): "though great
men feele not those losses, yet Gardiners, Carpenters, and Smiths
doe pay for it" (3:220). Smith sympathized with the plight of ship
passengers and advised commanders of vessels to lay in sufficient
supplies and medicines: "you cannot be too carefull to keepe your
men well, and in health at Sea: in this case some masters are very
provident, but the most part so they can get fraught enough, care
not much whether the passengers live or die, for a common sailer
regards not a landman, especially a poore passenger, as I have
seene too oft approved by lamentable experience" (3:292).

On the other hand, Smith commiserated with the lot of the
common seamen and advised ship commanders to care for their
men, whose work, "especially in fowle weather . . . is so incredible I
cannot expresse it." Often "overstraining themselves they fall sick
of one disease or other, for there is no dallying nor excuses with
stormes, gusts, overgrowne Seas, and lee-shores." Besides, Smith
argued, commanders would be indirectly looking out for themselves in providing good food, well packed: for "when their victuall
is putrified it endangers all." Seamen have the worst labors of all
men: "Men of all other professions in lightning, thunder, stormes,
and tempests with raine and snow may shelter themselves in dry
houses by good fires, but those are the chiefe times Sea-men must
stand to their tackling, and attend with all diligence their greatest
labour upon the deckes" (3:112; also 3:28).

In general, the plight of the poor and oppression by the rich
(and by kings especially) aroused Smith's contempt: "But alas, what

is it, when the power of Majestie pampered in all delights of pleasant vanity, neither knowing nor considering the labour of the Ploughman, the hazard of the Merchant, the oppression of Statesmen; nor feeling the piercing torments of broken limbes, and inveterated wounds, the toilsome marches, the bad lodging, the hungry diet, and the extreme misery that Souldiers endure to secure all those estates, and yet by the spight of malicious detraction, starves for want of their reward and recompences" (3:179).

Smith's benevolence also appeared in his recommendations to ship captains. After his exciting description of a sea fight, Smith told how the victors should behave toward the losers: "examine them in particular, and then conclude your conditions, with feasting, freedome, or punishment, as you finde occasion"; but be certain, he admonished, to behave with responsible humanity: "alwayes have as much care to their wounded as your owne, and if there be either young women or aged men, use them nobly, which is ever the nature of a generous disposition" (3:103).

The obverse of Smith's sympathy with the plight of others was his contempt and disgust for those who treated humans sadistically. After telling of his journey up the James River in the winter of 1608:9 with forty men bartering for and raising provisions, Smith wrote: "Those temporizing proceedings [with the Indians] to some may seeme too charitable, to such a daily daring trecherous people: to others not pleasing, that we washed not the ground with their blouds, nor shewed such strange inventions in mangling, murdering, ransaking, and destroying (as did the Spanyards) the simple bodies of such ignorant soules" (2:206). In fact, Smith treated all people fairly. Among his proudest achievements was that he had accomplished his governorship "with so little bloud shed" (1:257 2:206). Smith admired the perseverance of the Reverend Robert Hunt, "an honest, religious, and couragious Divine," who despite being "so weake and sicke" for six weeks "that few expected his recoverie" nevertheless stayed with the voyagers when he could have returned to England (1:204). The Jamestown fire burned his library and all his possessions "(but the cloathes on his backe,) yet none [did] ever see him repine at his losse" (1:217–18).

Smith's fairness and objectivity are sometimes surprising. Though Captain George Kendall, a member of the first council, became a malcontent (and possibly a Spanish spy) and was executed for mutiny (1:212), Smith nevertheless praised him for the "extraordinary paines and diligence" he took in erecting the colony's first defenses (1:206, 2:138). Certainly the London Company officers frequently exasperated Smith, yet he defended them from the charges made by the first colonists in the summer of 1607. To those who grumbled that "it was ill done of the Councel to send forth men so badly provided," Smith replied that "the fault of our going was our owne, what could bee thought fitting or necessary wee had." The colonists themselves volunteered. Moreover, he reminded them, they had all the provisions that they desired. How could they blame the London Company? The trouble lay in their own ignorance: "what wee should finde, what we should want, where we shoulde be, we were all ignorant." If there was another problem than their ignorance, it lay with the ship captains who transported them to Virginia. The colonists had expected to remain at sea only two months and to arrive in Virginia "with victuall to live, and the advantage of the spring to worke." But they spent five months on the voyage, consuming all "our victuall and lost the opportunity of the time, and season to plant" (1:210–11). Reprinting the passage in *The Generall Historie*, Smith placed the blame specifically. It lay with "the unskilful presumption of our ignorant transporters, that understood not at all, what they undertooke" (2:143). The primary reference, of course, was to Captain Christopher Newport, who commanded the tiny fleet that sailed from England in December 1606 for Virginia.

Despite his disgust with the Virginia councilors, Smith defended the London Council for choosing such councilors as Edward Maria Wingfield, John Ratcliffe, John Martin, and George Kendall: "As for the insufficiencie of them admitted in commission, that errour could not be prevented by their electors, there being no other choice, and all were strangers to each others education, quallities, or disposition" (1:213 2:152).

Smith respected and admired learning and specialized skills. Matthew Morton and Francis Nelson are among those praised as "expert" seamen (3:225 2:158). Smith marvelled at the success of five men who sailed from Bermuda to Ireland in a small boat without any instruments: "shee had sailed more then 3300. miles by a right line thorow the maine Sea, without any sight of land, and I thinke, since God made the world, the like navigation was never done, nor heard of" (2:364). He celebrated Captain William Norton for being expert in "Physicke and Chirurgery" (2:304). And Smith admired the jack-of-all-trades abilities of Captain Thomas

Nuce: he built two houses and "a faire Well of fresh water mantled with bricke . . . in all which things he plaied the Sawyer, Carpenter, Dauber, Laborer, or any thing" (2:310).

Smith was the first Jamestown colonist to become an Indian expert, but he appreciated others who learned the languages and customs of the Indians. He celebrated the Indian expertise of Samuel Collier and Nathaniel Powell. He also interjected a commendation of the early interpreter and Indian expert Thomas Savage within a passage borrowed from Thomas Pory: "it is sixteene yeeres since he went to Virginia, being a boy, hee was left with Powhatan, for Namontacke, to learne the language, and as this Author [Pory] affirmeth, with much honestie and good successe hath served the publike without any publike recompence, yet had an arrow shot through his body in their service" (2:290). He likewise applauded Captain Henry Spelman: "Oure Interpreter, a Gentleman had lived long time in this Countrie, and sometimes a prisoner among the Salvages, and done much good service, though but badly rewarded" (2:257). Later, telling of Spelman's death, Smith noted that he had been "one of the best Interpreters in the Land" (2:320).[5]

Honesty was another quality Smith commended (e.g., Thomas Savage, 2:290). He gathered together a group of favorite epithets when memorializing the fat Richard Fetherstone: "all the time he had beene in this Country, [he] had behaved himselfe, honestly, valiantly, and industriously" (2:174). The expert sailor Captain Francis Nelson was not only a survivor, he was generous to the colonists. Smith found it especially remarkable because Nelson was so unlike the usual cheating, rapacious sailors and commanders who visited early Virginia: "He had not any thing but he freely imparted it, which honest dealing (being a Marriner) caused us admire him" (2:158). Just as Smith thought well of some persons for faithfully keeping their word, so he scorned others for their lies and deceit. Governor George Yeardley promised one hundred bushels of corn to each soldier who accompanied him, "for a reward, but it was not performed" (2:257).

Humor

Throughout his writings, Smith employed and enjoyed humor, and he sometimes made himself its butt. He appreciated that archetypal American humor, the satire of the greenhorn. He reprinted

the story from *Mourt's Relation* about the two Plymouth Colony ten-
derfeet who went out into the woods, got lost, and, night coming
on, imagined "as they thought, two Lions roaring a long time together very nigh them, so not knowing what to doe, they resolved
to climbe up into a tree" (2:447).[6] On one occasion, he even portrays himself as a complete greenhorn. The passage plays with the
satiric idea of America as a land of Cockaigne, a lubberland, where
the streams flowed with milk and honey, where the trees were
loaded with food and candy, and where roasted fowl and fresh-
cooked fish cried "Eat Me!"

The lubberland satire of America was common, being the natural reply to the exaggerated accounts of the superabounding fertility of American nature.[8] American nature was certainly abundant, as Smith repeatedly witnessed, but skill was nevertheless
required to exploit nature's bounty. As he wrote the treasurer and
council of the London Company in late 1608, "Though there be
fish in the Sea, foules in the ayre, and Beasts in the woods, their
bounds are so large, they so wilde, and we so weake and ignorant,
we cannot much trouble them" (2:189). Smith recorded with wry
amusement and self-satire his attempt to catch the fish that sometimes surrounded them in schools during the first exploring trip
up the Chesapeake Bay. He found "in diverse places that abundance of fish lying so thicke with their heads above the water, as for
want of nets (our barge driving amongst them) we attempted to
catch them with a frying pan, but we found it a bad instrument to
catch fish with" (1:228).[8]

Ironic touches characterize Smith's writings. He called the colonists' earliest lodging at Jamestown "castles in the air." (Though
Edward Arber annotated the phrase as meaning "in the trees" [*AB*
95], I believe Smith was saying that the only shelters the whites had
were the ones they imagined.) His irony toward the foolish plans of
the London Company broke through time and again, perhaps the
most notable example being his scorn for the company's project to
sail a five-piece barge up the James River, take it apart, haul it over
the mountains, and sail it down the rivers flowing into the Pacific
Ocean (2:188). Like many other early Americans, he often found
humor in the contrast between English and Indian civilization.
During his captivity, he convinced Opechancanough to send messengers to Jamestown, ostensibly so that he could reassure the colonists that he had not been slain so that they would not revenge his

death, but actually to warn them of Opechancanough's plot against them. The Indians took his message to Jamestown but ran away when the troops sallied out from the fort. Smith had predicted what would happen and told them where to leave the message. When the Indians returned that night they found the goods he had said would be there. The Indians returned with the presents and related what had happened, "to the wonder of them all that heard it, that he could either divine, or the paper could speak" (2:150).

Smith repeated John Brereton's observation that the Indians "have no Beards but counterfeits." When they saw whites with great beards, the Indians offered to trade for them, thinking them false. Smith told the anecdote about the bag of gunpowder that the Indians saved until spring and then planted, because they wanted to "be acquainted with the nature of that seede." He also told of the Indian who attempted to dry powder as he had seen the English do. He dried it, however, too close to the fire. His Indian friends, "peeping over it to see his skill, it tooke fire, and blew him to death, and one or two more, and the rest so scorched, they had little pleasure to meddle any more with powder" (2:90, 211).

Smith also was capable of gruesome touches of realistic frontier/war humor, the kind of savage humor that breaks through the civilized surface and allows people to function in conditions of absolute horror. Describing the starving time during the winter of 1609–10, Smith recorded the colonists' reports of cannibalism in a straightforward fashion but at the end added his own ironic, ghoulish comment: "Nay, so great was our famine, that a Salvage we slew, and buried, the poorer sort tooke him up againe and eat him, and so did divers one another boyled and stewed with roots and herbs: And one amongst the rest did kill his wife, powdered her, and had eaten part of her before it was knowne, for which hee was executed, as hee well deserved; now whether shee was better roasted, boyled, or carbonado'd, I know not, but of such a dish as powdered wife I never heard of" (2:232–33).[9] Grotesque humor occurs repeatedly in later American literature, but this is its earliest American example. The same events as told by George Percy, acting governor of the colony at the time (who may have been Smith's source for the powdered wife anecdote), are without Smith's characteristic irony.[10]

Can one imagine Smith appreciating—or even tolerating—a braggart? He scorned people who pretended to know Virginia but who had practically never left Jamestown. Smith had the good qualities that he respected in others, and he was himself the most courageous, industrious, persevering, skilled, benevolent, and humane person in early Virginia. He had not in him the stuff of which braggarts are made.

6

Smith and the American Indian

The next night being lodged at Kecoughtan; six or seaven dayes the extreame winde, rayne, frost and snow caused us to keepe Christmas among the Salvages, where we were never more merry, nor fed on more plentie of good Oysters, Fish, Flesh, Wild-foule, and good bread, nor never had better fires in England, then in the dry smoaky houses of Kecoughtan.

—Smith's nostalgic recollection of sheltering from a blizzard in the Christmas season (December 26, 1609–January 6, 1609/10) with the Kecoughtan Indians. *The Generall Historie* (1624; 2:194).

VIRGINIA · MATOAKA ALS REBECCA FILIA POTENTISS PRINC : POWHATANI IMP : VIRGINIÆ ·

Ætatis suæ 21. Aᵒ
1616.

Matoaks alš Rebecka daughter to the mighty Prince
Powhatan Emperour of Attanoughskomouck alš virginia
converted and baptized in the Christian faith, and
wife to the worᵖᵗ Mʳ Joh Rolff.

Si:Paß:sculp: Compton Holland excud:

ɔcahontas, from Smith's *Generall Historie* (1624)

IN THE Introduction I claimed that Smith was the Indians' best friend in early Virginia. No other colonial Virginia governor treated the Indians as well as Smith, and I doubt that any other governor became as great an Indian authority. Of course, one can take an ahistorical point of view and say that Smith and the whites violated the Indians' rights when they "invaded" North America. The various Indian confederations that Smith encountered had a better appreciation of the situation: the whites were one more group of people who might be allies to fight against the Indians' traditional enemies. None of the Indian tribes or the whites foresaw the future—though each hoped to dominate. To single out Smith or the Virginia Company for blame ignores Renaissance realities. Within the early seventeenth-century context, Smith's behavior was not only fair, he was surprisingly kind and humanitarian. He treated Indians as he treated whites. Though early Jamestown was run according to military discipline, Smith tortured no Indians, executed none, and saved Indians when others wanted to slay them.[1] Smith, however, knew perfectly well that many Indians (and sometimes whole tribes) would be glad to murder him given a chance. If necessary to survive, he would slay them in battle. Yet, because he was a werowance—a chieftain among the whites—the Powhatan tribes treated him well the one time they had Smith at their mercy. But dozens of other times various Indians (including the Powhatan tribes) tried to ambush and kill him. They failed, but their numerous attempts to slay Smith and repeated successful attacks upon other whites and other Indian tribes proved their relative contempt for the life of others. In contrast, Smith prized all human life.

Smith's Fundamental Attitude

Experienced in various world cultures, including English, European, Middle Eastern, and African, Captain John Smith regarded the American Indian as one more example of the differences among human beings. Unlike the aristocrats and genteel councillors of early Virginia, Smith had been a commoner and a slave. He held no secret belief in his own innate superiority by reason of class and was, indeed, used to being scorned by supercilious aristocrats of his own time. He was in a better position to appreciate individual Indians and Indian culture than most of his English contempora-

ries. Smith's attitude toward the American Indian reflected his belief in the comparative method and stage theory of civilization.[2]
Smith knew and echoed Thomas Harriot's *A Briefe and True Report
of the New Found Land of Virginia.* In the 1590 folio version of *A Briefe
and True Report*, Theodore De Bry printed as an appendix five engravings of John White's drawings of primitive Picts and other early
Britons. Harriot wrote in introducing the appendix that the pictures were included "to showe how that the Inhabitants of the great
Bretannie have bin in times past as saufage as those of Virginia."
The engravings (from John White's pictures copying the French
artist Jacques Le Moyne de Morgues) were the most dramatic visual
representation of the comparative method and stage theory in the
Renaissance. Since the cheaper quarto edition (1588)[3] of Harriot's
Virginia did not contain the engravings, one could argue that Smith
was unfamiliar with them, but most of the illustrations in Smith's
various books were based upon De Bry's engravings.[4] One could
also argue that Smith only became aware of the Harriot folio edition and its illustrations[5] after returning to England in 1609. The
1590 edition, however, provides so much more information about
Virginia, both in the engravings and in Thomas Harriot's commentary on them, that if Smith saw the book at all before sailing for
Virginia in 1606, he would have studied it.

It is nearly impossible to think that in his two to three years in
London preparing for the Virginia expedition, he did not come
across the most important single volume then existing concerning
Virginia. But even if he did not see Harriot's folio, he must have
repeatedly come across statements expressing both the essential
sameness of human beings and the socioeconomic stages of development. The travel literature was filled with such observations.
While Smith was in London preparing for his expedition to the
New World, José de Acosta's *The Naturall and Morall Historie of the
East and West Indies* (1604) appeared in translation—another classic
work containing numerous observations on the stage theory and
comparative method.[6] John Smith no doubt read Acosta as well as
Harriot's *Briefe and True Report* (1590), and he must also have encountered the theory in numerous other writers.[7]

Discussing the idea of the planter or colonist in chapter 1, I
pointed out that Smith viewed the colonists as latter-day evangelists
and as "the greatest Princes on earth" because they planted "civilitie and humanitie" among ruder nations. Though Smith found de-

grees of civility existing in different nations and different parts of the world, he believed in the essential identity of all humans. Smith acknowledged the differences among Indian tribes. No North American Indian tribe was as savage as some described in Hakluyt. Smith noted that all East Coast Indians had some form of religion and used bows and arrows in hunting (1:168, 2:121). They were more civilized than the "blacke brutish Negers" of Africa's "fryed Regions" that he had read about. Some American Indian tribes and some nations in Asia were reported to eat their enemies, but a few African tribes exceeded them in brutality, for they "are knowne to be so mad, as to eat their slaves and friends" as well as their enemies (1:327, 3:210–11). The Powhatans, whom Smith came to know better than any other Indians, were his standard against which to measure other tribes. Though Smith found that many of their "countrie people" were "very barbarous, yet" he judged their government to be reasonable and in some ways superior to Europeans: "their Magistrats for good commanding, and their people for du subjection, and obeying, excell many places that would be counted very civill" (1:173).

He noted that the Wighcocomoco Indians were smaller, ruder, and spoke a different dialect than the Powhatans (2:107). The Accomack Indians were the "best husbands [i.e., farmers] of any Salvages we know." They raised enough corn to supply their wants for more than a year (2:291), whereas the Powhatans only raised enough to see them through the winter (2:113). For the other "three parts of the yeare, they onely observe times and seasons, and live of[f] what the Country naturally affordeth from hand to mouth" (2:113). Smith observed, "It is strange to see how their bodies alter with their diet, even as the deare and wilde beastes they seeme fat and leane, strong and weake," but he also noted that Powhatan and "some others that are provident" roasted and dried their fish, meat, and corn, keeping it for "scarce times" (*JV* 357). He judged the Powhatans to be more civilized than the Monacans and their confederates, for the latter practiced less agriculture and lived "for the most part of[f] wild beasts and fruits" (2:119). The Accomacks impressed Smith as the "most civill and tractable people we have met with" (2:291). After he met the Massawomekes (2:119), an Iroquois tribe, he thought that they enjoyed a higher stage of culture than the Powhatans or the Accomacks. The Susquehannocks were larger than other Indians, "for they seemed like Giants to the English, yea and to their neighbors." But for all their large size, they were like innocent children. They "seemed of an honest and simple disposition, with much adoe restrained from adoring us as Gods" (2:106).

From what he had read, Smith inferred that the Mexican and South American Indians had a higher stage of culture than the East Coast Indians. The Virginia Indians, like "meere Barbarians as wilde as beasts," had nothing to compare to the Mexican Indians who "dwelled in strong houses," "were a civilized people, [and] had wealth" (2:316). They had, however, many skills that Smith and the Europeans generally lacked. When Pocahontas saved his life, Powhatan said that Smith should live with them "to make him hatchets, and her bells, beads, and copper." Of course, he could not do so, and he explained, "For the King himselfe will make his owne robes, shooes, bowes, arrowes, pots; plant, hunt, or doe any thing so well as the rest" (2:151). Europeans were more specialized but less skilled in supplying the whole range of their needs.

Smith never doubted that the Indians were essentially the same humans as the whites: "Had the seede of Abraham, our Saviour Christ, and his Apostles, exposed themselves to no more daungers to teach the Gospell, and the will of God then wee; Even wee our selves, had at this present been as Salvage, and as miserable as the most barbarous Savage yet uncivilized" (1:360). Smith pointed out that at the time of Christ, the Romans then used "the Spaniards to work in those Mines, as now the Spaniard doth the Indians" (1:332, 2:410). Smith judged the degrees of civility among Indians according to religion, weapons, agriculture, vocabulary, and government—among other standards—but he never thought that they were inferior. Like the different nations of Europe, they were at different stages of socioeconomic, religious, and cultural development.

Individual Indians

Smith respected Indians as individuals. He valued their kindness. When first taken captive, Smith was comparatively well treated, but the nights were cold for his scanty clothing. In an appreciation added to *The Generall Historie*, he recorded: "Yet in this desperate estate to defend him from the cold, one Maocassater brought him his gowne, in requitall of some beads and toyes Smith had given

him at his first arrivall in Virginia" (2:149). Smith thought the Accomack werowance was "the comliest, proper, civill Salvage we in-
countred" (2:163). *The Generall Historie* copied a passage from John
Pory calling the werowance the "laughing King at Accomack"
(2:291). Following Pory, Smith expressed admiration for both the
laughing king and his brother Kiptopeke. Though Kiptopeke was
chief, he saw that the tribe preferred his brother, so Kiptopeke
"freely resigned him the moitie of his Countrie" and helped his
brother, even "bearing the greater burden in government, though
the lesser honour." Smith ironically noted that hardly any white
ruler would have behaved as well (2:291).

Kemps and Tassore, whom Smith imprisoned early in 1608 and
whom he at first thought "the two most exact villaines in the country," gradually became loyal confederates (1:261, 263, 265). Another Indian, "Amocis the Paspaheyan," whom Smith at first believed was "kept amongst us for a spie" (1:93), became such a friend
to the English that the Indians killed him "for loving us" (2:145).
Smith later mentioned Sakaweston, an accultured New England
Indian, who "after he had lived many yeeres in England went a
Souldier to the warres of Bohemia" in defense of the Protestant
religion (2:399). Smith especially appreciated Powhatan's courageous son Nantaquoud, "the most manliest, comeliest, boldest
spirit, I ever saw in a Salvage" (2:258). Though Smith generalized
that Indians "were inconstant in everie thing, but what feare con-
straineth them to keepe," he found exceptions to the generalization
and praised particular Indians. Choapoc was an "honest, proper,
good promise-keeping king" (1:266); and the king of Mangoaks
was similarly described: "This honest proper good promise-
keeping king, of all the rest did ever affect us" (2:215).

Smith's Indian ally Mosco, "a lusty Salvage of Wighcocomoco,"
guided the colonists up the Potomac River on their first exploration
of the upper Chesapeake. Though not mentioned in *The Proceedings* (generally compiled from others' writings), Mosco received an
extended appreciation in Smith's *The Generall Historie*. The additions in *The Generall Historie* devote more attention to Mosco than
to any other single individual. Smith "supposed him [Mosco] some
French mans sonne, because he had a thicke black bushe beard,
and the Salvages seldome have any at all." Smith noted that Mosco
"was not a little proud, to see so many of his Countrymen" (2:173).
Smith and his party encountered Mosco again on their second ex-

ploring expedition up the Chesapeake Bay, this time on the Rappahannock River. He was with the Moraughtacund Indians who "kindly entertained" Smith and his party. Mosco warned them against the Rappahannock Indians, "for they would kill us for being friends with the Moraughtacunds that but lately had stolne three of the [Rappahannock] Kings women." A day or two later, while Smith attempted to negotiate with the Rappahannocks, hostage Anas Todkill performed his heroic act, warning the whites of the ambush (2:173–74), but Smith devoted much more space to Mosco's exploits. After the Rappahannocks surprised the whites, "shot more then a thousand Arrowes," and were beaten off, Smith rewarded Mosco by giving him most of the Rappahannocks' arrows and their canoes. The next day, in a signal gesture of acceptance, Smith took Mosco aboard the barge as they went farther up the river. Again the Rappahannocks attacked. This time they disguised themselves with branches, "as we tooke them for little bushes growing among the sedge." But as soon as arrows started striking the boat, Mosco cried out, "the Rappahannocks, which presently we espied to be the bushes." Having beat off the Rappahannocks' second ambush, the whites went up the river as far as the barge could go (2:174).

There, at the falls at present-day Fredericksburg, the whites explored the land for an hour until a sentinel "saw an arrow fall by him." About one hundred Mannahoacks attacked. "But Mosco did us more service then we expected . . . the Arrowes of Mosco at the first made them pause upon the matter, thinking by his bruit and skipping, there were many Salvages." When the Mannahoacks retreated and left the wounded Amoroleck behind, Smith could hardly restrain Mosco from killing him. Smith appeased Mosco, however, by giving him all the arrows shot by the Mannahoacks (2:175).

After Amoroleck had been treated and had somewhat recovered, Smith interrogated him about the surrounding area. The "poore Salvage mildly answered," giving the little information about the geography and the neighboring Indian tribes that he knew. Amoroleck said that because of "his good usage," the Mannahoacks would be friends, for he was the brother of the king of Hassinnunga. Mosco, however, advised that they depart immediately before the Mannahoacks returned with reinforcements. Since the river was narrow and the cliffs on one side so high, Smith thought the Indians might be able to attack them with impunity in daylight. Therefore he waited for night before setting out (2: 175–76).

"It was not long before we heard their arrowes dropping on every side the Boat." Amoroleck and Mosco yelled to the attackers to forbear, "but such a yelling and hallowing they made that they heard nothing." The Indians followed, shooting at them all night. At dawn, the whites came to a broad bay, where they anchored and breakfasted. Then Amoroleck made a speech to the Mannahoacks gathered at the shore, explaining: "how good wee were, how well wee used him, how wee had a Patawomek with us, loved us as his life, that would have slaine him had we not preserved him, and that he should have his libertie would they be but friends; and to doe us any hurt it was impossible." Consequently two Mannahoacks swam out, one with a bow and another with a quiver of arrows. Smith gave them presents and "told them the other three Kings should doe the like, and then the great King of our world should be their friend, whose men we were." Consequently they met on a "low Moorish poynt of Land." The Indian kings submitted their personal bows and arrows, and Smith gave them presents. The ceremony concluded with trading. "Our Pistols they tooke for pipes, which they much desired, but we did content them with other Commodities, and so we left foure or five hundred of our merry Mannahoacks, singing, dauncing, and making merry, and set sayle for Moraughtacund" (2:176–77).

Before Smith returned to the Rappahannocks, other Indians had told them of the whites' fight and subsequent peace with the Mannahoacks. When Smith reached the Rappahannocks, he declared that they had twice assaulted him who "came onely in love to doe them good, and therefore he would now burne all their houses, destroy their corne, and for ever hold them his enemies, till they made him satisfaction." Asked what terms he demanded, Smith replied, "they should present him the Kings Bow and Arrowes, and not offer to come armed where he was; that they should be friends with the Moraughtacunds his friends, and give him their kings sonne in pledge to performe it, and then all King James his men should be their friends." Both sides agreed to meet at the place where the Rappahannocks had first attacked Smith. There the werowances of Nantaughtacund, Pisacack, and Rappahannock met. The subtle werowance of Rappahannock "presented his Bow and

Arrowes, and confirmed all we desired, except his sonne, having no more but him he could not live without him, but in stead of his sonne he would give" Smith the three women that the werowance of Moraughtacund had stolen from him. Smith appreciated the Indian's subtle strategy, giving away what he did not have. But the werowance of Rappahannock had initially been the injured party, and Smith evidently thought he saw a way that would satisfy the warring Rappahannocks and Moraughtacunds and, at the same time, bind them to the English (2:177).

Smith accepted the substitution and asked Mosco to go to Moraughtacund and bring back the three women. There the now-diplomat Mosco "made them such relations, and gave to his friends so many Bowes and Arrowes, that they no lesse loved him then admired us" (2:177). Mosco returned with the three women. They "were brought our Captaine, to each he gave a chaune of Beads: and then causing Moraughtacund, Mosco, and Rappahannock stand before him, bid Rappahannock take her he loved best, and Moraughtacund chuse next, and to Mosco he gave the third." Then the celebration began. The following day, "there was of men, women, and children, as we conjectured, six or seaven hundred, dauncing, and singing, and not a Bow nor Arrow seene amongst them." Mosco, recorded Smith, "changed his name [to] Uttasantasough, which we interpret Stranger, for so they call us." Both sides promised forever to be friends, the Indians "to plant Corne purposely for us; and we to provide hatchets, beads, and copper for them." The whites "departed, giving them a Volley of shot, and they us as loud shouts and cryes as their strengths could utter" (2:178).

Would any other governor of early Virginia have accomplished these feats of fighting or these triumphs of diplomacy? The answer is not only no—it is indeed inconceivable to think that they would. Smith's most characteristic action, however, was his reward to Mosco. The "king" of Moraughtacund and the "king" of Rappahannock might possibly have been reconciled by, say, Thomas Gates (though it seems to me extremely unlikely), but who among England's aristocratic governors of Virginia would have lined up the isolato Mosco with the two kings for a reward? True, Smith gave him the last—and therefore no—choice. But each Rappahannock Indian maiden was a prize. After all, the werowance of Moraughtacund had gone to war to abduct them.

Smith admired a good speech and recorded several by Powhatan. He also appreciated and recalled in detail one by Ocanindge, "whose worthy discourse deserveth to be remembred"
(1:261). After the king of Paspahegh, "a most strong stout Salvage,"
tried to kill Smith in the spring of 1609 and Smith captured him
(1:200), the king escaped. Thereafter the Paspaheghs repeatedly
waylaid the English. Captain Peter Winne took to the field and in-
effectually combated them. Smith was then president and trying to
do everything. His actions contrast with Winne's inconclusive en-
deavors. Smith set out against the Indians. When the Paspaheghs
saw Smith leading the fighting party, they "threw down their armes
and desired peace." Their "stout young" orator Ocanindge declared their situation. Beginning with a rhetorically beautiful invitation to appreciate the Indians' position, Ocanindge apologized
for the escape of the Paspahegh werowance:

> if hee have offended you in escaping your imprisonment;
> the fishes swim, the fowles flie, and the very beastes strive
> to escape the snare and live; then blame not him being a
> man, hee would entreat you remember, your being a pris-
> oner, what paines he tooke to save your life; if since he
> hath injured you he was compelled to it, but howsoever,
> you have revenged it with our too great losse. We perceive
> and well knowe you intend to destroy us, that are here to
> intreat and desire your friendship, and to enjoy our houses
> and plant our fields, of whose fruit you shall participate,
> otherwise you will have the worst by our absence, for we
> can plant any where, though with more labour, and we
> know you cannot live if you want our harvest, and that re-
> liefe wee bring you; if you promise us peace we will beleeve
> you, if you proceed in reveng, we will abandon the Coun-
> trie. [1:261–62]

Warrior Smith immediately transformed into the diplomat. Ever
practical as well as humane, Smith pledged friendship—so long as
the Indians kept their word.

When Smith in England encountered Uttamatomakkin (or
Tomocomo), Powhatan's councillor and brother-in-law of Pocahan-
tas, he wryly recorded that the Indian had attempted, at Powhatan's
direction, to count all the Englishmen. Tomocomo reported to
Smith that he had got a long stick when he arrived at Plymouth in

order to make a notch on it for "all the men he could see, but he was quickly wearie of that taske" (2:261). Smith noted too that Tomocomo was disappointed in his treatment. He had instructions from Powhatan to meet the king and queen. Smith knew and convinced Tomocomo that he had indeed been presented to the king. After Tomocomo realized that he had in fact met James I, he was offended. Smith recorded his touching observation: "You gave Powhatan a white Dog, which Powhatan fed as himselfe, but your King gave me nothing, and I am better than your white Dog" (2:261).

Pocahontas was Smith's special favorite among the Indians. He described her in the first extant reference, *A True Relation* (1608), as "a child of tenne yeares old, which not only for feature, countenance and proportion, much exceedeth any of the rest of his people, but for wit, and spirit, the only Nonpariel of his Country" (1:93). But along with Pocahontas, Powhatan sent "his most trustie messenger, called Rawhunt, as much exceeding in deformitie of person, but of a subtill wit and crafty understanding," to negotiate with Smith (1:93). Smith recognized and appreciated both aspects of Powhatan's strategy—the innocent, appealing, beautiful Pocahontas and the subtle, crafty, and ugly Rawhunt.

Smith revealed his embarrassment when he saw Pocahontas in London in the late autumn of 1616. "Hearing shee was at" Brentford "with divers of my friends," Smith "went to see her." He recorded her reaction: "after a modest salutation, without any word, she turned about, obscured her face, as not seeming well contented." Smith was nonplussed. So he, John Rolfe, and others left Pocahontas alone for "two or three houres." Smith wryly wrote that he was "repenting my selfe to have writ" Queen Anne that Pocahontas "could speake English." Finally Pocahontas came and told him of her anger for his neglect. Smith uncomfortably recorded her charge against him. In Virginia, she said, "you did promise Powhatan what was yours should bee his, and he the like to you; you called him father being in his land a stranger, and by the same reason so must I doe you." Smith thought it would be inappropriate in English society for Pocahontas, a king's daughter, to call him father, but as he tried to explain this to her, Pocahontas charged him with moral cowardice. To Smith's credit, he savored and recorded her reaction. She said: "Were you not afraid to come into my fathers Countrie, and caused feare in him and all his people (but mee) and feare you here I should call you father; I tell you then I will, and you shall call mee childe, and so I will bee for ever and ever your Countrieman. They did tell us alwaies you were dead, and I knew no other till I came to Plimoth; yet Powhatan did command Uttamatomakkin to seeke you, and know the truth, because your Countriemen will lie much" (2:261.

As Smith wrote Queen Anne, Pocahontas was small of stature but of great spirit (2:261). He was chagrined by his last meeting with Pocahontas. She made him feel guilty for not coming to see her sooner. But the anecdote, more than any other evidence, gives the reader an indication of the personality and character of Pocahontas. And knowing well that the statement attacked the English but appreciating its truth, Smith recorded Powhatan's opinion of the English, "your Countriemen will lie much."

Smith found Pocahontas attractive physically as well as mentally ("which not only for feature, countenance, and proportion, much exceedeth any of the rest of his people, but for wit, and spirit, the only Nonpariel of his Country" [1:93]), and his later account of her and two Indian maidens who came with her to England shows that he approved of intermarriage both personally and as policy. The two Indian maids were sent to Bermuda in 1621 "to be married to some would have them, that after they were converted and had children, they might be sent to their Countrey and kindred to civilize them" (2:384, 386).[8] Did Smith ever consider courting and marrying her? In 1612 he recorded that his enemies circulated the rumor that "hee would have made himselfe a king, by marrying Pocahontas." In fact, he was probably too busy running the colony, and she may still have been only fourteen when Smith was "blowne up with powder" in September 1609 and, his genitals mutilated, left the colony (1:274, 272).

More evidence could be added, but I believe that the information given above should convince any impartial person that Smith knew and appreciated Indians as individuals and that he treated them well when they deserved it and circumstances allowed.

Indian Warfare

Indians, probably a group subject to Powhatan, attacked the whites at their first landing at Cape Henry, April 26, 1607 (1:27).[9] Several weeks later, on May 18, the Paspaheghs, with about one hundred warriors, assaulted Jamestown but retreated after a fight (*JVJV* 139). On May 26, while Newport, Smith, Archer, and twenty others were exploring the James River, the Paspaheghs, now reinforced with warriors from Powhatan's other tribes to perhaps three hundred, attacked and nearly wiped out Jamestown. Only the ship's ordnance saved the whites (1:31; *JV* 95).[10]

For several months thereafter, the Indians kept up a constant warfare. Though many Indians were happy to trade with strangers, most automatically assumed unknown humans to be enemies. No Indians wanted the whites to settle permanently on their land. Smith could not blame them. He sympathized with the plight of the Indian—and even with their reasons for wanting to annihilate the whites. In some cases, it was because the whites had mistreated or killed them (1:361). When a captive, Smith was taken before the Rappahannock Indians to see whether he was the captain who had abducted several Rappahannocks a year or more before (1:51–52).[11] He had not, of course, and he scorned whites like Captain Thomas Hunt who kidnapped Indians (1:433). Smith wanted to include some soldiers in his projected New England colony "because of the abuses which have beene offered the poore Salvages" by people like Hunt and by the French (1:335). Indeed, Squanto of Plymouth colony fame was probably an Indian whom Smith repatriated to New England in 1614.[12]

The Indians also would kill the whites if a good occasion offered, "for their weapons and commodities, that were rare commodities." Once they realized that the whites were gradually taking over their lands, they resolved to fight. Writing after the 1622 massacre, Smith judged their attitude natural: "now they feare we may beate them out of their dens, which Lions and Tygers would not admit but by force" (1:432). He was struck by Amoroleck's explanation why the Mannahoacks ambushed the whites: "They heard we were a people come from under the world, to take their world from them" (2:175). Smith identified with the "poore salvages, whose Countrie wee challenge, use and possesse" (1:361, 2:437), but he knew if the early whites were to survive, they must have food from the Indians—by trade, if possible; by force, if necessary. If, however, he found force necessary, Smith always gave something in exchange for what the whites took.

In spring 1608, after most Indians had eaten their stored corn, they began frequently stealing from and even bullying the whites at Jamestown who were under orders from the Virginia Company at home not to abuse them. In *A True Relation* Smith told some incidents that he had forgotten by the time he wrote *The Generall Historie*. One particularly audacious Indian stole two swords. Smith asked for and received permission to set him in the stocks. The punishment, however, failed to deter him. The very next day, he returned with three more Indians and attempted to wrestle tools out of the whites' hands within the fort at Jamestown. "Their custome," said Smith, "is to take any thing they can ceaze off." Smith ordered the group to leave the fort. The same audacious Indian made the mistake of attempting to hit Smith (who was probably smaller than he), "which I prevented, striking him first." And then Smith, with a half-dozen men, chased the group off the peninsula (1:81–83).

Smith was pleased that the Indians generally seemed to like and trust him: "Such acquaintance I had amongst the Indians, and such confidence they had in me, as neare the Fort they would not come till I came to them, every of them calling me by my name, would not sell any thing till I had first received their presents, and what they had that I liked, they deferred to my discretion: but after acquaintance, they usually came into the Fort at their pleasure" (1:61–63). These exchanges took place during January and February 1607/8, before the local Indians had exhausted the last harvest's supply. By April or May, however, even the Indians within Jamestown stole from and threatened the whites. When Smith and Matthew Scrivener were out planting corn, two Indians, "each with a cudgell, and all newly painted with Terrasigillata, came circling about mee as though they would have clubed me like a hare." Smith refrained from attacking them but called Scrivener and retired to the fort. Proclaiming their friendship, the two Indians accompanied Smith and Scrivener to Jamestown and "asked me for some" Indians "whom they would beate." Encountering Amocis the Paspaheghan (who had adopted the whites and lived with them at Jamestown), "they offered to beat him." Two more Indians joined the first two. When Smith attempted to persuade "them to forbeare, they offered to beginne with me" (1:87; cf. 1:82–83). Too much! Smith ordered the gates of Jamestown shut and imprisoned all the Indians therein (1:87).

The next day, the Paspaheghs outside the fort captured two whites and demanded that the incarcerated Indians be released.

The council refused and voted to attack the Paspaheghs. The latter, however, then brought back the two captives and "freely delivered them" (1:89). Or so declared *A True Relation*. *The Proceedings* and *The Generall Historie*, however, said that Smith "sallied out amongst them, and in lesse then an houre, he so hampred their insolencies, they brought them his two men, desiring peace" (2:159; cf. 1:220). (That makes much better sense to me than the causeless delivering up of the two whites.) Thereupon President Ratcliffe released one Indian.

The whites wondered what was going on. Sometimes the local Indians were friendly and then sometimes they were hostile, without, so far as the whites could perceive, any reason for the change. "The Council concluded that I should terrifie them with some torture" in order to learn their intentions (1:89). Smith did not actually physically torture any Indians; he did, however, threaten them. Using age-old interrogation tactics, he took out the first Indian, questioned and threatened him, and then had his men fire off a volley of shots, so that the remaining Indians thought their comrade had been slain (2:159; cf. 1:89, 93, 220). The next Indian was bound to the main mast of the *Phoenix* and a firing squad of "sixe Muskets with match in the cockes" took aim at him while Smith questioned him. This Indian proclaimed that he did not know the strategy of the Indians but that another prisoner, Macanoe (1:93), who was a counselor of the Paspaheghs, was privy to all their strategy. Macanoe was brought out, and Smith threatened him with the rack and with a firing squad. Macanoe revealed that Powhatan directed all the actions of the Indian tribes who came to Jamestown and that he received the weapons and tools carried off by the Indians (1:89–90).

In reprinting the writings of authors who insulted the Indians, Smith sometimes silently suppressed affronts and sometimes replied to them. Edward Waterhouse wrote in 1622 that Opechancanough's traditional home was "onely . . . a cottage, or rather a denne or hog-stye."[13] Smith copied the passage but omitted the insult (2:295).[14] When writers condemned the Indians as cowards, Smith contradicted them: "But I must tell those Authors, though some might be thus cowardly, there were many of them had better spirits" (2:298). As he said in his general evaluation of Indian culture: "Some are of disposition fearefull, some bold, most cautelous, all Savage" (1:160). Smith appreciated the fact that the Indians did not want to lose lives in warfare. Neither did Smith. He recorded Powhatan's strategy in surprising and conquering the Payanka-tanks (a neighboring Indian village) in 1608: "First he sent diverse of his men to lodge amongst them that night, then the Ambusca-does invironed al their houses, and at the houre appointed, they all fell to the spoile, 24 men they slewe, the long haire of the one side of their heades with the skinne cased off with shels or reeds, they brought away. They surprised also the women and the children and the Werowance. All these they present to Powhatan. The Werowance, women and children became his prisoners, and doe him service" (1:175, 2:128).

Smith also witnessed a mock war between large groups of Indians and recorded their strategy (2:120). J. Frederick Fausz, seizing upon this example, has claimed that before the whites came Indians fought in "massed battle formations and open-field heroics" and that it was only the musket warfare that drove them to "hit-and-run guerilla tactics."[15] That seems to me, however, to put the Indians into a foolish straitjacket of tactics. They were not so simple. Indian tribes sometimes used battle formations (the Kecoughtans marched out in a "square order" [2:144]), but most Indian fighting parties that Smith encountered did not (recall the two ambushes set up by the Rappahannocks). Smith generalized, "Their chiefe attempts are by Stratagems, trecheries, or surprisals" (2:119). Like the Indians, Smith was an adaptable fighter, and he trained his soldiers to imitate, when possible, the Indian method of taking advantage of all cover the terrain offered. When the Mannahoacks attacked Smith's party in August 1608, Smith noted that "there was about an hundred nimble Indians skipping from tree to tree, letting fly their arrows so fast as they could: the trees here served us for Baricadoes as well as they" (2:175).[16]

Just as Smith judged the Turks superior to the Europeans as fighters "by reason of their hardness of life and constitution" (3:199), so too he appreciated the Indians' stoicism and physical toughness. When they waded through the freezing oozy mud to help the whites, Smith noted that they "seemed to take a pride in shewing how litle" they "regarded that miserable cold and durty passage, though a dogge would scarce have indured it" (1:73). In December 1607, while Smith was a captive, he persuaded Opechancanough to have a letter taken to Jamestown: "This he granted and sent three men, in such weather, as in reason were unpossible by any naked to be indured" (1:49). Smith noted, "They are very strong, of an able body and full of agilitie, able to endure to lie in the woods under a tree by the fire, in the worst of winter, or in the weedes and grasse, in Ambuscado in the Sommer" (2:114–15). He thought perhaps their early training was partly responsible. "To make" the children "hardie," the Indian mothers washed their infants "in the coldest mornings . . . in the rivers," but he also said that grease and painting helped inure them: "painting and oyntments so tanne their skinnes, that after a yeare or two, no weather will hurt them" (2:116).

When the Virginia authorities apologized for their inability to avenge the 1622 massacre ("for the Salvages are so light and swift, though wee see them [being loaded with armour] they have much advantage of us though they be cowards" [2:110–11]), Smith scoffed. He reminded them that "by reason, art and vigilancy, courage and industry," the Indians could be "slaine, subjected or made tame." The Indians were "still but Salvages as they were, onely growne more bold by our owne simplicities, and still will be worse and worse till they be tormented with a continuall pursuit, and not with lying inclosed within Palizados, or affrighting them out of your sights" (2:311).

Smith proposed building a series of forts near the fall line of the major rivers from the James to the Potomac and having several forces of forty soldiers patrol between the forts. Some Indians, Smith believed, would join the whites: "Now if but a small number of the Salvages would assist us, as there is no question but divers of them would; And to suppose they could not be drawne to such faction, were to beleeve they are more vertuous then many Christians, and the best governed people in the world" (2:317). With a series of forts and several roving forces of soldiers, it would be easy to kill Opechancanough's Pamunkeys and to deal "with any other enemies at our pleasure" (2:317). If warfare was necessary, Smith was an expert. Echoing Harriot, he wrote in the opening of *Advertisements*: "The Warres in Europe, Asia, and Affrica, taught me how to subdue the wilde Salvages in Virginia and New England, in America" (3:269).

Trade and Tribute

After Thomas Studley's death on August 28, 1607 (*JV* 144), Smith became cape merchant or supply officer. Smith ("whom no perswa-

sions could perswade to starve" [2:192]) was responsible for the
food. He therefore began trading with the Indians or, if necessary,
enforcing tribute (2:331). He told how he began "trade abroad" in
A True Relation. In November 1607, with food running out, most of
Jamestown's "chiefest men," the gentlemen, were willing to starve
and die. Smith wasn't. Taking half a dozen men, he went to Kecoughtan "to trade for Corne, and try the river for Fish." Storms
prevented the latter. "The Indians thinking us neare famished,
with carelesse kindnes offered us little pieces of bread and small
handfulls of beanes or wheat, for a hatchet or a piece of copper."
To these outrageous terms Smith replied "in like maner." "But the
Children, or any that shewed extraordinary kindeness, I liberally
contented with free giftes, such trifles as wel contented them"
(1:35). According to *A True Relation*, the Indians simply changed
their minds and began to trade the next day. (One may suspect that
the London editor expurgated Smith's account at this place.) But in
The Generall Historie Smith told what happened. Facing starvation,
Smith resolved to enforce tribute from the Indians. Expecting to
have to use weapons, Smith had his men load their muskets with
pistol shot so that they would not kill the Indians: "But seeing by
trade and courtesie there was nothing to be had, he made bold to
try such conclusions as necessities inforced, though contrary to his
Commission: Let fly his muskets, ran his boat on shore, whereat
they all fled into the woods. So marching towards their houses, they
might see great heapes of corne: much adoe he had to restraine his
hungry souldiers from present taking of it, expecting as it hapned
that the Salvages would assault them, as not long after they did with
a most hydeous noyse" (2:144).

The expert soldier Smith appreciated the force presented by
the Indians and recorded their massed formation, a "square order,"
probably with the foremost Indians carrying shields to protect
them from arrows—a good defense against traditional Indian enemies. But the shields were nearly useless against Smith's version of
buckshot aimed at the Indians' legs:

> Sixtie or seaventie of them, some blacke, some red, some
> white, some party-coloured, came in a square order, sing-
> ing and dauncing out of the woods, with their *Okee* (which
> was an Idoll made of skinnes, stuffed with mosse, all
> painted and hung with chaines and copper) borne before

them: and in this manner being well armed, with Clubs,
Targets, Bowes and Arrowes, they charged the English,
that so kindly received them with their muskets loaden
with Pistoll shot, that downe fell their God, and divers lay
sprauling on the ground; the rest fled againe to the woods,
and ere long sent one of their *Quiyoughkasoucks* to offer
peace, and redeeme their *Okee*. [2:144]

At such times Smith disclosed his reasonableness and even a bit of
diplomatic genius. Instead of trying to subject the Kecoughtan Indians to harsh terms, he made allies of them, giving them the items
he had at first offered to trade: "Smith told them, if onely six of
them would come unarmed and loade his boat, he would not only
be their friend, but restore them their *Okee*, and give them Beads,
Copper, and Hatchets besides: which on both sides was to their
contents performed: and then they brought him Venison, Turkies,
wild foule, bread, and what they had, singing and dauncing in
signe of friendship till they departed" (2:144–45).

Necessity dictated Smith's depredations, but he always attempted to make amends. Typically, the result of Smith's resort to
force was that the Indians and the whites celebrated a successful
trade and a new alliance. Smith's policy reflected not only the
whites' necessity but also his personal diplomatic skills, characteristic fairness, and decency. When the Indians ran out of food, Smith
had compassion for them, gave them "part againe in pittie," and
made sure that they had seeds to plant in the spring (1:432).
Searching the "countries of Youghtanund and Mattapamient" for
food, he found that "the people imparted what little they had, with
such complaints and tears from women and children, as he had bin
too cruell to be a Christian that would not have bin satisfied, and
moved with compassion" (1:256).

The amicable relations that Smith established with the Kecoughtan Indians in November 1607 continued throughout his
time in Virginia. Just after Christmas 1608 Smith set out to visit
Powhatan, but a blizzard came up, and Smith and his party of forty-
six men sought refuge at Kecoughtan. There they spent "Christmas among the Salvages" (actually the Christmas season from December 31 through Twelfth Night, January 6), where "we were
never more merry nor fed on more plentie of good Oysters, Fish
Flesh, Wild-foule, and good bread; nor never had better fires in

England, than in the dry smoaky houses of Kecoughtan" (2:194). Apparently Smith recalled the occasion with pleasure.

In early September 1608, returning from his second exploring expedition up the Chesapeake Bay, Smith sailed up the Nansemond River (which flows into the south side of the James River opposite Newport News) to make friends with those Indians and to trade. Though Captain Christopher Newport spent little time in the colony, he had during his second Virginia visit (January–March 1607:8) attempted to barter with the Nansemonds, but seeing they were preparing an ambush, Newport had attacked them, killing at least one and wounding several others (1:79). Smith hoped to make allies of these Indian "neighbours neare home, as [he had with] so many Nations abroad." The first Nansemond Indians Smith saw were "making their wires" (i.e., their weirs or fish traps), but they fled on seeing the whites. "Ashore we sent, and where they wrought we threw divers toyes, and so departed." The Indians caught up with them; one of them "desired us to goe to his house up that river, into our Boat voluntarily he came, the rest ran after us by the shore with all shew of love that could be" (2:178).

They sailed up the Nansemond River until they came to great cornfields on both sides and an island which also had cornfields. The Indian in their boat lived on the island. Smith visited his house, gave presents to his wife and children, and then sailed farther up the ever-narrowing river. Meanwhile the few Indians whom they had seen at first increased on each side of the river, all with their bows and arrows. Behind their barge appeared "seaven or eight Canowes full of men armed." When they reached a heavily wooded area, "presently from each side the river came arrowes so fast as two or three hundred could shoot them, whereat we returned to get the open" (2:179). The warriors in the canoes "let fly also as fast, but amongst them we bestowed so many shot, the most of them leaped overboord and swam ashore, but two or three escaped by rowing" (2:179). When Smith and his men got back down to the plains and cornfields on each side of the river, they seized all the canoes and moored them in the middle of the river. "More than an hundred arrowes stucke in our Targets, and about the boat, yet none hurt, onely Anthony Bagnel was shot in his Hat, and another in his sleeve."

Smith resolved to destroy the Indians' boats, take their corn, and then burn their houses on the island. The whites began "to cut in peeces their Canowes." When the Indians saw that, they lay down their bows and made signs of peace. "Peace we told them we would accept, would they bring us their Kings bowes and arrowes, with a chayne of pearle; and when we came again give us foure hundred baskets full of Corne, otherwise we would breake all their boats, and burne their houses, and corne, and all they had." The Indians agreed, brought as much corn "as we could carry," and so the whites departed "good friends" (2:179).

When Indians stole the whites' tools and weapons, Smith was sure to punish them, but he never used needless cruelty or killed them for theft (1:220–21, 2:160). The Indians came to accept Smith as the one white whom they could trust and rely upon. He became "their Market Clarke" (2:154) because they found that others would abuse or cheat them. Smith's authority, however, ceased in August 1609. Seven ships of the Gates-Somers fleet reached Virginia, carrying Smith's old enemies John Ratcliffe, John Martin, and Gabriel Archer. They triumphantly brought the news that a new charter (even though it was on the flagship carrying Gates and Somers, which had been caught in a hurricane and wrecked on the Bermudas) had been issued on May 23, 1609. The new charter superseded the old one, under which Smith had been elected president of the council. The flabbergasted Smith did not know what to do. His authority was gone, but the newcomers, lacking the ship carrying Gates and Somers, began quarreling among themselves. Smith offered to resign in favor of John Martin, who quickly refused the responsibility. Smith resolved to run the colony until September 10 unless Gates and Somers arrived sooner. September 10 was the scheduled time for the annual election under the old charter, and then all the persons who said they were councillors under the new charter could elect a new president.

Smith knew that the several hundred new colonists could not stay all huddled together at Jamestown with the more than one hundred colonists already there. In the previous spring, when he found that rats had devoured the corn, Smith sent one party with Ensign William Laxon "downe the river to live upon Oysters," another group "with lieutenant Percy to try for fishing at Poynt Comfort," and a third group with "Master West . . . went up to the falls" (2:213), while various individual whites "were billetted amongst the Salvages, whereby we knew all their passages, fields and habitations, how to gather and use there fruits as well as themselves; for they did know wee had a commanding power at James towne they durst not wrong us of a pin." The main party at Jamestown lived primarily on sturgeon and "Tockwhogh roots" (2:213), while rebuilding the town, constructing a good well, and planting "thirty or forty Acres" (2:212). Smith's policy worked well, with only seven colonists dying during the spring and summer of 1609. Though the new colonists disputed his authority, they reluctantly agreed to be guided by him until September 10 (*JV* 282–83).

Smith sent Francis West "with an hundred and twentie of the best he could chuse" to the falls (Richmond). And he sent Captain John Martin "with neare as many to Nandsamund." They were given "their due proportions of all provisions according to their number." George Percy stated that West went to the falls "with sixe monthes victewells to inhabitt there." Despite the evidence of Smith and Percy, J. Frederick Fausz blames Smith for the outbreak of Indian hostilities in August and September 1609, claiming that he sent "rude and raucous colonists to eat up the provisions of alienated local tribes."[17] It seems to me, however, that Smith chose the only practical course of action in dispersing more than two hundred colonists to other locations.[18] Though he no doubt expected the parties to supplement their diet with fish, fowl, game, and plants, they carried enough food to live until the spring without any additions.

Smith could not imagine that the whites would deliberately and causelessly attack the Indians, but these fools (thinking Smith was no longer in absolute authority) did just that. "The people [Indians] being contributors [paying tribute of corn to the whites] used him [Captain John Martin] kindly; yet such was his jealous feare, in the midst of their mirth, he did surprise this poore naked King, with his Monuments, houses, and the Isle he inhabited, and there fortified himselfe; but so apparantly distracted with feare, as emboldened the Salvages to assault him, kill his men, release their King, gather and carry away a thousand bushels of Corne, he not once offering to intercept them" (2:221).

Francis West and his men, also believing themselves free from the authority of Smith, were as bad as Martin. "That disorderlie company so tormented those poore naked soules, by stealing their corne, robbing their gardens, beating them, breaking their houses, and keeping some prisoners; that they dailie complained to Captaine Smith" (1:271). Smith sympathized and identified with the

Indians. The actions of the whites disgusted him. He claimed that "neither all the Counsels of Spaine, nor Papists in the world could have devised a better course to bring them all to ruine, then thus to abuse their friends" (2:314). Smith asserted that "there was more hope to make better Christians and good subjects" of the Indians "then the one halfe of those" with him in Virginia "that counterfeited themselves both" (2:215). Martin, West, and the other leaders simultaneously denied Smith's authority and called for his help. He chased up and down the James River, trying to placate the Indians and to impose order on the whites. As he sailed down the James, sleeping in exhaustion, he was "blown up with powder," and his Virginia career ended.

By his fighting ability, respect for life, shrewdness, lack of prejudice, practicality, and diplomacy, Smith managed to establish and preserve peace and friendly relations with the various Indian tribes he encountered around the Chesapeake Bay. That was an amazing accomplishment. Over three years after Smith had left Virginia, Samuel Purchas recorded in *Purchas His Pilgrimage* (1613) Smith's reputation and influence with the Indians: "*Powhatan* had aboue thirtie Commanders, or *Wirrowances*, vnder him, all which were not in peace onely, but seruiceable, in Captaine *Smiths* presidencie, to the English, and still as I have been told by some that have since beene there, they doe affect him, and will ask of him." [19] In prefatory verses for *The Generall Historie*, Edward Jorden said that he had heard the Indians praise Smith: "*Much traveld Captaine, I have heard thy worth / By* Indians, *in* America, *set forth*" (2:51). If Smith had remained in Virginia, he would have continued trying to keep the Indians not only from fighting the whites but also from constantly warring with one another. But when his authority ended with the arrival of the remnants of the Gates-Somers fleet in August 1609, his carefully constructed détente with the Powhatan Indians collapsed.

Psychology and Superstition

Returning from the first exploring trip up the Chesapeake Bay in mid-July 1608, Smith and his companions stopped at Kecoughtan, where the Indians, "seeing our captaine hurt [from a stingray], and another bloudy (which came by breaking his shin), [and] our number of bowes, arrowes, swords, targets, mantles and furs; would needs imagine we had bin at warres." When Smith found that "the truth of these accidents would not satisfie them," he made use of a basic psychology that served him well. He would let the Indians believe that he and the whites were great warriors. The ironic humor regarding "secret" in the following sentence reveals Smith's characteristic appreciation of the difference between idealism and practicality, appearance and reality: "finding their aptnes to beleeve, we failed not (as a great secret) to tel them any thing that might affright them, what spoile wee had got and made of the Masawomeckes. This rumor went faster up the river then our barge" (1:229). Attacked by the Tockwogh Indians on the Eastern Shore in early August, Smith again used "the invention of Kecoughtan" (1:231) to persuade the Tockwoghs that he was an enemy to the Massawomekes and thus their friend. The ploy worked again. Nor was Smith above using the Indians' superstitions to secure an advantage. His display and explanation of the "compasse diall" when captured in 1607 (1:47) probably gave him some celebrity as a medicine man. He wrote in *The Proceedings* that the cosmological explanation made the Indians admire "him as a demi-God" (1:213). And in *The Generall Historie* he said that they "admired him more then their owne *Quiyouckosucks*" (i.e., their lesser gods [2:146]).

Smith added greatly to his reputation as a medicine man in the spring of 1609 when he imprisoned two brothers whose confederate had stolen a pistol. Smith freed one, promising that if he did not return the pistol within twelve hours, his brother would hang. The night grew cold, and Smith, "pittying the pore naked Salvage in the dungeon, sent him victuall and some charcole for fire." But the prisoner used too much charcoal at once, smothered, and fell partially in the fire. His brother returned before midnight, but the captive appeared to be dead. The brother "most lamentably bewailed his death, and broke forth in such bitter agonies that the President [Smith], to quiet him, told him that if hereafter they would not steal, he wold make him alive again: but little thought hee could be recovered." Smith, however, did his best with "aquavitae and vineger," and the Indian rejuvenated, seemingly brought back to life. So much liquor had been poured down his throat, however, that he was "so drunke and affrighted that he seemed lunaticke, not understanding any thing hee spoke or heard; the which as much grieved and tormented the other, as before to see him dead." Smith promised to make him better, "and so caused him to be laid by a fire to sleepe: who in the morning having well slept, had recovered his perfect senses." The result was "that this was spread amongst all the Salvages for a miracle, that Captaine Smith could make a man alive that is dead" (1:262).

Smith tried to talk about the Christian God when he had a willing Indian audience, and he remained surprised at the Indians' failure to be converted. Smith thought that the Indians acknowledged the Christian God to be superior to their own. He cited Quiyoughcohanock, "whose devotion, apprehension, and good disposition much exceeded any in those Countries, who though we could not as yet prevaile withall to forsake his false Gods, yet this he did beleeve that our God as much exceeded theirs, as our Gunnes did their Bowes and Arrows; and many times did send to the president, at James towne, men with presents, intreating them to pray to his God for raine, for his Gods would not send him any" (1:172). The situation puzzled Smith. An anthropologist explains that the Indian "illustrated the common logic of polytheistic people who often have no objection to adding foreign deities to their pantheon if it seems to assure more efficient control of the natural universe." Quiyoughcohanock was not converting to Christianity: "The chief was not interested in changing his religious customs in emulation of the Europeans; he merely wished to improve his own culture by judicious borrowing—a gun at one time, a supernatural being at another."[20]

Smith gradually became reconciled to the Indians' lack of interest in Christianity. He recorded that Powhatan told Tomocomo to see the English God. Tomocomo was disappointed that he had not been able to do so. Smith again did his best to explain the Christian religion, but he must have realized that despite his repeated efforts, Powhatan, Tomocomo, and other Indians had little concept of Christianity (2:261). Smith even recorded the humorous reply given by the king of Pawtuxent: "Hee much wondered at our Bible, but much more to heare it was the Law of our God, and the first Chapter of Genesis expounded of Adam and Eve, and simple mariage; to which he replyed, hee was like Adam in one thing, for he never had but one wife at once." Smith noted that the king of Pawtuxent, like "all the rest, seemed more willing of other discourses they better understood" (2:289). Smith never, however, became reconciled to the London Company's official hypocrisy. The authorities proclaimed that the main reason for colonizing was to convert the Indians, but the company and its later officials behaved otherwise. Few whites were interested in the Indians. Smith scornfully said that the company and its officers made "religion their colour, when all their aime was nothing but present profit" (3:272).

Religion was one means of imposing order and discipline upon the small group of whites alone in a boundless pagan universe. Smith revealed in passing that during the 1608 exploring expeditions up the Chesapeake Bay, "our order was, dayly, to have prayer, with a psalm" (1:231). The whites' ceremony impressed the Susquehannocks. After witnessing the ritual, the Susquehannocks "were long busied with consultation." Then "they began in a most passionate manner to hold up their hands to the sunne, with a most feareful song, then imbracing the Captaine, they began to adore him in like manner, though he rebuked them, yet they proceeded til their song was finished, which don, with a most strange furious action, and a hellish voice, began an oration of their loves" (1:232). Though unwilling to go so far as to allow the Indians to think that he was a god, Smith was entirely willing to perpetuate superstitions about himself.

Smith knew that the fundamental reason for the 1622 massacre was that the Indians perceived the whites were gradually taking more and more of their traditional farmlands. Smith, however, also reported the immediate occasion of the war's origin. The Indian warrior/medicine man Nemattanow or Jack of the Feather killed a man named Morgan early in March 1622. Because of his courage and wisdom, Nemattanow was a leading werowance, and the Indians believed that he was "immortall from any hurt could bee done him by the English." But Nemattanow was subsequently killed by two of Morgan's servants. As he lay dying, he asked that they keep it a secret that "hee was slaine with a bullet" and asked that he be buried among the English. His death, however, became known, and Opechancanough "grieved and repined, with great threats of revenge" (2:293). Fourteen days later, on March 22, 1622, the Indians attacked.[21]

Smith as Ethnologist

Since the formal study of anthropology has existed, anthropologists have appreciated Smith's qualities as an observer of Indian culture. He frequently showed a surprising sensitivity about inter-

preting Indian culture in terms of postfeudal European civilization. When he explained that the Indians had no "letters wherby to
write or read," he noted that customs were their only laws. But then
he added that their customs had the force of laws: the werowances
"are tyed to rule by customes." Lest the reader interpret the word
werowance as "king," Smith clarified: "But this word Werowance
which we call and conster [consider] for a king, is a common worde
whereby they call all commanders: for they have but fewe words in
their language, and but few occasions to use anie officers more then
one commander, which commonly they call werowances" (1:178).
Though Europeans wanted to believe that the Indians did not own
land and that whites could therefore settle in America without actually depriving Indians of their lands,[22] Smith flatly denied the
European belief: "They all know their several lands, and habitations, and limits, to fish, foule, or hunt in, but they hold all of their
great Werowance Powhatan, unto whom they pay tribute of
skinnes, beads, copper, pearle, deere, turkies, wild beasts, and
corne" (1:174, 2:127). Smith realized that like most tribes and nations, the Powhatans were self-centered and surprisingly ignorant
of the surrounding tribes. The Powhatan Indians thought they
lived in the center of the world, and they knew only a few neighboring Indian tribes. Likewise, the Susquehannocks "knowe no more
of the territories of Powhatan then his name, and he as little of
them" (1:232). Amoroleck, the Mannahoack, said that the only Indians he knew were the Powhatans, the Monacans, the Massawomekes, and the Nantaughtacunds (2:175). Smith appreciated the
generosity of Indians, gave examples of it, and sometimes explained their beneficence to his readers: "victuals you must know is
all there wealth, and the greatest kindnes they could shew us"
(1:67).

Unfamiliar systems were difficult for the Europeans to grasp,
but Smith came to understand such different ones as matrilineal
inheritance. He explained in *A True Relation* that "each of his breth-
eren succeeded other" and then added: "For the Crowne, their
heyres inherit not, but the first heyres of the Sisters, and so succes-
sively the weomens heires: For the Kings have as many weomen as
they will, his Subjects two, and most but one" (1:61). Describing the
Indians' inheritance in *A Map of Virginia*, he was clearer: "His kingdome descendeth not to his sonnes nor children, but first to his
brethren . . . and after their decease to his sisters. First to the eldest

sister then to the rest and after them to the heires male and female of the eldest sister, but never to the heires of the males" (1:174).

Smith's increasing knowledge and understanding of Indian customs may be found in his differing accounts of their burial customs and ideas of afterlife. In *A True Relation* he wrote: "The death of any they lament with great sorrow and weeping: their Kings they burie betwixt two mattes within their houses, with all his beads, jewels, hatchets, and copper: the other in graves like ours. They acknowledge no resurrection" (1:59). An anonymous early seventeenth-century annotator of Smith's *A True Relation*, who seems to have had some knowledge of Virginia and its Indians, criticized Smith's account: "This Author I fy[nde] in many errors w[hich?] they doe impute to h[is?] not well understa[n]ding the language[,] for they doe Ackno[w]ledge both God [&] the Devill and that af[ter] thei are out of this world they shall r[ise?] againe in anothe[r] world where the[y?] shall live at ea[se] and have great[e] store of bread a[nd] venison and other [????]" (1:59). In *A Map of Virginia*, however, Smith gave more details about both the burial of the kings and the ordinary people (1:169). He had learned, furthermore, that the Indians believed in an afterlife—at least for the leaders and medicine men: "They thinke that their Werowances and Priests which they also esteeme *Quiyoughcosughes*, when they are dead, doe goe beyound the mountaines towardes the setting of the sun, and ever remaine there in forme of their *Oke*, with their heads painted with oile and copper, and tobacco, doing nothing but dance and sing, with all their Predecessors. But the common people they suppose shall not live after death" (1:172).

One could list numerous further examples of Smith's ethnographic observations. Some have been given in chapter 2, describing his individual publications, and others have been discussed in chapter 3, in the section on exoticism. Smith was an extremely curious, intelligent, and accurate observer of the American Indians. The columns of entries under his name in the index to John R. Swanton's *The Indians of the Southeastern United States* amply prove the extraordinary number and exactness of his observations. Though I agree with Carville V. Earle that "the full story of Smith's ecological and ethnographic sensitivity and his application of this knowledge remains untold,"[23] I hope that material presented herein justifies my opinion that Smith was the most careful observer of Indian customs, manners, language, religion, and individuals of his day.

Smith's relations with tribes other than the Powhatans commonly followed a regular pattern. Smith's overtures of friendship and trade by the whites, an attack by the Indians, a vigorous defense by Smith's men, a parlay between the two sides, and, finally, trade and a declaration of friendship. During the time he spent in Virginia, Smith became a comparative Indian expert, learning to speak the Powhatans' Algonquian and to know more of the various Indian tribes around the Chesapeake Bay area than the tribes themselves knew. Smith's relationships with the Powhatans embody two opposing myths. On the one hand, after the Powhatans realized that the whites intended to remain in Virginia, Smith's relations with Powhatan, Opechancanough, and the Powhatan tribes were a constant ritual of death. As I will prove in the next chapter, genocide was clearly the intent of the Powhatan Indians, and preservation of the whites while getting food from the Indians was Smith's purpose. Suspicion, fear, treachery, and death typify his encounters with the Powhatans. On the other hand, the Pocahontas/Smith meetings have all the allure of the Romeo/Juliet story, the star-crossed lovers from warring families. They embody the pastoral dream of love, of the lion lying down with the lamb, of the peaceable kingdom. Pocahontas/Smith is the mythic American Dream; Powhatan/Smith is the nightmare reality. In his relations with the Indians, Smith accomplished the impossible task of balancing with ease on a seesaw of terrorism and utopianism. Powhatan and he were well matched, and their relations deserve a separate chapter.

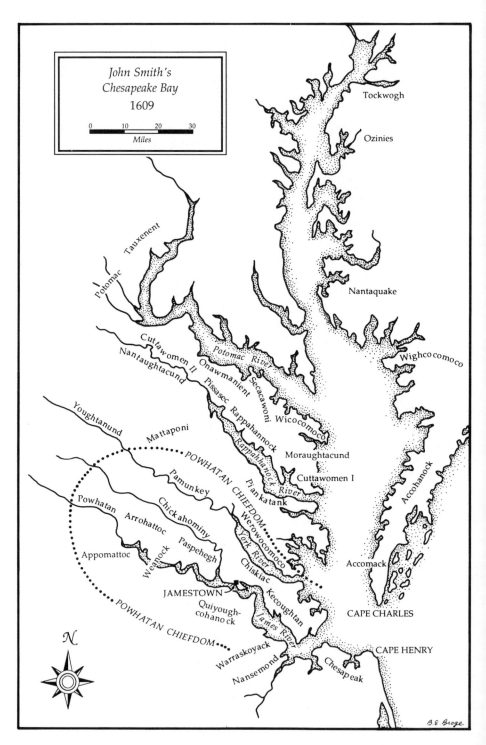

John Smith's Chesapeake Bay, 1609

7

Powhatan and Smith

Think you I am so simple not to knowe, it is better to
eate good meate, lie well, and sleepe quietly with my
women and children, laugh and be merrie with you, have
copper, hatchets, or what I want, being your friend; then
bee forced to flie from al, to lie cold in the woods, feed
upon acorns, roots, and such trash, and be so hunted by
you, that I can neither rest, eat, nor sleepe; but my tired
men must watch, and if a twig but breake, everie one crie
there comes Captaine Smith.

—From Powhatan's speech to Smith at their last meeting,
January 1608/9. *The Proceedings* (1612; 1:247).

S MITH wrote more about Powhatan, the great creator of the
Powhatan Confederacy, than any other Indian. The two leaders were well matched. They respected each other and, at
first, tried to manipulate one another. Powhatan regarded Smith as
a werowance, a leader among his people, and as a bit of a medicine
man. Half a dozen years after Smith had left Virginia—and after
the whites had repeatedly assured Powhatan that Smith was dead—
the Indian leader instructed his adviser Uttamatomakkin (called
Tomocomo by the English) and his daughter Pocahontas to look
for Smith in England. Evidently Powhatan could hardly accept the
death of the indomitable young white. When Smith sought out Pocahontas in 1616, she said: "They did tell us alwaies you were dead,
and I knew no other till I came to Plimoth; yet Powhatan did command Uttamatomakkin to seeke you, and know the truth, because
your Countriemen will lie much" (2:261). On his side, Smith com-
prehended Powhatan's role as overlord and strategist for the surrounding Indian tribes. He knew and esteemed the "subtle salvage" chief as a worthy and dangerous adversary.

Though their meetings usually lasted several days, Powhatan
and Smith only met on five occasions. The first encounter occurred
at the end of 1607, after Smith had been captured by Opechancanough's warriors. The captive described Powhatan's appearance in *A
True Relation*:

> Arriving at Werawocomoco, their Emperour proudly lying
> uppon a Bedstead a foote high upon tenne or twelve
> Mattes, richly hung with manie Chaynes of great Pearles
> about his necke, and covered with a great Covering of *Ra-
> haughcums* [raccoon skins]: At his heade sat a woman, at his
> feete another, on each side sitting uppon a Matte uppon
> the ground were raunged his chiefe men on each side the
> fire, tenne in a ranke, and behind them as many yong
> women, each a great Chaine of white Beades over their
> shoulders, their heades painted in redde, and [he] with
> such a grave and Majesticall countenance, as drave me into
> admiration to see such state in a naked Salvage. [1:53]

A True Relation provides a good description, but *The Generall Historie*
version is clearer. Each rendering contains a detail or two not present in the other (*The Proceedings* omits Smith's first meeting with
Powhatan [cf. 1:213]):

Before a fire upon a seat like a bedsted, he sat covered with
a great robe, made of Rarowcun skinnes, and all the tayles
hanging by. On either hand did sit a young wench of 16 or
18 yeares, along on each side the house, two rowes of men,
and behind them as many women, with all their heads and
shoulders painted red; many of their heads bedecked with
the white downe of Birds; but every one with something:
and a great chayne of white beads about their necks. At his
entrance before the King, all the people gave a great
shout. [2:150–51]

Neither *The Proceedings*'s (1612) skimpy account of Smith's captivity nor *The Generall Historie*'s longer one details Powhatan's interest in Western technology or Smith's description of the world.
A True Relation (1608), however, tells that Powhatan "much de-
lighted" in Opechancanough's relation of Smith's explanation of
the universe with the aid of a compass (1:47, 49) and "oft examined
me upon the same" (1:53). On the other hand, Opechancanough's
fascination with Smith's "round Ivory double compass Dyall" is presented at greater length in *The Generall Historie* (2:147) than in *A
True Relation* (1:47). The two later accounts (*The Proceedings* and *The
Generall Historie*) also omit Smith's first fascinating conversation
with Powhatan.

Powhatan asked why the English had come to Virginia. The
London Company's council knew that the Indians would resent the
English intention to settle in Virginia permanently. In their "Instructions given by way of advise," the council said that the colonists
should trade with the Indians "before that they perceive you mean
to plant among them" (*JV* 51–52). Smith realized that Powhatan
would want to kill the colonists if he knew that they planned to
settle there. Smith made up a story about the English being in a sea
fight with the Spanish and coming ashore for fresh water (1:53).
Powhatan then asked why the English had explored so far into the
interior with their boat. Smith said that on the other side of the
mountains, where there was salt water (at the time Smith, like all
other Europeans, still hoped to find the Pacific Ocean just over the
mountains), the Monacan Indians (enemies of Powhatan) had slain
Newport's child, "whose death we intended to revenge" (1:55).

On his side Powhatan told him that several days' journey beyond the falls, there was a great ocean. There were also to the west

"people with short Coates, and Sleeves to the Elbowes, that passed that way in Shippes like ours." And inland to the south there was "a countrie called Anone, where they have abundance of Brasse, and houses walled as ours" (1:55). As Wesley Frank Craven observed, Powhatan "resorted at times to the familiar trick of assuring them [the whites] that everything they hoped to find on the upper James, where resided his enemies the Monicans, was there to be found."[1]

Thus the very first exchange between the two began with Powhatan trying to learn why the whites had come to his country and with Smith's lie, though a lie Smith judged necessary both for his own life and that of the colony. Powhatan, in turn, told his lies, thus trying to make use of the whites.[2] Smith replied by telling of England's empire (1:55–57).

Smith omitted many incidents in divulging the story of his captivity in *A True Relation*, including Pocahontas's saving his life. Smith also skipped (see 1:53, 55 [the information, however, was indirectly revealed when Smith described his next meeting with Powhatan]) Powhatan's promise to release Smith in exchange for four "Demy Culverings" (large cannons [1:65]). During his captivity, Smith agreed to the exchange, knowing that the Indians would be unable to carry the cannons. In *The Proceedings*, Smith said that at his return, Powhatan sent "divers of his men loaded with provision, he had conditioned, and so appointed his trustie messengers to bring but 2 or 3 of our great ordenances, but the messengers being satisfied with the sight of one of them discharged, ran away amazed with feare, till meanes was used with guifts to assure them our loves" (1:213). In *The Generall Historie*'s expanded account, Smith told of a religious ritual carried out by Powhatan, his werowances, and medicine men to determine Smith's (and the colonists') intentions. The ritual's results were favorable:

> Two dayes after [Pocahontas saved Smith], Powhatan having disguised himselfe in the most fearefullest manner he could, caused Captaine Smith to be brought forth to a great house in the woods, and there upon a mat by the fire to be left alone. Not long after from behinde a mat that divided the house, was made the most dolefullest noyse he ever heard; then Powhatan more like a devill then a man with some two hundred more as blacke as himselfe, came unto him and told him now they were friends, and pres-

ently he should goe to James towne, to send him two great
gunnes, and a gryndstone, for which he would give him
the Country of Capahowosick, and for ever esteeme him as
his sonne Nantaquoud. [2:151]

Instead of *A True Relation*'s four cannons (1:65) or *The Proceedings*'s
two or three "great ordenances" (1:213, the trade was now for two
cannons and a grindstone (2:151. Obviously Smith did not think
the exact details of the supposed trade were important and did not
reread *A True Relation* to refresh his memory—or to try to be con-
sistent. Powhatan's and Smith's first encounter, with Smith a captive, lasted three or four days, concluding with the above ritual, on
Friday, January 1, directly after which Powhatan sent Smith back to
Jamestown, where he arrived on Saturday morning, January 2,
1607/8.

The second meeting with Powhatan occurred about seven
weeks later, in late February 1607/8 when Smith visited Werowocomoco on the Pamaunk (York) River. Invited by Powhatan to come
to trade, the whites set out following the guides Powhatan supplied.
Smith and twenty men, constituting the lead party, took the short-
cut overland, while Newport (who had arrived back in Virginia on
January 2, 1608, with the first supply) and a large group sailed by
the circuitous river route. Namontack and the werowance of Kis-
kiak led. They seemed to Smith, however, to pretend to be unfamiliar with the route, thus rousing his suspicions. They took the colonists through a valley "intercepted by a great creek over which they
had made a bridge of grained stakes and railes." Viewing the
treacherous bridge, Smith warily thought that the exposed and
dangerous situation that the whites must traverse was reason "to
suspect some mischiefe" (1:63). Therefore Smith "intermingled
the Kings sonne [Nantaquoud], our conductors, and his chiefe
men amongst ours, and led forward, leaving halfe at the one ende
to make a guard for the passage of the Front." Smith recorded that
the Indians, "seeing the weaknesse of the Bridge, came with a
Canow, and tooke me in of the middest, with foure or five more:
being landed, wee made a guarde for the rest till all were passed"
(1:63).

No comparable passage exists in *The Proceedings*. Though *The
Generall Historie* omits much of the material included in *A True Relation*, Smith nevertheless recalled in 1624 the treacherous Indian

bridges he had crossed some fifteen years earlier: "made of a few cratches, thrust in the ose, and three or four poles laid on them, and at the end of them the like, tyed together only with barkes of trees, that it made them [the whites] much suspect those bridges were but traps." By 1624 Smith had forgotten that the Indians took him partway over in a canoe, but he remembered his suspicions. Seeing the precarious bridge, Smith made "diverse Salvages to goe over first, keeping some of the chiefe as hostage till halfe his men were passed to make a guard for himselfe and the rest" (2:155).

Finally, Smith and his men arrived at Werowocomoco. He presented Powhatan with a red suit, a white greyhound, and a hat: "as Jewels he esteemed them, and with a great Oration made by three of his Nobles, if there be any amongst Salvages, kindly accepted them, with a publike confirmation of a perpetuall league and friendship" (1:65). Smith recorded that Powhatan appreciated the trick that Smith had played upon him in promising to let the Indians have cannons when he returned from captivity: "with a merrie countenance he asked me for certaine peeces which I promised him, when I went to Paspahegh. I told [him] according to my promise, that I proffered the man that went with me foure Demy Culverings, in that he so desired a great Gunne, but they refused to take them; whereat with a lowde laughter, he desired [me] to give him some of less burthen, as for the other I gave him them, being sure that none could carrie them" (1:65). The exchange occurs neither in *The Proceedings* nor in *The Generall Historie* (cf. 1:216, 2:156).

Now began the ritualistic dance of death that characterized all Powhatan's and Smith's subsequent dealings. Powhatan constantly tried to get the English to leave their arms behind. Smith knew that if the English did, the Indians could massacre them with impunity. And Smith thought that Powhatan planned to. After Powhatan greeted Smith and his advance party, the chief said that, "he expected to have all these men lay their armes at his feet, as did his subjects." Smith replied that only the whites' enemies desired that ceremony, "but never our friends" (1:65, 67). Smith added that Newport would give him "a child [i.e., a hostage] of his, in full assurance of our loves."

The next day (about the end of February 1607/8), Newport arrived by boat with his party, proceeding ashore "with a trumpet before him." Powhatan again asked, "Why we came armed in that sort, seeing he was our friend, and had neither bowes nor arrowes"

(1:69). (Of the armed Indian warriors in the surrounding area [2:155], Powhatan said nothing.) Newport gave Powhatan Thomas Savage, "whom Newport called his sonne; for whom Powhatan gave him Namontack his trustie servant, and one of a shrewd, subtill capacitie" (2:156). In *A True Relation*, Smith said that Powhatan gave Namontack to Newport to go with him to England in place of his son Thomas Savage, adding that Powhatan's reason "was to know our strength and countries condition" (1:79). Powhatan later—and perhaps at this time—suspected that the English had come to America because they lacked food and timber.

When the actual trading began, Powhatan "desired to see all our Hatchets and Copper together, for which he would give us corne." The crafty trader Smith, however, knew that gambit: "with that auncient tricke the Chickahomaniens had oft acquainted me." He asked what Powhatan would give for one copper kettle, but the chief said that such bickering was beneath him: "Hee seeming to despise the nature of a Merchant, did scorne to sell, but we freely should give him, and he liberally would requite us." Captain Newport agreed to Powhatan's terms and set out at once "twelve great Coppers" (i.e., large copper pots). In return, Smith reported, Powhatan gave Newport as much corn as Smith received for one small copper pot at Chickahominy. Powhatan further insisted on trading for hatchets at his own rate (1:71).

Retelling the story in *The Proceedings* (repeated in *The Generall Historie*), Smith made the exchange more dramatic. Smith gave Powhatan a brief speech: "Captaine Newport it is not agreeable with my greatnes, in this pedling manner to trade for trifles, and I esteeme you a great werowans. Therefore lay me down all your commodities together; what I like I will take, and in recompence give you what I thinke fitting their value" (1:217). Smith, who interpreted, warned Newport that Powhatan's intent was only "to cheat us." But Newport, "thinking to out brave this Salvage in ostentation of greatnes, and so to bewitch him with his bounty," agreed to Powhatan's terms. Smith grew angry with Newport, for "we had not 4 bushells" of corn in exchange for trade goods that Smith hoped to barter for "20 hogsheads" (1:217, 2:156). The food was insufficient to feed the colonists until the summer, but Newport would not starve, for he would soon sail back to England (he left on April 10 1608. *The Proceedings* reported that the difference "bred some unkindnes betweene our two captaines, Newport seeking to please the humor of the unsatiable Salvage; Smith to cause the Salvage to please him" (1:217, 2:156).

Obviously Powhatan was a better negotiator and businessman than Newport. But Smith was not quite through. He displayed some blue beads, pretending to have only a few and to set great store by them. Powhatan wanted them. *The Generall Historie* account is dramatic and engaging: "A long time he importunately desired them, but Smith seemed so much the more to affect them, as being composed of a most rare substance of the coulour of the skyes, and not to be worne but by the greatest kings in the world. This made him halfe madde to be the owner of such strange Jewells" (2:156). In the end, Powhatan traded two or three hundred bushels of corn for a pound or two of blue beads (1:71, 217).

The third morning, Powhatan sent his son to the Englishmen's barge to tell them not to bring their weapons with them, "least his weomen and children should feare." Captain Newport obliged Powhatan, but Smith and his followers took their arms. When Powhatan saw Smith, he again asked him to leave his weapons, "much misliking my sword, pistol and target," but Smith replied that the Monacans who had slain Newport's child, Smith's brother, had persuaded him to do so, and once they were unarmed, "shot at us, and so betraide us" (1:71). Powhatan appealed to Newport, asking him to have his men leave their weapons, but Smith refused. Thus ended the second meeting between Powhatan and Smith. Years later, when Smith retold the story in *The Generall Historie* (2:155–57) from the bare-bones account in *The Proceedings*, he had forgotten most of the details and generally omitted Powhatan's incessant requests that the whites abandon their arms. During the second meeting, Smith spent at least five days with Powhatan, two or more before Newport arrived and at least three afterwards. Newport and his party returned to Jamestown on March 9, 1607/8 (*JV* 228).

When Newport was about to depart for England in early April, Powhatan "presented him with 20 Turkies, conditionally to returne him 20 Swords, which immediately were sent him." Smith noted in a marginal heading that it was "an ill example to sell swords to Salvages" (1:220; cf. 1:79, 2:159). After Newport's departure, Powhatan "presented Captaine Smith with the like luggage," but Smith refused to trade for weapons, whereupon Powhatan ordered his people to steal the whites' weapons whenever they could (1:220). Growing gradually bolder, the Indians finally would "surprise us at work, or any way," wresting tools and even weapons from the colonists' hands within the fort. Orders from England, Smith explained, were "so straight not to offend them as our authority bearers (keeping [i.e., hiding out within] their houses) would rather be any thing then peace breakers." Soon, however, Smith could no longer stand such insolence and began imprisoning thieving Indians (1:220).

As a result of interrogating Indian captives in the spring of 1608, Smith learned from Macanoe, one of the "counsell of Paspahegh," that Powhatan had devised a plan for the eventual annihilation of the whites. Smith recorded in *A True Relation* that the Paspaheghs and the Chickahominies were to harass the whites at work, steal their tools, and capture any stragglers. Meanwhile, Powhatan's closest allies would pretend to be friends until Captain Newport returned and Newport's hostage Namontack was safely returned. Then, Powhatan would hold a great feast for Newport, and when he was least prepared, Powhatan would "ceaze on him" (1:89, 91). *The Proceedings*'s version (1:220) is skimpy. Other incidents confirmed Powhatan's inimical strategy. The Patawomeke Indians attacked Smith on June 16, 1608, "commaunded to betray us, by Powhatans direction" (1:227, 2:167).

The third and fourth meetings with Powhatan occurred in October 1608. Since Smith had sent off the manuscript of *A True Relation* with Captain Francis Nelson of the *Phoenix* on June 2, reports of these meetings only appear in *The Proceedings* and *The Generall Historie*. With four white men and Namontack (just returned from England with Newport),[3] Smith (who disagreed with the action requested by the Virginia Company but was outvoted by the other councillors) invited Powhatan to come to Jamestown to receive the presents Newport had just brought from England and to be crowned. Powhatan, however, was away on a hunting trip. That night Pocahontas and the other Indian women staged a "Virginia Maske" for Smith (1:235–36). When Powhatan returned the next day, the subtle savage was as suspicious as the wily white. Powhatan said he would not go to their fort: "neither will I bite at such a baite" (1:236). Powhatan had evidently resolved by this time never to put himself into the hands of the English.[4] The news from his spy Namontack would only have further alarmed him. Powhatan had hoped to make use of the English for his own purposes. But Namontack surely told him that the white invaders were a mighty

people, with as many warriors as sand on the shores and with great
and mighty cities. Namontack's intelligence probably strengthened
Powhatan's resolve to eliminate the whites as soon as possible.

Powhatan agreed to wait eight days to receive Newport. Smith
returned to Jamestown with the message. Newport shortly sailed
for Werowocomoco. The presents were delivered and the farce of
coronation enacted. With Smith's help Captain Newport crowned
Powhatan. Namontack persuaded Powhatan that the scarlet cloak
and other English dress would not hurt him. Smith wrote: "a fowle
trouble there was to make him kneele to receave his crowne, he
neither knowing the majestie, nor meaning of a Crowne, nor bend-
ing of the knee, indured so many perswasions, examples, and instructions, as tired them all. At last by leaning hard on his shoulders, he a little stooped, and Newport put the Crowne on his head."
(The English were behind in the coronation: Powhatan's adoption
of Smith into the Powhatan Confederacy at the end of December
1607 had the same purpose.) Smith drove home his attitude toward
such flummery by noting that Powhatan, in return for the numerous gifts from the whites, "gave his old shoes and his mantle to
Captain Newport" (1:237). "His old shoes and his mantle"—such
was the stuff of kingship. One could argue that the passage indirectly reveals Smith's reverence for "the majestie" and "meaning of
a Crown." But it would have been impolitic if not treasonable for
Smith directly to satirize either the idea or the trappings of royalty.
Smith objected to the foolish coronation because it made Powhatan
"so much overvalue himselfe, that he respected us as much as nothing at all" (just like a king!) and because the "strange Coronation"
took so much time and valuable resources (2:181). One suspects
these criticisms were as true, in Smith's opinion, for European royalty.

How different was William Strachey's response to Powhatan!
Writing two years later, Strachey echoed Smith but added that Powhatan's majestic bearing must be attributed to "an infused kynd of
diviness, and extraordinary (appointed as it shal be so by [the] king
of kings) to such who are his ymediate instruments on earth (how
wretched soever otherwise vnder the curse of misbelief and Infidelity)."[5] Strachey clearly believed in and echoed Hamlet's expression
about that "divinity which doth hedge a King . . . how wretched
soever otherwise under the curse of misbelief and infidelity"
(4.5.124). Whether Smith knew *Hamlet* or not, he would never have

echoed the sentiment. These two encounters with Powhatan, Smith's third and fourth, probably lasted one and four days, respectively.

When Smith went to Chickahominy in November 1608 to trade, the Indians refused, "with as much scorne and insolencie as they could expresse" (1:239, 2:186). Smith surmised that they were following Powhatan's orders and that Powhatan intended to starve the English. He told the Chickahominies that "he came not so much for their corne, as to revenge his imprisonment, and the death of his men murdered by them" (1:239, 2:186). Landing his men in military order, matches burning to fire the muskets, Smith prepared to charge. The Indians fled but shortly after sent back spokesmen loaded with food. Naturally Smith traded. The following month, when Smith attempted to trade with the Indians at Nansemond, he found that at first they refused to do so, "excusing themselves to bee so commanded by Powhatan" (1:242, 2:191). Smith resorted to a threat, marching his men toward the Indians, who decided "they would rather sell us some, then wee should take all" (1:242). And so he bartered for 100 bushels of corn, leaving the Indians as friends. According to the more specific account in *The Generall Historie*, after pleading that Powhatan had commanded them not to trade, the Indians fled. Smith set one Indian house on fire, and the Indians reappeared, promising to give half their corn, and so "loaded our three Boats" (2:191).

The fifth and last time that Smith met Powhatan was in January 1608/9, when Smith journeyed to Werowocomoco at Powhatan's invitation. David Beers Quinn has argued that at their last meeting Powhatan confessed to Smith that he had killed the remnants of the "Lost Colonists" along with their Chesapeake Indian allies. Quinn claimed that all the prior contacts between the whites and Powhatan show that the whites did not then know that Powhatan had killed the remnants of the Roanoke colonists.[6] Quinn especially stressed that the London Company could not have known this information when Newport left for Virginia, about August 1608, with the second supply and with instructions to crown Powhatan. Yet the company's instructions to Thomas Gates, issued before May 15, 1609, referred to Powhatan's killing the lost colonists "vppon the first arrivall of our Colonie" and ordered Gates either to make Powhatan a prisoner or to make him pay tribute.[7] The dramatic change in the company's attitude toward Powhatan means that Captain Newport must have carried back to England the news that Powhatan had killed the lost colonists when he left Virginia, about December 1, 1608.

If Smith, who objected to crowning Powhatan but was outvoted by the other councillors, had known about the massacre of the lost colonists before October 1608, he would surely have used the information. But he failed to convince Newport and the other councillors, and the crowning went off without any especial trouble. Therefore it seems likely that Newport and Smith only learned about the killing in November 1608. Quinn theorized that William White, who had lived with the Powhatans for some time, was a good possibility for the information. Or perhaps some Indian, now friendly to Smith, told of the slaughter. At any rate Smith certainly checked out the information with various sources, for neither the Virginia Company nor William Strachey expressed any doubt that Powhatan killed the lost colonists, though there were multitudinous rumors and the London Company's silence on most matters was deafening. Quinn concluded, "A full report to the king by Smith, the remaining councillors, and Newport, with strict injunctions to secrecy on those who knew about the matter, would be the obvious policy to pursue. This would accord with what is told by Strachey of a report made to the king on Powhatan's killing of the lost colonists."[8]

Quinn's thesis makes good sense. Every one of the first four meetings between Smith and Powhatan ended with Smith seemingly content with the course of events. Samuel Purchas stated that Powhatan himself told Smith he had killed the lost colonists: "Powhatan confessed to Cap. Smith that hee had beene at their [the lost colonists'] slaughter, and had divers utensills of theirs to shew." Purchas elsewhere noted that "Powhatan confessed that hee had bin at the murther of that Colonie: and shewed to Cap. Smith a Musket barrell and a brasse Morter, and certaine peeces of Iron which had bin theirs."[9] Smith evidently did not know during the first four meetings with Powhatan that the overlord had been responsible for the death of the lost colonists. But his attitude toward Powhatan was different during this last meeting. He said nothing directly about the Roanoke colonists, perhaps trying to maintain friendly relations with the Powhatan Indians (if not with Powhatan) even after the London Company had given up.

When Powhatan invited Smith to come to trade, he promised that if Smith would send him men to build a house, bring him a grindstone, fifty swords, some pieces [i.e., guns], and a cock and a hen, with copper and beads, that he would load Smith's ship with corn (1:242). Smith sent four Dutchmen to build the house, asking one especially to spy upon Powhatan (1:243–44). Several days after the Dutchmen left on the short overland route, Smith "set forth with the Pinnas, 2. barges, and six and forty men" by the circuitous water route (1:243). Evidently Smith was now prepared for trouble. In the previous October, he had gone to see Powhatan to arrange for the coronation with just four men. Now in January 1608/9 he took a strong force. The first night of the journey by water, Smith stopped at Warraskoyack (on the south side of the James below Jamestown) where the Warraskoyack chief warned him that Powhatan intended to kill him: "bee sure hee hath no opportunitie to seaze on your armes; for hee hath sent for you only to cut your throats" (1:244, 2:193).

When Smith arrived at Werowocomoco, the sight of twenty-four fresh scalps hanging on a line between two trees greeted him. For some unknown reason, Powhatan had recently slaughtered the Payankatank warriors, "his neare neighbours and subjects," and proudly showed the scalps to the whites, supposing "to halfe conquer them, by this spectacle of his terrible crueltie" (1:175). Powhatan denied that he had sent for Smith, but after Smith pointed out the Indians who had brought the message, "the king concluded the matter with a merry laughter." Powhatan, however, would only trade for "gunnes and swords," refusing the usual copper, "saying he could eate his corne, but not his copper" (1:246). After Smith replied that he had no superfluous swords or guns and vowed friendship, "except you constraine mee by your bad usage," Powhatan promised within two days to trade what he could spare (1:246, 2:194).

At this, their last meeting, Powhatan again brought up the subject of why the whites were in his country. By now, he knew the answer. Powhatan said, "many doe informe me, your comming hither is not for trade, but to invade my people, and possesse my Country" (2:195). Smith's silence is telling. He did not relate his reply. Perhaps he said some few Englishmen were going to stay in Virginia to supply a base against the Spanish—or to find a route to the South Sea—but whatever he said, I am sure that he was not honest. Neither, of course, was Powhatan. Powhatan said that since Smith and his men were armed, the Indians were afraid to come to trade with them. Powhatan urged them to "leave abord your weapons, for here they are needlesse" (1:246, 2:195). Smith noted that the Dutchmen, "finding his plenty, and knowing our want" and perceiving Powhatan's preparation to betray Smith, "little thinking wee could escape both him and famine," cast their lot with Powhatan. They told him everything they knew about the colonists (1:246, 2:195). When Powhatan questioned Smith, he knew the colonists intended to settle permanently in his land. In making spies of the Dutchmen, Powhatan was only going Smith one better, for Smith counted on a Dutchman to spy on Powhatan (2:195).

Smith and Powhatan lied to one another. Powhatan tried to use Smith and the whites in his strategic warfare. The English, however, led by Smith, had instead formed alliances with other Indian nations. They had not been defeated by Powhatan's enemies and had gradually become a formidable enemy. Powhatan knew the reddish-blonde, bristly-haired Englishman well, for all his subordinate tribes reported their actions—and their submissions to Smith—to Powhatan, no doubt asking the overlord, What else could we have done? If they had not traded, Smith would have taken all their corn (rather than some of it) and would have ruined their villages as well. The task of killing Smith was referred to Powhatan. But Powhatan's artifices failed. Unable to kill Smith and the whites with impunity, Powhatan tried diplomacy. He made a brilliant speech on the difference between peace and war. Smith obviously appreciated it, though he must have doubted the sincerity of Powhatan's conclusion:

> Captaine Smith you may understand, that I, having seene
> the death of all my people thrice, and not one living of
> those 3 generations, but my selfe, I knowe the difference
> of peace and warre, better then any in my Countrie. But
> now I am old, and ere long must die, my brethren, namely
> Opichapam, Opechankanough, and Kekataugh, my two
> sisters, and their two daughters, are distinctly each others
> successours, I wish their experiences no lesse then mine,
> and your love to them, no lesse then mine to you; but this
> brute from Nansamund that you are come to destroy my

Countrie, so much affrighteth all my people, as they dare
not visit you; what will it availe you, to take that perforce,
you may quietly have with love, or to destroy them that
provide you food? what can you get by war, when we can
hide our provision and flie to the woodes, whereby you
must famish by wronging us your friends; and whie are
you thus jealous of our loves, seeing us unarmed, and both
doe, and are willing still to feed you with that you cannot
get but by our labours? think you I am so simple not to
knowe, it is better to eate good meate, lie well, and sleepe
quietly with my women and children, laugh and be merrie
with you, have copper, hatchets, or what I want, being your
friend; then bee forced to flie from al, to lie cold in the
woods, feed upon acorns, roots, and such trash, and be so
hunted by you, that I can neither rest, eat, nor sleepe; but
my tired men must watch, and if a twig but breake, everie
one crie there comes Captaine Smith, then must I flie I
knowe not whether, and thus with miserable feare end my
miserable life; leaving my pleasures to such youths as you,
which through your rash and unadvisednesse, may quickly
as miserably ende, for want of that you never knowe how
to find? Let this therefore assure you of our loves and everie yeare our friendly trade shall furnish you with corne,
and now also if you would come in friendly manner to see
us, and not thus with your gunnes and swords, as to invade
your foes. [1:247–48, 2:195–96]

Smith recognized Powhatan's skilled oratory, his point of view, and
his duplicity.

Smith replied that he and his men had kept their vow of love
and peace, but that Powhatan's promises were "everie daie violated"
by some of his subjects. Smith could lie as well as Powhatan: "for
your sake only," Smith had not exacted revenge. He said that "had
wee intended you anie hurt, long ere this wee coulde have effected
it." Finally trade began. But Powhatan remained unhappy that
Smith retained his weapons, that he always kept some men with
him on guard, and that the whites would not abandon their defenses. Powhatan recriminated with him, saying that he had never
used any other werowance as kindly as Smith. And yet "from you I
receave the least kindnesse of anie." Powhatan reminded Smith

that Captain Newport gave him whatever he desired and sent away weapons when he was asked (but Smith knew that he himself was present, with weapons, when Newport did so). All other chiefs did the same—except Smith. "Captain Newport you call father, and so you call me, but I see for all us both, you will doe what you list, and we must both seeke to content you." Powhatan continued on to request that if Smith was really friendly, he should "sende hence your armes that I may beleeve you" (1:248–49, 2:197).

Smith, of course, refused, believing that Powhatan "but trifled the time to cut his throat." Since Smith wanted to allay Powhatan's suspicions, he promised that "to content you, tomorrow I will leave my armes, and trust to your promise." Smith lied. Powhatan, however, was not to be fooled. The trading ended. While some Indians were breaking the ice so that Smith's boat could come to shore and take on the corn and men, Powhatan slipped away with the women and children, but "to avoid suspition, left 2 or 3 of his women talking with" Smith in the longhouse. Hearing some noise, Smith looked out and found the fields around the house filling up with warriors. Seizing his pistol, sword, and shield, Smith rushed through the surrounding Indians down to the guards at the shore. Retelling the incident in *The Generall Historie*, Smith added the information that he fired his pistol and that John Russell accompanied him in the flight through the warriors to the boat (1:249, 2:197).

"To dissemble the matter," to excuse his absence, and to apologize for the sudden appearance of a mass of Indian warriors, Powhatan sent Smith a great bracelet and a chain of pearls. The orator who presented the gifts explained that "fearing your guns," Powhatan had fled with the women and children, but he was still Smith's friend. If Smith would have his company send away their weapons, "which so affrighteth his people," Powhatan would return. But Smith would not relinquish his safeguards. Powhatan and Smith never saw one another again. The Indians provided baskets for Smith's men to carry the corn to the pinnace, and, Smith added ironically, "they kindlie offered their service to gard our armes" while the whites carried the corn. "A great manie they were, of goodlie well appointed fellowes as grim as divels," but Smith and his men cocked their muskets and prepared to fire. He then ordered the Indians to carry the corn to the boat. "Wee needed not importune them to make quick dispatch" (1:250).

Caught by the low tide, the whites had to remain at Werowo-comoco till dawn. The following incident, briefly mentioned in *The Proceedings* (1:250), contained no reference to Pocahontas, but in *The Generall Historie* Smith told a fuller story. As Smith and his men waited in the early night, Pocahontas appeared and told Smith that Powhatan was preparing a feast for the whites, but that while they were eating, Powhatan and several hundred warriors would attack. Smith pressed some presents upon her, "but with the teares run-ning downe her cheekes, shee said shee durst not be seene to have any: for if Powhatan should know it, she were but dead, and so she ranne away by her selfe as she came." Less than an hour later, the feast arrived, borne by "eight or ten lusty fellowes" who were "very importunate to have us put out our matches (whose smoake made them sicke) and sit down to our victuall." But Smith made them taste every dish and then sent several Indians as messengers to Powhatan, "to bid him make haste for hee [Smith] was prepared for his comming." Smith had only two or three of his men eat at a time; the rest stayed prepared with their musket matches burning. All night long, various Indian messengers came "to see what newes." "Thus wee spent the night as vigilantly as they, till it was high-water" (2:198–99).

Smith's attitude toward Powhatan was different during this last meeting, for Smith intended to return to Werowocomoco, "with a purpose, to have surprised him and his provision" (1:256, 2:205–6). Smith's knowledge that Powhatan had killed the lost colonists would explain why, for the first time, he intended to kill Powhatan. But Powhatan moved inland to Orapakes, a more remote and secure location. Both Smith and Powhatan knew that they were now playing a more dangerous game. Something had caused the change. David Beers Quinn's thesis makes good sense. Knowing that Powhatan had killed the lost colonists would be cause for Smith to seize or kill Powhatan, and Powhatan's realization that the whites now knew of his slaughter of the lost colonists and the Chesapeakes would have been reason for him to move.

When Smith left Werowocomoco, Powhatan sent two Dutch-men (Adam and Francis) overland to Jamestown, where they claimed that Smith had sent them for more arms. By this strata-gem, Powhatan secured "a great many swords, pike-heads, peeces, shot, powder, and such like." When Smith learned of the Dutch-men's perfidy, Smith asked for volunteers to find and kill them, but

Powhatan protected them (1:250). After Smith left Virginia in October 1609, the Dutchmen returned to spy upon the whites, but in the starving time they fled back to Powhatan. When Lord De La Warr arrived in Jamestown in June 1610, the Dutchmen asked to return to Jamestown, telling Powhatan "what wonders they would doe" for him. The chief, however, replied, "You that would have betrayed Captaine Smith to mee, will certainly betray me to this great Lord for your peace: so caused his men to beat out their braines" (2:226). Succeeding colonists had not Smith's caution. When the queen of Appomattoc invited fourteen whites "to feast and make merry" with her, they were persuaded "to leave their Armes in their boat." The queen "said how their women would be afrayd ells of their pieces." The result was a "treacherous Massacre."[10] Captain John Ratcliffe, who returned to Virginia in August 1609, was too proud and opinionated to learn from Smith. Asked by Powhatan to come to trade, Ratcliffe did not keep "a proper and fitting Courte of Guarde." He and thirty men were killed (2:232).[11]

An examination of Smith's attitude toward Powhatan reveals Smith's fundamentally egalitarian views. Almost all observers agreed that Powhatan was extraordinary. Smith furnished the best descriptions. He wrote that Powhatan conducted himself with "such a Majestie as I cannot expresse" and noted his "grave and Majesticall countenance" (1:65, 53). Despite his standard usages of the words *majesty* and *majestical*, Smith was not impressed with Powhatan because he was a king. Smith elsewhere referred scornfully to the laziness of royalty ("like a valiant Prince asketh what's the matter, when horrour and death stood amazed each at other" [3:174]; cf. "where they would be Kings before their folly" [3:298]) and to their ignorance and pampered condition (3:179). Smith found Powhatan striking as a person. He carefully detailed Powhatan's posture and situation, whether lying on an elevated bed on "ten mats" or sitting on a "throne," and commented on the respectful positions and attitudes of the surrounding Indians (1:53, 65). Smith also noted that "Powhatan carried himselfe so proudly, yet discretely (in his salvage manner) as made us all admire his naturall gifts, considering his education" (2:156, 1:216). Smith attributed Powhatan's extraordinary dignity and impressiveness to his appearance and bearing, the respect and fear with which the other Indians regarded him, his position as the area's greatest Indian chief, and his personal character. Smith obviously thought Powhatan a well-matched opponent.

There exists a comparatively subtle (and hitherto unremarked) indication of Smith's respect for Powhatan (and his comparative lack of respect for James I). In his great map of Virginia of 1612, Smith named the river on which the whites settled "Powhatan Flu." In doing so, Smith deliberately ignored the name that the whites had already given the river—the King's River or the James River. The colonists had named the river in 1607. Writing a "Description of the River and Country" in May or June 1607, Gabriel Archer said, "This River . . . we have named our kinges River" (*JV* 98). George Percy, in a diary of the first explorations, described Newport's setting up a cross at the falls of the river (the site of present-day Richmond): "The foure and twentieth day [Sunday, May 24, 1607] wee set up a Crosse at the head of this Riuer, naming it Kings Riuer, where we proclaimed Iames King of England to haue the most right vnto it." Samuel Purchas, printing Percy's account in his *Pilgrimes* (1625), chose to follow Smith's name (he also reprinted Smith's map of Virginia in the book) and added the marginal heading "Riuer of Pohatan" (*JV* 141).

In his apologia of 1608, Edward Maria Wingfield called it "the kinges river" (*JV* 221). The Virginia Company's "Instructions, Orders, and Constitutions . . . To Sir Thomas Gates, Knight, Governor of Virginia," of May 1609, twice referred to the "Kings River."[12] Gabriel Archer again used the appellation "the Kings Riuer" on August 31, 1609 (*JV* 281). The London Company's *A True And Sincere Declaration* (London: I. Stepney, 1610), which was entered for publication at Stationers Hall on December 14, 1609, called it the "*Kings River*."[13] Thomas Dale, writing on August 17, 1611, from Jamestown, identified it as "the Kings River."[14] William Strachey, whose *Historie of Travell into Virginia Britania* copied "about four-fifths of Smith's work [*A Map*] and included every passage actually describing the people, the country, or its products,"[15] followed Smith's name, the Powhatan River, once when actually copying Smith (p. 43), but twice Strachey added to Smith's name the phrase "or the Kings River" (pp. 41, 63). In a passage not taken from Smith, Strachey called it the "Kings River" (p. 37). Introducing a "Dictionary of the Indian Language," Strachey noted that the dictionary applied primarily to the area of the river "called by them

Powhatan, and by us, Kings River."[16] Finally, in *A Brief Declaration of the Present State of Things in Virginia*, the Council for Virginia referred to "the Lands lying along the Kings River."[17]

In the Zuniga copy (surreptitiously obtained by Zuniga and forwarded to Spain) of the map that Smith sent back from Virginia with Francis Nelson on June 2, 1608, along with the manuscript of *A True Relation*, the river is unnamed (*JV* 238–40).[18] But in the text of *A True Relation* (1608), Smith himself called it "the King's river" (1:81). Further, though he did not record Newport's ceremonial erecting of a cross and naming of the river, he was present on the occasion and described the exploring trip in *A True Relation* (1:31). The evidence testifies beyond a reasonable doubt that the commonly accepted name among the colonists for the river from 1607 to approximately 1617 was the King's (i.e., King James's) River. A few people besides Smith, however, referred to it as the Powhatan River. Henry Spelman, in his "Relation" written in England about 1613 (*AB* ci), refered to "the Powhatan River" (*AB* cii)—perhaps reflecting the influence of Smith's map and pamphlet.[19] The Reverend Alexander Whitaker, in *Good News from Virginia* (London, 1612), said that the river was "commonly called Powhatans River" (38).[20] On November 11, 1619, the governor and council in Virginia referred to "these three rivers of Roakoake Powsatan and Pamunky."[21]

Smith could have been following the Indian practice in 1612 when he named the river the "Powhatan river,"[22] but he knew that he was subverting the common white name and deliberately slighting King James. Smith explained that the river was not named for the Indian Powhatan but for "the name of a principall country that lieth upon it" (1:145, 2:102). Though Smith later explained that Powhatan's real name was Wahunsonacock (1:173, 2:126) and that he took the name Powhatan from his "principall place of dwelling" (1:173, 2:126), Smith certainly realized that for whites and Indians alike, the name Powhatan automatically called up the great Indian chief, not the area of that name. He may even have made an ironic reference to the honor actually due to King James. In the very paragraph that named the river "Powhatan," he described the situation of Jamestown and said that it was named "in honour of the Kings most excellent Majestie" (1:146, 2:103). I suspect that Smith thought that naming the miserable settlement "Jamestown" was sufficient honor for King James—and that Powhatan, not James, deserved to have the great river perpetuate his fame.

During the latter 1610s the name James River gradually superseded the earlier name, Kings River. By 1621 only the name James River appears commonly in the records of the Virginia Company.[23] During the time he composed *The Generall Historie* (1622–24), Smith must have known that James River was now the standard name, but he nevertheless persisted in calling it the Powhatan River in passages reprinted from *A Map of Virginia* (1:145, 147, 2:102, 104). In paraphrasing Virginia Company documents, however, he slipped and automatically used the name James River at least once in *The Generall Historie* (2:296). By the end of his life, even Smith seems to have realized that his effort to honor and perpetuate Powhatan by affixing his name to Virginia's major river had finally failed. In *The True Travels* Smith referred to the river with an awkward circumlocution, "the river of James Towne" (3:25). His Indian name may have failed, but Smith evidently preferred not to honor King James by calling Powhatan's river after the English king.

As long as Smith's map or its derivatives were current (to the late seventeenth century), the name Powhatan appeared on the river,[24] but the names King's River or James River surfaced on a few other maps. On June 22, 1607, Robert Tindall wrote to Prince Henry enclosing the first known map of Virginia drawn by a Jamestown colonist. A revised version, drawn by Tindall between March 9 and April 10, 1608, is extant. For the first time on a map, the river was labeled "King James's River" (*JV* 104–6).[25] The Velasco map (1611) called it "the Kings Riuer" (*JV* 336).[26] Lord Baltimore's map, published in Andrew White, *A Relation of Maryland* (London, 1635), was the first printed map to designate it the "Iames flu."[27] John Farrer's 1650 manuscript map used "James River" and his 1651 printed map "James His River."[28] The great Augustine Herrman map of 1673—the map that finally superseded Smith's map of 1612—settled the matter even so far as maps were concerned. Herrman used the name that had been standard among the locals since the late 1610s, the James River. Even the John Speed *Map of Virginia and Maryland* (London: Basset and Chiswell, 1676), which persevered in following the geography of Smith's map, used the Herrman map's toponymy.[29]

Though Smith's effort to memorialize Powhatan could be seen

as a part of his general policy of preserving Indian names on his maps, the local Indians may not have called the river the Powhatan.[30] Moreover, we positively know that the James River, unlike all the other rivers that flowed into the Chesapeake Bay, had a well-established name among the whites before 1612—a name that complimented the king of England—when Smith deliberately attempted to subvert that name and call the river "Powhatan."[31]

8

Dissatisfaction with
the Social Order

I am sure many would take it ill, to be abridged of the
titles and honors of their predecessors; when if but truly
they would judge themselves, looke how inferior they are
to their Noble Vertues, so much they are unworthy of
their honors and livings, which never were ordained for
shewes and shadowes, to maintaine idleness and vice, but
to make them more able to abound in honor, by
Heroicall deeds of action, judgement, pietie, and vertue.

—Smith on titles and honors, reprinted in *The Generall Historie*
(1624; 2:427) from his *A Description of New England* (1616; 1:350)

From *True Travels* (1630), last compartment

TH Killeth the BASHAW,
its and on his   horse
th·Chap·   17·

London Printed
by Iames Reeue

Gentlemen

SMITH believed that social conditions should be different and more egalitarian in the New World. He frequently revealed his impatience with the traditional social order. From his first publication in 1608 to his last in 1631, Smith castigated mere "gentlemen." The Cambridge historian H. C. Porter claimed that Smith "was not at all against gentlemen as such."[1] Perhaps Porter forgot that the primary characteristic of a Renaissance gentleman was someone who did not work—and who, indeed, disdained manual labor. As Theodore K. Rabb wrote, "the essence of their [the aristocrats'] social distinction was their contempt for such demeaning activity" as "manual labor."[2] Smith, however, prized work as meritorious in itself and scorned those gentlemen and others who "never did know what a dayes worke was" (2:225).

Smith often ignored the early seventeenth-century realities and used the word *gentleman* to mean "useless parasite." Smith found exceptions in Virginia (some gentlemen were brave), and he praised individuals for their achievement even if they were gentlemen, but in Smith's usage, the word *gentleman* usually had negative connotations. Few gentlemen could do anything. Describing the second exploring expedition up the Chesapeake Bay, Smith complained that the party had "not a marriner or any that had skill to trim their sayles, use their oares, or any businesse belonging to the Barge, but 2 or 3, the rest being Gentlemen or as ignorant in such toyle and labour" (1:149, 2:106). Though William Strachey copied Smith's information concerning geography and Indians that surrounded this passage, he omitted Smith's slurs on gentlemen.[3]

In his letter to the Virginia Company of London (c. December 1, 1608), Smith expressed his disgust with the persons sent over. Including the second supply's seventy people, Smith now had about 227 men and 2 women in Virginia (2:325 n.1) "but not twentie work-men" (2:324). Send over no more gentlemen! They were worthless! America needed, Smith said, good workers—a point he drove home with an awkward coinage that concluded the categories of laborers and craftsmen the plantation especially required: "When you send againe I intreat you rather send but thirty Carpenters, husbandmen, gardiners, fisher men, blacksmiths, masons, and diggers up of trees, roots, well provided; then a thousand of such as we have" (2:189–90). Needless to say, England had no such specialists as "diggers up of trees, roots"—but the phrase well expressed Smith's point. Virginia needed people who could do hard manual labor. It did not need and could not use more gentlemen.

In *The Generall Historie of Virginia* (1624), the knight-errant Smith even attacked the usual run of brave knights. The trouble was that they were gentlemen: "in Virginia, a plaine Souldier that can use a Pick-axe and spade, is better than five Knights, although they were Knights that could breake a Lance" (2:263). With acute psychology, Smith also explained why gentlemen were less suited than laborers to be colonists: "for men of great place, not inured to those incounters, when they finde things not sutable, grow many times so discontented, they forget themselves, and oft become so carelesse, that a discontented melancholy brings them to much sorrow, and to others much miserie" (2:263). Using comparisons to Vietnam prisoners of war, Karen Ordahl Kupperman confirmed Smith's shrewd evaluation: "The colonists' unwillingness to help themselves, their surrender to melancholy resulted from the complex interaction of environmental and psychological factors."[4] In a statement that must have shocked his religiously xenophobic Western contemporaries, Smith confessed he not only respected the Turks but even thought that in war or other hardships they had an advantage over the Christians "by reason of their hardnesse of life and constitution" (3:199).

Recording his achievements as president, Smith apologized for not building more substantial "houses . . . Forts and Plantations." He explained that there was "but one Carpenter in the Countrey, and three others that could doe little, but desired to be learners" (2:225). The published lists of colonists were, he said, deceiving. For "those we write labourers were for the most part footmen, and such as they that were Adventurers brought to attend them, or such as they could perswade to goe with them, that never did know what a dayes worke was: except the Dutch-men and Poles, and some dozen other." But most colonists were simply incapable of work, "for all the rest were poore Gentlemen, Tradsmen, Servingmen, libertines, and such like" (2:225). When Smith discovered in the spring of 1609 that rats had eaten most of the colonists' food supply, he divided the Jamestown colonists into smaller groups and sent them to various locations, so that they could subsist on oysters, fish, and edible wild plants; "but such was the strange condition of some 150, that had they not beene forced *nolens, volens,* perforce to gather and prepare their victuall they would all have starved or eaten one another" (2:213). Such was the condition of gentlemen.

Contrasting the Massachusetts Bay planters with the group that sailed for Virginia in 1607–10, Smith praised the 1630 emigrants, "men of good meanes, or Arts, Occupations, and Qualities," not "such as flye for debt, or any scandall at home." The Bay Colony had people "more fit for such a businesse, and better furnished of all necessaries if they arrive well, than was ever any Plantation went out of England" (3:270). After thoroughly condemning the Virginia Company's policies, Smith warned the Massachusetts Bay Company to avoid the Virginia Company's example. Do not have "such change of Governours, nor such a multitude of Officers, neither more Masters, Gentlemen, Gentlewomen, and children, than you have men to worke, which idle charge you will finde very troublesome, and the effects dangerous, and one hundred good labourers better than a thousand such Gallants as were sent me, that could do nothing" (3:272). (Of course, Smith did not spell out the implication that England, as well as the colonies, would be better off without such drones.) Fortunately, the recent New England emigrants were as "well bred in labour and good husbandry as any in England" (3:275). Laborers and farmers, not gentlemen or aristocrats, were necessary for new plantations.

Smith repeatedly violated the standard social code that demanded deference and even servility from those of a lower social rank. Naturally the gentlemen objected to his attitudes and his opinions. Edward Maria Wingfield, first president of the council in 1607, told Smith that "though wee were equall heere [in Virginia], yet if he [Wingfield] were in England, he would thinck scorne his man [i.e., Wingfield's servant] should be my Companyon" (*JV* 220). Concluding his narrative, Wingfield added that he would prefer his name not be associated in any way with Smith: "to such I would not my name should be a Companyon" (*JV* 231). Captain Gabriel Archer complained that Smith "gaue not any due respect to many worthy Gentlemen"—meaning, of course, that Smith did not especially respect Archer (*JV* 282). George Percy, the ranking aristocrat of the earliest colonists, called Smith a radical "fellow" who attempted "to take all men's authorities from them"—but it was Smith, the councillor and then the president of the council, who rightfully had authority in Virginia.[5]

Smith knew that his supposed superiors considered him insubordinate and that they resented both his attitudes and (when he was in power) his treatment of them as ordinary men. He occasionally replied to such criticism. In *The Proceedings* (1612) he wrote that while president, he took thirty men from the fort at Jamestown out into the woods about five miles, "to learn to make clapboard, cut downe trees, and ly in the woods." The group included Gabriel Beadle and John Russell, "the only two gallants of this last supply, and both proper gentlemen." Smith acknowledged that the "pleasures" of work were "strange" to "their conditions, yet lodging eating, drinking, working, or playing, they doing but as the President, all these things were carried so pleasantly, as within a weeke, they became Masters, making it their delight to heare the trees thunder as they fell." Then Smith answered the anticipated criticism: "By this, let no man think that the President, or these gentlemen spent their times as common wood-hackers at felling of trees, or such like other labours, or that they were pressed to anything as hirelings or common slaves, for what they did (being but once a little inured) it seemed, and they conceited it only as a pleasure and a recreation. Yet 30 or 40 of such voluntary Gentlemen would doe more in a day then 100 of the rest that must bee prest to it by compulsion" (1:238–39).

Edwin C. Rozwenc thought this passage proved that Smith was not "responding to the wilderness environment by instituting a rough-and-ready frontier egalitarianism." (Actually, Smith said that the new surroundings in America allowed gentlemen to ignore their former condition and to learn to enjoy work and achievement.) Rozwenc claimed that "Smith was too proud of his coat of arms acquired by valorous exploits in Transylvania to war upon a social system based on honor and distinction."[6] Smith, however, was not praising "Gentlemen" in opposition to the "rest." He was defending himself from an evidently frequently repeated criticism and pointing out that volunteers (even gentlemen volunteers) worked harder than those who were compelled to labor. No doubt he also meant to criticize the Virginia Company policy whereby all worked for the common store, rather than every individual for himself. When Smith reprinted the above passage in *The Generall Historie of Virginia* (1624), he added a clause that made it abundantly clear he was not praising gentlemen. He wrote, "but twentie good workemen had been better than them all." And since the earlier marginal heading in *The Proceedings* (which the printer may have added)[7] had read "One gentleman better than 20 lubbers," Smith changed it to read "3 Men better than 100" (the text makes it clear that Smith was saying that three good workmen would be better than one hundred gentlemen [1:239; cf. 2:185]).

Describing the regime imposed by Lord De La Warr, William Strachey praised the role of gentlemen in Virginia: "How contentedly do such as labor with us go forth when men of rank and quality assist and set on their labors! I have seen it and I protest it, I have heard the inferior people with alacrity of spirit profess that they should never refuse to do their best in the practice of their sciences and knowledge when such worthy and noble gentlemen go in and out before them, and not only so but, as the occasion shall be offered, no less help them with their hand than defend them with the sword."[8] Smith never used such expressions (common among his contemporaries) as "inferior people," and he repeatedly said that gentlemen were worthless as workers, but he tried to accommodate himself to the seventeenth-century social order and to find something praiseworthy to say of gentlemen. In one passage in *The Generall Historie*, he followed Strachey, but he could not quite bring himself to give gentlemen unalloyed praise: "Nor should it bee conceived that this businesse excludeth Gentlemen, whose breeding never knew what a daies labour meant, for though they cannot digge, use the Spade, nor practice the Axe, yet may the staied spirits of any condition, finde how to imploy the force of knowledge, the exercise of counsell, the operation and power of their best breeding and qualities" (2:235–36; cf. 2:225). But his attempt to find a role for gentlemen was a minor note in his chorus of contempt.

He repeated his opinion of gentlemen's worthlessness in his May 1623 testimony before the king's commissioners. All gentlemen, the commissioners must have seethed at Smith's blunt disregard for the decorum of early seventeenth-century social structure. Smith told them that one hundred "good labourers and mechanicall men . . . would have done more then a thousand of those that went, though the Lord Laware, Sir Ferdinando Waynman, Sir Thomas Gates and Sir Thomas Dale were perswaded to the contrary, but when they had tried, they confessed their error" (2:328). Actually, so far as is known, De La Warr, Wainman, Gates, Dale, and the council of the Virginia Company never acknowledged their mistake. Only Smith thought so. Smith echoed his old position in his last publication, *Advertisements* (1631): "one hundred good labourers [would have been] better than a thousand such Gallants as were sent me, that could doe nothing but complaine, curse, and despaire" (3:272). In one way Rozwenc was right. Smith believed in a discriminating social system, but he thought that rewards should be based upon the individual's own achieved "honor and distinction"—not upon his inherited position or background. That belief completely undercut the seventeenth-century structure of society.

Smith even thought that people of supposed quality were more covetous and selfish than others. In his *True Travels* he noted how few gentlemen were now employed in the noble endeavour of colonization, and those few, he commented, were generally seeking some trade monopoly. He quipped that gentlemen "seldome seeke the common good, but the commons goods" (3:223).

The Council

In Virginia the members of the council constituted the official aristocracy. As the most famous English soldier of his day, Smith was appointed to the council (indeed, only the Virginia Company's leaders' knowledge of Smith's incredible eastern European adventures could explain why he, a young social nonentity, was made a councillor), but he repeatedly expressed contempt for his fellow councillors. The first council consisted of Bartholomew Gosnold (c.1572–1607), Edward Maria Wingfield (c.1553–1613), Christopher Newport (1560–1617), John Smith (1580–1631), John Ratcliffe (fl. 1606–9), John Martin (c.1667–1632?), and George Kendall (c.1570–1607)—listed in that order (1:205).[9] The selection of that whippersnapper Smith (not only was he the son of a yeoman but he was also, at age twenty-seven, the youngest council member); the omission of the ranking aristocrat George Percy (1580–1632), younger brother of the ninth earl of Northumberland and the same age as Smith; the omission of Gabriel Archer (c.1579–1609/10); and the order of ranking (with Gosnold before Wingfield and with Newport and Smith before Martin and Kendall) must have surprised many of the gentlemen—and especially upset Percy, Wingfield, and Archer. The listing shows that the leaders of the Virginia Company were at first trying to ensure success by making men of proven ability (though they were not the ranking aristocratic families) leaders of the colony. They changed their tactics, however, in 1609, when they made Lord De La Warr governor, Sir Thomas Gates lieutenant governor, and Sir George Somers admiral. With the new charter, they reverted to the traditional approach. The selection of councillors in 1606 was a different matter. Newport and Smith both came from nonaristocratic backgrounds. But Newport was among the most experienced sea captains of the Atlantic American regions, and Smith had demonstrated his extraordinary abilities in eastern Europe.

The colonists recognized that Newport, the captain of the fleet, would be in charge as long as he remained in the colony. Three council members played minor roles in Virginia. Gosnold, named first in the commission and an obvious choice as leader, deferred to his older cousin Wingfield and died in the first summer. Kendall (possibly a Spanish spy) was executed in the fall for mutiny (1:41; *JV* 225).[10] And Newport was often absent from the colony because his primary responsibility was to captain the ships supplying Virginia. Nevertheless, Smith grew more and more disgusted with Newport. Finally in his letter of approximately December 1, 1608, to the treasurer and council of the Virginia Company in London, Smith accused him of peculation: "The Souldiers say many of your officers maintaine their families out of that you send us: and that Newport hath an hundred pounds a yeare for carrying newes. For every master you have yet sent can find the way as well as he, so that an hundred pounds might be spared, which is more then we have all, that helpe to pay him wages" (2:189). Smith said nothing negative about Gosnold, but he called all the other councillors "factious" or "malicious" (1:211) and variously judged them to be lazy, stupid, petty, vain, avaricious, or simply contemptible (e.g., 1:181–89).

The "overweening jealousie" of the council's first president, Edward Maria Wingfield, prevented the company from exercising "at armes" or building "fortifications." (The diction makes me suspect that Smith was named in the first instructions to be in charge of the colony's military preparations, but the instructions, unhappily, are not extant.) Consequently the colony barely escaped annihilation in an Indian attack on May 26, 1607 (1:31, 206, 2:138). Wingfield had been one of the organizers of the Virginia Company and was named in its first charter as one of four key people to whom the Southern Virginia Company was granted (*JV* 25, 29). He was also an important contributor to the company, adventuring eighty-eight pounds.[11] But after Christopher Newport left for England in June 1607, Wingfield selfishly kept all the best food for himself while the colonists starved on scanty rations that contained "as many wormes as graines" (1:210, 2:143). He even planned "to escape these miseries in our Pinnas by flight" (1:210, 2:143). His actions quickly made him "generally hated" by the colonists (1:35). The councillors still living and present in Virginia on September 10, 1607 (Ratcliffe, Martin, and the recuperating Smith, who had been ill in the first summer at Jamestown), voted to depose Wingfield and elected Ratcliffe president.

Wingfield's successor as president, Captain John Ratcliffe, was no better. The fainthearted Ratcliffe had wanted to turn back when the ships did not find Virginia as soon as they expected (1:205, 2:138). He attempted to hide his true identity, and Smith later asserted that "Ratcliffe is now called Sicklemore, a poore counterfeited Imposture" (2:189). He may have been trying to conceal a connection with Robert Cecil, earl of Salisbury. In a letter to Salisbury, Ratcliffe proposed "dividing the Country" (2:188), probably into great baronies. Whoever he was, Ratcliffe had some money. He invested fifty pounds in the Virginia Company, in comparison to Smith's paltry nine pounds.[12] Ratcliffe had the same aristocratic (and cowardly) pretensions about the president's role as Wingfield. Ratcliffe maintained that "the dignitie of his place" required that he not "leave the Fort" at Jamestown (2:158). By "the sale of the Stores commodities" (which Smith, as cape merchant or supply officer, was in charge of throughout Ratcliffe's presidency and which were supposed to be held in common), Ratcliffe "maintained his estate, as an inheritable revenew" (2:158). He entertained himself and his cronies lavishly until the whole company was disgusted with him. Finally, in the late spring of 1608, Smith and newly arrived council member Matthew Scrivener "tyed" Ratcliffe "to the rules of proportion" (1:224, 2:162).

But when Smith went off on his first exploring trip up the Chesapeake (June 2–July 21), "the Presidents authoritie so overswayed Master Scriveners discretion as our store, our time, our strength and labours was idly consumed to fulfill his phantasies" (1:224, 2:162–63). When Smith returned on July 21, he found the colonists in despair and confusion: the last supply were "al sicke, the rest, some lame, some bruised, al unable to do any thing, but complain of the pride and unreasonable needlesse cruelty of their sillie President, that had riotously consumed the store, and to fulfill his follies about building him an unnecessarie pallace in the woods had brought them all to that miserie; That had not we arrived, they had as strangely tormented him with revenge" (1:229). Smith provisionally assumed the presidency, put Scrivener in as acting president, appointed a number of old soldiers to assist him, and set out on July 24 on his second expedition up the Chesapeake Bay. When he returned on September 7, he found Ratcliffe imprisoned for "muteny" (1:233). Having spent a year as a do-nothing governor, Ratcliffe was officially deposed on September 10, 1608. Complaints about Ratcliffe had reached the Virginia Company, and it instructed Sir Thomas Gates in the spring of 1609 to look into his "diuers iniuries and insolences" (*JV* 267). About December 1, 1608, Smith sent Ratcliffe back to England with Newport "least the company should cut his throat." Smith warned the Virginia Company that if Ratcliffe and Archer returned, "they are sufficient to keepe us alwayes in factions" (2:189). Nevertheless the company sent Ratcliffe, Martin, and Archer back with the Gates and Somers fleet. Escaping the worst of the hurricane, they arrived in August 1609. After Smith was "blowne up with powder" (1:272), Ratcliffe was one of the men left in charge. He was soon killed by Powhatan.[13] Ralph Hamor agreed that Ratcliffe was "not worthy remembering, but to his dishonor."[14]

Smith conclusively evaluated Captain John Martin (along with Ratcliffe), as "little beloved, of weake judgment in dangers, and lesse industry in peace" (1:211, 2:144). Martin's father was lord mayor of London, and Martin invested ninety-five pounds in the Virginia Company.[15] Further, his brother-in-law, Sir Julius Caesar, was chancellor of the exchequer in 1606 when the Virginia Company was chartered. No doubt because of his family, Martin was appointed to the council. Though he knew nothing of minerals, Martin caught gold fever and insisted on filling the ships returning to England with worthless dirt that he believed to be gold (1:219, 220). Then he succumbed to a "never-mending sicknes" (1:212; cf. 1:221) and so, to the disgust of his servant Anas Todkill, remained almost always at Jamestown. A sarcastic marginal heading, "The adventures of Captaine Martin," appeared in *The Proceedings* by the following sentence: "hee went twice by water to Paspahegh a place neere 7. miles from James towne, but lest the dew should distemper him, was ever forced to returne before night" (1:221). Because Virginia no longer had "neither pepper, sugar, cloves, mace, nor nugmets [nutmegs], ginger, nor sweat meats," Martin returned to England with Captain Francis Nelson on June 2, 1608, "to injoy the credit of his supposed [mining] Art" (2:160). After he came back to Virginia in mid-August 1609, Martin went to Nansemond with nearly 120 men. There he revealed "his jealous feare and cowardise," attacking and slaughtering the friendly Indians and then fearfully hiding himself and his men in the Indians' fortification (1:269–70). Writing in 1608, even Edward Maria Wingfield also scorned Martin: he "never stirred out of our Towne tenn scoare, and how slack hee was in his watching and other dutyes, it is too well knowne" (*JV* 231).

Smith held these miserable councillors in contempt because they daily violated every idealistic and practical behavior that a commander should personify. When his men on the first exploring expedition up the Chesapeake Bay (after enduring two fierce storms, nearly dying of thirst, and being frightened by continuing further explorations into the unknown) demanded to return, Smith made a speech which encapsulated his own ideals as a leader (and incidently demonstrated that he had read Hakluyt's *Principal Navigations* with great attention):

> Gentlemen if you would remember the memorable historie of Sir Ralfe Lane, how his company importuned him to proceed in the discoverie of Morattico, alleaging, they had yet a dog, that being boyled with Saxafras leaves, would richly feed them in their returnes; what a shame would it be for you (that have beene so suspitious of my tendernesse) to force me returne with a months provision scarce able to say where we have bin, nor yet heard of that wee were sent to seeke; you cannot say but I have shared with you of the worst is past; and for what is to come of lodging, diet, or whatsoever, I am contented you allot the worst part to my selfe; as for your feares, that I will lose my selfe in these unknowne large waters, or be swallowed up in some stormie gust, abandon those childish feares, for worse then is past cannot happen, and there is as much danger to returne, as to proceed forward. Regaine therefore your old spirits; for return I wil not, (if God assist me) til I have seene the Massawomekes, found Patawomeck, or the head of this great water you conceit to be endlesse. [1:226–27]

Such was Smith's spirit. The men gained heart and sailed on with him.

The members of the earliest governing aristocracy of Virginia were generally do-nothing sycophants. Smith repeatedly castigated them. No wonder a divine-right aristocrat like George Percy judged Smith a radical.[16] Percy knew his man. Under Percy's inept leadership after Smith's departure, the colony declined from 500 to "not many more than 60 most miserable and poore creatures" (1:276). The fault, according to the authors of *The Proceedings*, lay with Percy and others in authority: "had we beene in Paradice it selfe (with those governours) it would not have beene much better with us." The aristocrats and gentlemen in power had not sufficient ability; those with ability would not be selected as leaders by such people as Percy, Ratcliffe, Archer, Martin, and Francis West. "Yet was there some amongst us, who had they had the governement, would surely have kept us from those extremities of miseries, that in 10 daies more would have supplanted us all by death" (1:276). Evidently others beside Smith realized that ability, not hierarchical place, determined capable leadership. But these are the opinions of Smith's men, who had learned the lesson from the former yeoman.

Hierarchic Order

A structure of offices and places mirroring the social hierarchy characterized England's postfeudal social order. Naturally the London Company set up a microcosm of England's hierarchic system in Virginia. The very idea disgusted Smith. In *The Proceedings* Smith printed an account (presumably written by Anas Todkill) satirizing the uselessness of Edward Maria Wingfield and Captain Gabriel Archer: "wee not having any use of Parliaments, plaies, petitions, admirals, recorders, interpreters, chronologers, courts of plea, nor Justices of peace, sent Master Wingfield, and Captain Archer . . . for England, to seeke some place of better imploiment" (1:219). Reprinting the passage in his *Generall Historie*, Smith added a clause ("that had ingrossed all those titles" [2:158; cf. 2:325]) making it clear that such superfluous positions existed in Virginia when less than two hundred settlers lived there.

Nevertheless, the Virginia Company increased the formalized structures in its new charter of 1609. Smith sarcastically reported:

"Sir Thomas West, Lord de la Warre, to be Generall of Virginia; Sir Thomas Gates, his Lieutenant; Sir George Somers, Admirall; Sir Thomas Dale, high Marshall; Sir Fardinando Wainman, Generall of the Horse; and so all other offices to many other worthy Gentlemen, for their lives: (though not any of them had ever beene in Virginia, except Captaine Newport, who was also by Patent made vice Admirall)" (2:218). Summarizing later, Smith said that the 1609 council "appointed us neere as many offices and Officers as I had Souldiers." Of course, the new group "neither knew us nor wee them," and the change was made by the council in London "without our consents or knowledge" (2:325).

In its new patent the Virginia Company claimed that hierarchic "fourmes and ensignes" would "begett" more "reverence to . . . authority." The company advised its new lieutenant governor Sir Thomas Gates to "use such fourmes and ensignes of government as by our lettres pattents wee are enabled to grant unto you; as also the attendance of a guarde uppon your person." The company assured Gates that such "fourmes" would ensure "more regard and respect of your place." Attempting to devise a system that would define the exact status of every person in the colony, the company instructed Gates to "devide your people into tennes, twenties and so upwards, to every necessary worke a competent nomber, over every one of which you must appointe some man of care and [skill] in that worke to oversee them and to take dayly accounte of their laboures, and you must ordaine that every overseer of such a nomber of workemen deliver once a weeke an accounte of the wholle committed to his Charge."[17]

Gates took the advice. William Strachey's *For the Colony in Virginia: Lawes Divine, Morall, and Martiall* (1612) describes the new Virginia regime. Strachey's dedicatory poem, "To the Right Honorable, the Lords of the Councell of Virginia," proclaimed his (and the company's) reactionary conservatism:

> Noblest of men, though tis the fashion
> > Noblest to mix with basest, for their gaine:
> Yet doth it fare farre otherwise with you,
> > That scorne to turn to Chaos so again,
> And follow your supreme distinction still,
> > Till of most nobel, you become divine.[18]

Strachey's *Lawes* spells out detailed instructions for every rank: captain of the watch, other captains, lieutenants, ensignes, sergeants, corporals, and privates (pp. 53–92). All male colonists were included within the hierarchic structure.

After returning to England in the fall of 1609, Smith followed Virginia developments closely. He thought the discipline too severe and the military structure ridiculously rigid. He indirectly criticized the Virginia colony's martial regime in *A Description of New England* (1616). A new colony, he said, "must be cherished as a childe, till it be able to goe, and understand it selfe, and not corrected nor oppressed above its strength, ere it knowe wherefore" (1:349). Smith recurred to the Virginia Company's excessive discipline and to his child metaphor in *The Generall Historie of Virginia* (1624). For an infant colony, "all the content, rewards, gaines, and hopes, will be necessarily required, to be given to the beginning, till it be able to creepe, to stand, and goe, and to encourage desert by all possible meanes; yet time enough to keepe it from running, for there is no feare it will grow too fast, or ever to any thing, except libertie, profit, honor, and prosperitie there found, more binde the Planters of those affaires in devotion to effect it; then bondage, violence, tyrannie, ingratitiude, and such double dealing, as bindes free men to become slaves" (2:426).

The Virginia Company did not intend to advocate "libertie" for the planters. In its 1609 "Instructions" to Gates, the council specifically ordered him not to proceed "uppon the nicenes and lettre of the lawe" according to English traditions but to "proceede by martiall lawe accordinge to your comission as of most dispatch and terror and fittest for this government."[19] In 1615 Ralph Hamor apologized in his *True Discourse of the Present Estate of Virginia* for the supposed necessity of martial law in Virginia.[20] Smith reprinted Hamor's words in *The Generall Historie of Virginia*, but he absolutely disagreed. When Hamor claimed that Jeffrey Abbot's "dangerous" attempted "subversion" of the colony proved that such regulations were necessary, Smith exploded:

> This Jeffrey Abbots, how ever this Author censures him, and the Governour executes him, I know he had long served both in Ireland and Netherlands, here hee was a Sargeant of my Companie, and I never saw in Virginia a more sufficient Souldier, lesse turbulent, a better wit, more hardy or industrious, nor any more forward to cut off them that sought to abandon the Countrie, or wrong the

Colonie; how ingratefully those deserts might bee rewarded, envied or neglected, or his farre inferiors preferred to over-top him, I know not, but such occasions
might move a Saint, much more a man, to an unadvised
passionate impatience, but how ever, it seems he hath
beene punished for his offences, that was never rewarded
for his deserts. [2:240]

Jeffrey Abbot, whom Smith recorded as a sergeant, had volunteered to accompany Smith on his journey to visit Powhatan and
Opechancanough to bargain for food in January 1608/9. The out-
look for the trip, Smith reported, "was censured very desperate," so
that a number of those Smith asked found "excuses to stay behind"
(1:243–442, 2:192–93). Abbot also volunteered to go and kill the
traitorous Dutchmen living with Powhatan (1:267, 2:216). Abbot
evidently kept some notes on Virginia: he appears on the title page
of *A Map of Virginia* as an author of *The Proceedings* (1:131; cf.
2:207).

In remonstrating against the action of Gates, Smith evidently
saw Abbot as a version of himself. Abbot, a hardy and industrious
old soldier, had risked his life numerous times in England's wars
and in Virginia; but then (Smith surmised) his "farre inferiors" in
merit were promoted over him because they were from a higher
social class. I find it revealing that Smith, who evidently did not
know exactly why Abbot was executed, supposed that it must have
been because of his resentment over being treated contemptuously
by aristocrats and because undeserving gentlemen were promoted
over him. Was Abbot one of the old settlers that Smith's adherents
had in mind who would have been a better governor than the miserable aristocrats imposed upon the colonists in the fall of 1609? If
he believed himself such, that might explain his execution.

Telling of the death of Thomas West, Baron De La Warr, in
1618, Smith again complained of the Virginia Company's excessive
hierarchy: "Yet this tender state of Virginia was not growne to that
maturitie, to maintaine such state and pleasure as was fit for such a
personage, with so brave and great attendance." All that was
needed, said Smith, was "some small number of adventrous Gentlemen to make discoveries, and lie in Garrison, ready upon any occasion to keepe in feare the inconstant Salvages." But instead, early
Virginia had "more commanders and officers than industrious la-

bourers" and "more to wait [upon gentlemen] and play than work" (2:263).

In May 1623 a royal commission appointed to investigate the affairs of the London Company interviewed Smith. When he was asked "How thinke you it [Virginia's troubled situation] may be rectified?" (2:330), he condemned Virginia's hierarchic structure. The London Company, he said, wasted funds "maintaining one hundred men [servants and guards] for Governour, one hundred for two Deputies, fifty for the Treasurer, five and twenty for the Secretary, and more for the Marshall and other Officers who were never there nor adventured any thing, but onely preferred by favour to be Lords over them that broke the ice and beat the path, and must teach them what to doe" (2:330; cf. 2:268–69). The opinion of John Rolfe, husband of Pocahontas, was just the opposite. He thought that a large number of servants would ensure that the Virginia Company's chief officers would not engage in the practice of hiring indentured servants (2:268). But the practical Smith thought it ridiculous to create a complete hierarchy of offices on the frontier: "For the government I think there is as much adoe about it as the Kingdomes of Scotland and Ireland, men here conceiting Virginia as they are, erecting as many stately Offices as Officers with their attendants, as there are labourers in the Countrey, where a Constable were as good as twenty of their Captaines, and three hundred good Souldiers and labourers better then all the rest, that goe onely to get the fruits of other mens labours by the title of an office" (2:330–31; cf. 3:214).

One could argue that Smith only objected to a hierarchic governmental structure in Virginia because the colony was comparatively unpopulated (neither Smith nor the London Company nor the English establishment included the Amerindians in their reckoning), but such an interpretation ignores the whole tenor of Smith's objections. Besides, his use of the usual radical commonplaces concerning official appointees—undeserving parasites who received "the fruits of other mens labours by the title of an office"— places him in the antiestablishment traditions of the Renaissance.[21] But, of course, to make his argument as effective as possible and to make it acceptable to the royal commissioners before whom he was testifying, Smith emphasized the absurdity of having such a complicated hierarchy in a barren wilderness: "Thus they [the Virginia Council] spend Michaelmas rent in Mid-summer Moone, and would rather gather their Harvest before they have planted their Corne" (2:331).

In his last book (1631), written seven years after the London Company's dissolution, Smith again lampooned the company's hierarchic structures in Virginia: "appointing the Lord De-la-ware for Governour, with as many great and stately officers, and offices under him, as doth belong to a great Kingdome, with good summes for their extraordinary expences; also privileges for Cities; Charters for Corporations, Universities, Free-schooles, and Glebe-land, putting all those in practice before there were either people, students, or schollers to build or use them" (3:272; cf. 2:263). Smith pointed out that the few colonists present in Virginia in the 1600s lacked "provision or victuall to feed" themselves—and yet the company created all these foolish "officers and offices" (3:272). Throughout his writings, Smith condemned the whole hierarchic system of offices and the "superfluity of officers" (3:275) in Virginia. They only impeded the colony's progress.

Radical Traditions

During the sixteenth and seventeenth centuries, radical thought is comparatively hard to document except during the Interregnum, but indications of protodemocratic ideas surface in the Tudor and Stuart drama, in popular clichés, proverbs, songs, and ballads, in mock rituals and reverse coronations, in occasional riots and the creation of new words, and in the writings of some religious groups. Altogether, these bits and pieces of folklore and writings furnish a background of ideas for the English Revolution of the 1640s and prove that a continuous tradition of discontent with the social order existed throughout Captain John Smith's life.

Other early Virginia governors naturally reserved the best food and choicest dainties for themselves and their favorites, but when Smith became governor, he shared the very worst with all the colonists, reserving the choice fare for the sick (1:226, 238, 264–65, 2:143). After succeeding Smith as president, George Percy naturally reverted to the traditional forms. In a letter to his brother Henry, the ninth earl of Northumberland, Percy wrote on August 17, 1611: "the place which I hold in this Colonie (the store affording no other means than a pound of meale a day and a little Oatemeale) cannot be defraied with smale expence, it standing upon my reputation (being Governour of James Towne) to keep a continuall and dayly Table for Gentlemen of fashion aboute me."[22] To maintain this foolish form for "Gentlemen of fashion," Percy gradually borrowed over 430 pounds from his older brother.[23] Meanwhile, most Virginia colonists died of starvation.

Just over two years earlier, Smith as president revealed his different attitude by choosing to base his practices upon the radical biblical text 2 Thessalonians 3:10. Smith knew and used the Geneva Bible (first printed 1560; the King James Bible was not published until 1611). The "argument" or summary of 2 Thessalonians in the Geneva Bible concluded: "he [Paul] willeth them to correct suche sharply, as liue idelly of other mens labours, whome, if they do not obey his admonitions, he commandeth to excommunicate." The Geneva Bible glossed the "instruction" (at 2 Thess. 3:6) that Paul gave: "Which is, to travail, if he wil eat." Line 3:10 says: "For euen when we were with you, this we warned you of, that if there were anie, which wolde not worke, that he shulde not eat." The marginal heading by this line comments: "Then by the worde of God none oght to liue idelly, but oght to giue him self to some vocacion, to get his liuing by, and to do good to others." Line 3:10 was a rallying cry of social unrest during the Interregnum.[24] Its antiaristocratic implications were certainly apparent earlier. Smith used it to proclaim his doctrine as president of the Virginia Council that "he that will not worke shall not eate (except by sicknesse he be disabled)" (1:259).

Smith's text became famous in Virginia. After rats devoured the common storehouse of food in the late spring of 1609, some colonists fled to the friendly Indians Kemps and Tassore. They had been captured by Smith early that year and imprisoned at Jamestown where they learned the colonists' ways before being freed. The runaway colonists found that Kemps and Tassore had mastered Smith's practices. "Kemps first made himselfe sport, in shewing his countrie men (by them) how he was used, feeding them [the runaways] with this law, who would not work must not eat, till they were neere starved indeede" (2:214; also 1:265). Years later, in the starving time after the massacre of 1622, the people "became so faint no worke could be done; and where the Law was, no worke, no meat, now the case is altered, to no meat, no worke" (2:311).

Even in writing a special dedication to Edward Seymour, the earl of Hertford, inserted in a copy of *A Map of Virginia* (1612)

Smith could not refrain from sarcasm at the general idea of aristocracy. He wrote: "Though riches now, be the chiefest greatnes of the great: when great and little are born, and dye, there is no difference: Vertue onely makes men more then men; Vice, worse then brutes. And those [virtue and vice] are distinguished by deedes, not words; though both be good, deedes are best" (1:133). Smith echoed the Christian and humanist traditions in judging that "the chiefest greatnes of the great" resided in the virtue of an individual's actions.[25] Though lip service to such Christian and humanist ideals characterized the age, Smith went far beyond the mere praise of virtue. He knew as well as the London Company that religion normally supported the status quo.[26] But Smith followed through, in words and deeds, the logical consequences of his belief in the common man. He directly satirized those who merely inherited "titles and honours." Too often, he claimed, inherited honors only resulted in displays of "showes and shadowes, to maintaine idlenesse and vice." Aristocrats must justify their superior position. Their status obligated them to "abound in honor, by heroycall deeds of action, judgment, pietie, and vertue." If they did not excel by their personal actions, they were "unworthy of their honours and livings" (1:350). Smith granted that "it is a happy thing to be borne to strength, wealth, and honour," but he maintained that an individual's own achievements "by prowesse and magnaminity" are "the truest luster" (3:299). Reading between the lines, one sees that the soldier Smith was evidently not "borne to strength" but that his prowess was won by exercise and discipline. Further, one wonders how an aristocrat like the earl of Hertford felt about being harangued by Smith on the nobility's duties. It hardly seems a good way to win a patron.

In the same dedication to Seymour, Smith echoed a common Renaissance proverb—one that Benjamin Franklin later judged suitable for popularization in *Poor Richard*—"Help, hands, for I have no lands."[27] The meaning was clear. If you did not have an inherited estate, then you must work with your hands. Smith alluded to the proverb when he wrote, "my hands hath been my lands this fifteene yeares in Europ, Asia, Afric, or America" (1:133). Smith's reference to the proverb explains the puzzling dedication "To the Hand" in *A Map of Virginia*. "T. A." (Thomas Abbay), who added a paragraph expounding the dedication, was obviously a friend and admirer of Smith. He compared Smith to Columbus but

added that Smith lacked a patron comparable to "that ever renowned Queene Izabell of Spain" who befriended Columbus.
Since Smith had no patron, "T. A." dedicated the book to no one.
"I found it only dedicated to a Hand, and to that hand I addresse
it" (1:135). Evidently Smith had in mind the proverb (and his lack
of patrons) and so ironically dedicated the book "To the Hand."
"T. A." supplied a partial explanation for the puzzling dedication.
Smith's ironic statement "my hands hath been my lands" in his dedication of one copy to Seymour amplified and glossed the cryptic
but straightforward dedication "To the Hand." Smith thought the
proverb expressed his own situation. He echoed it later. In *A Description of New England* (1616—repeated in *The Generall Historie*),
he announced that if an immigrant to America had "nothing but
his hands," he could nevertheless "by industry quickly grow rich"
(1:332, 2:410).

The opinions voiced by agrarian figures like the plowman in
the anonymous interlude *Of Gentylnes and Nobylyte* (c. 1525) are similar to Smith's usual sentiments: "suffycyency is ever noblenes . . .
Nor I thynk it not reasonable nother, / For ych man is borne to
labour tryly."[28] During the medieval and Renaissance periods,
expressions of dissatisfaction with the social order were common.
Everyone knew the proverb "When Adam delved and Eve span, /
Who was then the gentleman?"[29] The plowman in the interlude *Of
Gentylnes*, like Smith, and like Paul in 2 Thessalonians, respected
and admired hard work and held idleness in contempt. The Middle
English "Song of the Husbandman" beautifully presented the
agrarian radicalism of its day.[30] A ballad printed in 1630 echoed
these same themes of resentment for the rich and idle and celebrated the labor of the poor. Indeed, "The Poore Man Payes for
All"[31] anticipated the late nineteenth-century American populist
folksong "The Farmer Is the Man."[32] Instead of the American refrain, "The farmer is the man who feeds them all," the English ballad's refrain was "But poore men pay for all." In the year the Virginia colony was established, rioters in England's Midlands tore
down the hedges and fences that were beginning to dot the com-
munal lands, and the word *leveller* first appeared in its later meaning—a radical.[33]

The vogue of Robin Hood, which dates back to the Middle
Ages but became increasingly popular during the Renaissance, attests to the growing reputation of the English yeoman. One of the
oldest Robin Hood ballads begins:

> Lythe and listin, gentilmen,
>   That be of frebore blode;
> I shall you tel of a gode yeman,
>   His name was Robyn Hode.[34]

The later songs and legends often portray a more common person, with Robin's longbow (used by aristocrats and commoners alike) and sword (especially the weapon of the aristocrat) even being occasionally replaced by a staff. J. C. Holt has noted that the hero "and his men suffered progressive social decline" in the sixteenth and seventeenth centuries.[35] The common reversal in the Robin Hood tales and ballads, wherein the hero is bested by an unknown opponent, is an interesting version of "The World Turned Upside Down" motif, common to mock coronations and reverse rituals from ancient times to the present.[36]

In an age when nearly everyone automatically used the expressions "the better sort" and the "common" or "vulgar sort" of people, Smith had his own definition of the *best*. The "best" were those who worked and achieved. Smith was enough a citizen of his age to use the terms *common sort* and *better sort* almost automatically when discriminating among Indians (1:160–61, 171), though he at one time in *A True Relation* cast doubt upon the automatic transference of the European hierarchic system to Indian culture: "Nobles, if there be any amongst Salvages" (1:65). Smith chafed at the common phrase and sarcastically referred to "them we cal the better sort" (1:214, 2:153). Smith rarely used the cliché in connection with whites, and when he did, he usually defined the meaning of the term by an individual's personal characteristics, not his social position. Thus he once defined the *better sort* as those who were "constant in their resolutions" (3:294; cf. 3:216). The *best* were defined as "the most worthy in Judgement, reason or experience" (1:170); and elsewhere the "best" were the hard workers who "preserved in Christianitie by their industrie the idle livers of neare 200 of the rest" (1:176; also 2:129).

Smith's Historiography

Smith reinforced his protodemocratic philosophy of individualism with the lessons of history. Although justly famed as a man of action, Smith prepared for his various roles by an extensive and intensive training—intellectual as well as physical. After his first experiences as a teenage soldier in the Lowlands, he returned home to Lincolnshire and studied books like Machiavelli's *The Arte of Warre* and Antonio de Guevara's *The Diall of Princes*, learning them so well he could, years later, recall the principles set forth in the latter, devising and using a system of fire signals (3:156, 164 n.5) and a complex system of explosives he called "Fierie Dragons" (3:349; cf. 3:166). All the while, he was strenuously perfecting his physical prowess in warfare and practicing horsemanship and jousting "with his lance and Ring" (3:156). At first he created his own course of self-study and exercises, but later "his friends perswaded one Seignior Theadora Polaloga [Paleologue], Rider to Henry Earle of Lincolne, an excellent Horse-man, and a noble Italian Gentleman" to tutor him, so he left his "Pavillion of boughes" in Lord Willoughby's Lincolnshire woods and went off to live and study at the earl of Lincoln's Tattershall Castle (3:156).

Throughout his writings, Smith referred to the Spanish historians of empire. They provided inspiration, on the one hand, and examples of miserable difficulties and failures: "let them [the English doubters of empire] peruse the histories of the Spanish discoveries and plantations, where they may see how many mutinies, discords, and dissentions, have accompanied them and crossed their attempts" (1:213–14). Smith believed that the Virginia and New England explorations and colonization were the greatest achievements of his own day.

Smith knew many of the most famous contemporary historians. He must have met the greatest historian of colonization, Richard Hakluyt (1552?–1616), in 1604–6 when in London preparing to voyage to the New World. Hakluyt was a patentee of the Virginia Company and may originally have intended to go to Virginia himself (*JV* 22–25). Smith obviously read Hakluyt carefully. Beside Hakluyt, Smith was probably also introduced to Thomas Harriot (1560–1621), Sir Walter Ralegh's scientific expert who had voyaged to Roanoke and who wrote *A Briefe and True Report* (1588) of the English explorations and observations there. Smith studied Harriot's writings on Ralegh's attempted colonies so thoroughly that he echoed him—word for word, on one occasion—in writing of his own experiences in Virginia.[37] His knowledge of Harriot's writings may have saved his life. When first captured by the Indians in December 1607, he recalled Harriot's mystifying the North Carolina Indians in 1585 with his compass and used the example to explain cosmology and European civilization to Opechancanough (1:47, 102 n.99, 2:215, 147).

Smith knew Bartholomew Gosnold well, the captain who had explored New England in 1602 and who sailed with Smith for Virginia in 1606. Smith and Gosnold must have been accumulating their own collection of maps for the Virginia area from Hakluyt, Harriot, and the English mapmakers. When Smith studied navigation and mapmaking we do not know, but clearly he was an expert in both before journeying to Virginia in 1606. Of course, some knowledge of mapmaking is essential for a military officer, so Smith may have studied cartography with Theodore Paleologue. His extended periods at sea in the Mediterranean in 1601 and 1604 (during the latter period he was driven by a storm from the North African coast to the Canaries [1:204 n.4, 3:212 n.1]) would have afforded him both time and opportunity for the practical study of navigation. At any rate, as his writings (especially the treatises on seamanship [3:27, 65–66, 111, 112]), his explorations in Virginia and New England, and his maps prove, he was a thorough master of early seventeenth-century navigational and cartographic skills.[38] Smith met Henry Hudson in 1605 or 1606. Emanuel van Meteren recorded that Smith sent Hudson maps and letters from Virginia. Hudson may (but it seems to me extremely unlikely) have been the person to whom Smith addressed *A True Relation*. Smith evidently sent Hudson manuscript versions of his early map of the Chesapeake and of the letter that was printed as *A True Relation* (*JV* 238–39, 274).

Smith may have met the other great celebrant of English overseas explorations, Samuel Purchas (1575?–1626), before leaving for Virginia in 1606, but certainly Smith became a close friend of Purchas after returning from Virginia in late 1609. Purchas not only used Smith's manuscript writings and his draft of a map of Virginia in *Purchas His Pilgrimage* (1613 and later editions), but he also reported incidents that Smith told him in conversation (3:314–18).[39] Purchas admired Smith and found his life story fascinating. He featured a briefer version of Smith's *True Travels* in his *Hakluytus Posthumus, or Purchas His Pilgrimes* (1625 [3:328–67]). Purchas and Smith referred to one another familiarly, and Smith in many ways surpassed Purchas as a compiler and editor. Smith's great work *The Generall Historie of Virginia, New-England, and the Summer Isles* (1624) imitated the grand compilations of Hakluyt and Purchas, but in its

personal tone and urgency it took the compilation of travel literature to a new height. The year after Purchas's death, Smith praised
him in *A Sea Grammar* (1627) as a "Gentleman whose person I
loved, and whose memory and vertues I will ever honour" (3:96).

What Hakluyt, Harriot, and Purchas were to the history of English overseas expansion, Sir Robert Bruce Cotton (1571–1631)
was to the history of England. The greatest collector of early English manuscripts, Cotton certainly knew Hakluyt, Harriot, and
Purchas, and perhaps met Captain John Smith through them. One
of Cotton's areas of expertise was the navy. In 1608 and again in
1626, he was appointed to investigate abuses in the navy, and he
roundly condemned the patronage system whereby appointments
were made by favor rather than merit. Cotton, like his historian
friends William Camden (who had been Cotton's teacher at West-
minster) and John Speed, believed that the study of history proved
that empires rose and flourished by virtue, valor, and right judgment—not by patronage.[40] As a naval expert, Cotton would have
been especially interested in the appearance of Smith's treatises on
seamanship, *An Accidence, or The Path-way to Experience* (1626) and
its revised, expanded reprint, *A Sea Grammar* (1627).

Cotton's beliefs and theories found a welcome admirer in
Smith; Cotton, in turn, respected Smith. Cotton, "that most
learned Treasurer of Antiquitie," urged Smith to write his autobiography (3:141). Cotton was therefore responsible for *The True
Travels*, to which Cotton's librarian, Richard James, contributed a
prefatory poem (3:146–47). In the dedication of *The True Travels*,
Smith praised Cotton, no doubt to the embarrassment and chagrin
of the three patrons to whom he dedicated the book. When the
book appeared in 1630, the great antiquary was in prison and in
disgrace. Smith might have expected to suffer from the association
with Cotton, and certainly the three patrons must have feared that
they too would be associated with Cotton. But Smith was not one to
abandon his beliefs and his friends for political reasons. Not only
did he possess valor on the battlefield, he had the courage of his
convictions. He stood by his friends. Smith was sensitive to the political currents of the day. He suppressed a reference to Sir Walter
Ralegh in revising *A Map* (1612) into *The Generall Historie* (see 1:150
and n.5). But Ralegh, who had been beheaded in 1618, was not
Smith's friend. Indeed, Ralegh was identified with the search for
gold mines in Guiana, an expectation that Smith scorned (1:406,

441, 2:474); choosing to follow the model of Holland, Smith recommended fishing, farming, trade, and work as the basis for successful colonization. Unlike Sir Walter Ralegh, Robert Cotton won Smith's entire approval. The testimony to Cotton would have been judged, at best, imprudent by any conscientious courtier. But Smith's experiences in Scotland in 1599 had convinced him that he did not have the personality "to make him a Courtier" (3:155).

As his study and his writings demonstrate, Smith loved history. Perhaps his most memorable single aphorism celebrated it.[41] History, he said, was "the memory of time, the life of the dead, and the happinesse of the living" (3:288). As the epigraph to this chapter proves, Smith thought that the reason for giving titles and honors was to make people even better "able to abound in honor, by Heroicall deeds of action, judgment, pietie, and vertue." He brought his reading to bear upon his incipient social theories and used his own historiography to prove that rewards for individual merit finally determined the success or failure of civilizations. Past empires had collapsed under the weight of idleness, luxury, and a useless aristocracy. England was repeating the cycle.

He set forth his theory in *A Description of New England* (1616) and repeated it in *The Generall Historie* (1624). The decline and fall of past empires resulted from "the excesse of idlenesse, the fondnesse of Parents, the want of experience in Magistrates, the admiration of their undeserved honours, the contempt of true merit, their unjust jealosies, their politicke incredulities, their hypocriticall seeming goodnesse, and their deeds of secret lewdnesse" (1:344, 2:421). These vices now characterized England. Further, great past civilizations had all risen because of "the adventures of her youth, not in riots at home; but in dangers abroad." And when, in the heyday of Chaldea, Syria, Greece, and Rome, such persons "grewe aged," they used "the justice and judgment" provided by "their experience" to run their empires. Thus those past civilizations had become "Lords of the world" through the "pains and virtues of their adventurous youths" (1:344, 2:421). "The Hebrewes, and Lacedaemonians, the Goths, the Greceans, the Romanes, and the rest, what was it they would not undertake to inlarge their Territories, enrich their subjects, resist their enemies? Those that were the founders of those great Monarchies and their vertues, were no silvered idle golden Pharises, but industrious iron-steeled Publicans: They regarded more provisions, and necessaries for their people, then jewels, riches, ease, or delight for themselves. Riches were their servants, not their Maisters" (1:360). But when Chaldea, Syria, Greece, Rome, and other countries no longer rewarded "adventurous youths," those civilizations degenerated and "lost in a few daies" all that their citizens had achieved throughout "many years." Great empires fell through "ease and vices" (1:344, 2:421). Constantinople fell to the Turks because of "the effects of private covetousness" (1:345, 2:422).

Similar causes produced similar results. England was no longer rewarding its "adventurous youths." Thus, if England did not change its policies and begin again to reward merit, it would decline and fall. Though the theory that luxury caused the degeneration of empires was a historiographical commonplace, Smith's belief that civilizations grew and flourished because of rewards for individual merit was unusual. Smith's theories of history may have been inspired by conversations with Cotton or by reading in Camden and Speed, but they certainly also reflected his experiences and characteristic beliefs. For Smith, the study of history confirmed his experience and his belief that the greatest achievements of all past empires finally depended upon the efforts of striving, aspiring, young individuals—like numerous ones he had known and like himself.

9

The New American Order

Let all men have as much freedome in reason as may be, and true dealing, for it is the greatest comfort you can give them, where the very name of servitude will breed much of ill bloud, and become odious to God and man.

—Smith's final opinion on the social order. *Advertisements* (1631; 3:287).

"Adam and Eve" from Thomas Harriot, *A Briefe and True Report of the New Found Land of Virginia* (Frankfort: T. De Bry, 1590), frontispiece to appendix of illustrations

America as Possibility

A MERICA, the empire of the future, offered an individual the opportunity to re-create himself. That was Smith's vision and the primary reason he loved colonization. By 1616, when he wrote *A Description of New England*, his American experiences had validated his incipient social philosophy. In the postfeudal society of Renaissance England and Europe, most farmers worked for the local gentry in a state of semivassalage with little hope of controlling their own labor or owning their own land. But America, Smith wrote, afforded "us that freely, which in England we want" (1:347). Smith said that in America "every man may be master and owner of his owne labour and land" (1:332). Smith's contemporaries disagreed. The Virginia Company (like its predecessors) intended to create a fiefdom in America where the aristocrats would own thousands of acres of land and where the mass of the colonists would work for the great baronial landowners.[1]

Fundamental differences in attitudes between some leaders of the Virginia Company and Captain John Smith emerged on the voyage to America, and they are apparent in Smith's earliest surviving writing, *A True Relation* (1608). On the voyage, when the ships stopped at the Canary Islands on February 22, 1606/7, Smith was accused of mutiny and imprisoned (1:204 n.4, 206–7, 2:139 n.2). At Nevis, between March 28 and April 2, Edward Maria Wingfield and his supporters erected "a paire of gallows" to hang Smith, but evidently captains Christopher Newport and Bartholomew Gosnold were not convinced of Smith's guilt, and so Smith simply continued to be confined (3:236). Arriving in Virginia on April 26, the colonists opened their box of sealed instructions, which disclosed that Smith had been appointed to the council. After the colonists' initial explorations, the council decided (over Gosnold's objections [1:29]) to settle at Jamestown. Then, May 13, the council members (except Smith, still under arrest) took the oaths of office. Wingfield was elected president.[2] In his first official action, President Wingfield explained why Smith was not sworn in as a councillor.

Smith evidently remained under some form of confinement until he accompanied Newport on an exploring expedition up the James River (May 21–27). By June 10, with Newport planning shortly to return to England, Wingfield had decided upon his course of action. Smith reported that Wingfield and his confederates intended to "referre him to the Councell in England, to receave a check," pretending that they would prefer not to expose his heinous crimes out of tender consideration for him. Smith sarcastically reported that they claimed that "particulating his designes" would "make him so odious to the world, as to touch his life, or utterly overthrowe his reputation" (1:207, 2:140).

Smith, however, petitioned to be sworn to the council in Virginia and requested a hearing. "So wel he demeaned himselfe in this busines, as all the company did see his innocencie, and his adversaries malice, and those suborned to accuse him, accused his accusers of subornation" (1:207, 2:140). The hearing exonerated Smith. He said that then the Reverand Robert Hunt made a speech reconciling the councillors and "caused Captaine Smith to be admitted of the Councell" (1:207, 2:140). Archer's account confirms Smith's. He wrote that "the Counsell scanned the Gentlemans [Smith's] Petityon." Though he attributed the reconciliation to the efforts of Captain Newport rather than the Reverand Mr. Hunt (probably both men asked for reconciliation and cooperation from the councillors), Archer also reported that the upshot of the hearing was to dismiss all charges against Smith and to take his oath as a councillor (*JV* 97).

No one knows for sure exactly what Wingfield charged against Smith. Smith probably reported the charges in *A True Relation*, but the editor evidently expunged this material and some other evidence of dissension among the councillors (1:98 nn.15–16). Smith, however, recapitulated the charges against him in *The Proceedings* (1612) and copied that brief characterization in his *Generall Historie* (1624). Wingfield and his supporters "fained he [Smith] intended to usurpe the governement, murder the Councell, and make himselfe king" (1:207, 2:139). The charges were proved groundless at Smith's trial—but why would Wingfield invent such slanders?

Although the particulars cannot be known, the underlying reasons for the animosity between the two can be gathered from a consideration of the personalities and characteristics of Wingfield and Smith. Wingfield was a gentleman of distinguished family (his middle name alluded to Queen Mary's sponsorship of his father, Thomas Maria Wingfield) who had served in the army both in Ireland and in the Netherlands. Approximately fifty-four years of age in 1607,[3] Wingfield considered himself superior to everyone else on the Virginia voyage. After all, not only was he the oldest and most experienced soldier, he was the only colonist whose name appeared among the patentees in the Virginia Company's first charter of 1606 (*JV* 24). In the *DNB* sketch, John A. Doyle judged that Wingfield "was evidently self-confident, pompous, and puffed up by a sense of his own superior birth and position, unable to cooperate with common men and unfit to rule them." Wingfield certainly would have expected respect and subservience from the young soldier (a yeoman's son!) Smith.

Smith, however, would hardly defer to Wingfield. Smith no doubt considered himself Wingfield's equal or superior as a soldier. Smith's feats in eastern Europe surpassed those of any contemporary. Even as a sailor, Smith was probably more knowledgeable than anyone except two of the ship captains—Christopher Newport, captain of the *Susan Constant*, and Bartholomew Gosnold, captain of the *Godspeed*. Smith had previously sailed to the Canaries (where Wingfield first presented charges against him and had him imprisoned), and Philip Barbour suggested that perhaps an outspoken opinion concerning the navigation to Virginia was responsible for Wingfield's slander (2:139 n.2). Smith favored a direct route to Virginia rather than the traditional roundabout way that touched on various islands between England and mainland North America. Smith said that this "unneedfull Southerly course, (but then no better was knowne) occasioned them in that season much sicknesse" (2:63). The colonists, however, had planned for the trip to Virginia to take only two months (1:210–11), and therefore they must have intended to take a more direct route.

Smith's attitudes and vision were anathema to the Virginia Company. The company feared possible criticisms. It instructed the council in 1606 "to Suffer no man to return but by passport from the president and Councel nor to write any Letter of any thing that may Discourage others" (*JV* 53–54). Eagerly read in London, Smith's long Virginia letter contained an enormous amount of fascinating information about the discovery and exploration of Virginia and gave an account of the actions of the Virginia colonists. *A True Relation* also, however, revealed constant bickering among the council members, showed that most Indian tribes were hostile and wanted to annihilate the whites, and frankly presented the miserable situation of the colonists, with many sick and dying and others trying to abandon the colony and flee to England. Smith's account was the best available, and the public wanted immediate news about Virginia, but it contained material unsuitable, in the Virginia Company's opinion, for distribution. So the Virginia Company hired an editor to cut out the unfavorable information and to see the manuscript quickly through the press. Conscious that some cuts resulted in nonsensical readings, the editor of Smith's *True Relation* (1608) apologized for butchering the manuscript: "somewhat more was by him written, which being as I thought (fit to be private) I would not adventure to make it publicke" (1:24). Philip Barbour's edition indicates where he believed cuts had been made; and in his notes, he sometimes guessed (and sometimes, by citing later versions of the same incidents, proved) that specific materials were deleted.[4]

Again in May 1609 the Virginia Company directed the new lieutenant governor, Sir Thomas Gates, to "take especial care what relacions come into England and what letters are written." The company emphasized that all letters and relations were to be sent "first to the Councell here, according to a former instructions."[5] Smith's *Map of Virginia* (1612) and *The Proceedings* were probably published in Oxford rather than London because the Stationers' Company refused to license the tracts.[6] Smith repeatedly defied the Virginia Company, and he consistently advocated ideals repulsive to the company's leaders—and later, ideals too radical for the leaders of Plymouth colony or the Massachusetts Bay Company. Ironically, the Virginia Company, Plymouth colony, the Massachusetts Bay Company, Calvert's Maryland, and all later organizers of American colonies were gradually forced to adopt Smith's recommendations, for industrious colonists would not emigrate on the company's terms.[7]

A key clause in *The Proceedings* (1:233), unremarked by previous scholars, dramatically demonstrates the difference between Smith and the other council members. The council's president was elected by the council annually, on September 10. Edward Maria Wingfield had been elected as soon as a permanent place of settlement had been chosen, May 13, 1607, probably by a unanimous vote (I assume his younger cousin Bartholomew Gosnold deferred to him and voted for him; Gosnold's deference and vote would have been decisive for all the other councillors),[8] except for Smith, who was a prisoner and not allowed to vote or to be admitted to the council, despite being named in the instructions. Less than four months later, September 10, 1607, only four members of the original council voted. Bartholomew Gosnold had died; George Kendall had been or was about to be executed; and Christopher Newport was on his way back from England. The four were Wingfield, Smith (admitted to the Council on June 10, 1607 [1:206–7, 2:139–40]), John Ratcliffe, and John Martin. The latter three deposed Wingfield and elected Ratcliffe president (1:35). A year later, September 10, 1608, only three members of the council were present in Virginia—Smith, Ratcliffe, and Matthew Scrivener. Wingfield and Martin had returned to England,[9] but Matthew Scrivener, who came over with the first supply in January 1607/8, had been appointed to the council in England (1:222). By the summer of 1608 Ratcliffe had been exposed as someone really named John Sicklemore and had, worse, proved to be incompetent as president. When Smith returned from his first exploring expedition up the Chesapeake Bay in July 1608, he found the colony in disarray. The colonists at large elected him president; but since only the members of the council technically had the right to vote, and since the annual election was not supposed to take place until September 10, the popular election of c. July 23 was unofficial. Smith left Scrivener in charge as acting president in Jamestown when he sailed off, July 24, on his second voyage exploring the Chesapeake. When Smith returned to Jamestown on September 7, he found Ratcliffe/Sicklemore had been imprisoned for mutiny (1:233). Technically, as president, Ratcliffe had two votes—and thus would have tied the two votes by Smith and Scrivener, but he was in prison, in disgrace. His vote, as a member of the council, probably did not count. Smith was therefore elected president on January 10, 1608, only by Scrivener—and, of course, himself.

In fact, however, Smith was the colonists' general choice as president: "The 10. of September 1608. by the election of the Councel, and request of the company, Captaine Smith received the letters patents, and tooke upon him the place of President, which till then by no meanes he would accept though hee was often importuned thereunto" (1:233). Smith was the popular choice as president. Of course, Smith had the good sense to abide by the letter of the law and to say that he was elected by the council on the date appointed. He could not, however, refrain from giving the unnecessary, irrelevant, irreverent, and even radical information that he was also elected by the "request of the company." A democratic election cast doubt upon the whole system of Virginia government. Smith, however, was no doubt proud of his popular election, and he may well have been suggesting that elections should be carried out by a democratic process. He repeated the clause in *The Generall Historie* (2:180). Smith believed that the colonists themselves should make the decisions that affected them, not the London Council. He was the only popularly elected governor of colonial Virginia. (Technically, he was president of the council, not governor of the colony; Smith himself, however, referred to the position on the title pages of his later publications as "Governor of Virginia.") All other governors were elected by the council or appointed by the crown. The Virginia Company and the aristocracy of England knew that Smith's democratic election repudiated the Renaissance world order.

Smith's Influence on New England

Charles M. Andrews wrote that Smith "was as much a 'founder' of New England as he was of Virginia."[10] That statement does Smith more credit than he deserves. Smith was among the first Virginia colonists, and he played the key role in preserving the Virginia colony during its early existence. He did not have a comparable role in New England: William Bradford, Edward Winslow, and Miles Standish did. But Smith had two other kinds of influence in Virginia that he later had in New England. First, as Wesley Frank Craven noted, though Smith's "methods and procedures" while president of the council in Virginia "were for the most part unauthorized," they were realistic and practical and provided the Virginia Company officials with policies they subsequently accepted and followed.[11] Second, his writings and map of Virginia were the most important literary and geographical contributions to the early settlement of Virginia (and later, Maryland). So, too, Smith's methods as colonial leader and his writings and map of New England had at least a comparable importance for New England colonization. After all, Smith's Virginia maps and writings appeared after the colony had been established (though it might well have failed at any time during the early years). But Smith's New England map and writings appeared before New England was colonized. And the extraordinary importance of his name for the area, "New England," could hardly be overestimated.

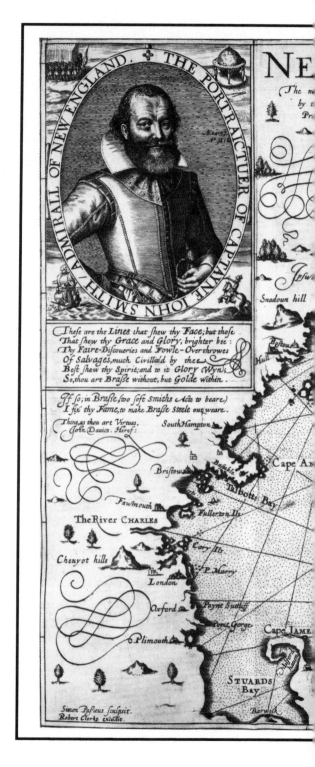

Smith's map of New England
(1616)

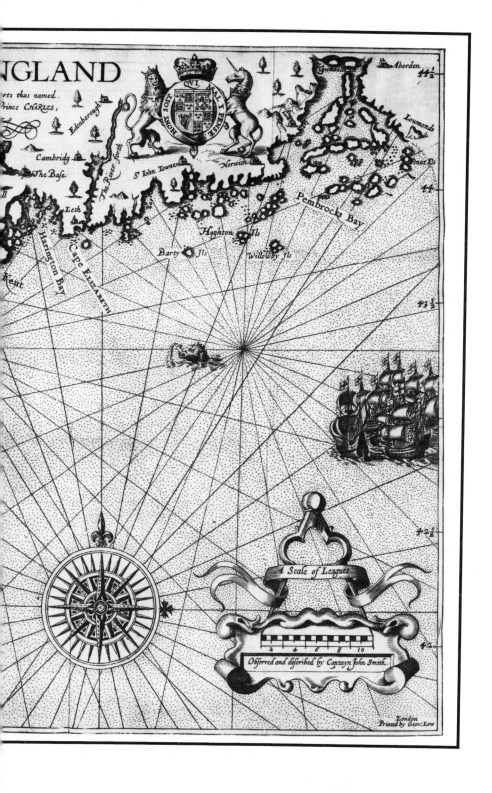

NGLAND

rts thus named.
Prince CHARLES,

Edenborough

Cambridg
The Bafe

Leth

The River forth

St Iohn. Towne

Norwich

Gunnilton

Aborden

Lowmonds

Pines Ils

Pembrocks Bay

Haughton Ilk

Barty Ils

Willowby Ils

Harington Bay

Cape Elizabeth

A Scale of Leagues

2   4   6   8   10

Obſerved and deſcribed by Captayn John Smith.

London
Printed by Geor: Low

Smith also, I suspect, was important to New England in two ways that have not hitherto been suggested. I believe that Smith was probably responsible for the Winthrop group's decision to take their charter with them to Massachusetts. And I hypothesize that John Winthrop's famous speech on board the *Arbella*, "A Modell of Christian Charity," replied to the hopes for a different social system in America that Smith had generated among some of the emigrants.

Before Smith explored New England in 1614, the area was generally regarded as too cold and inhospitable for the constitution of English people. The Popham colony's failure at the Sagadahoc (now Kennebec) River in 1607–8 made New England seem impossible as a site for colonization. When the Virginia Company council wrote the Plymouth Corporation on February 17, 1608/9, inviting the Plymouth group to join in the successful Southern Virginia colony, it mentioned the "Coldnes of the Clymate" as a reason for the Popham colony's failure.[12] Smith later reported that in 1608, "the Country [was] esteemed as a cold, barren, mountainous, rocky Desart" (2:399). Sir Ferdinando Gorges recalled its reputation at that time as being "over cold, and in respect of that not habitable by our nation."[13]

In 1614, however, Smith found New England attractive and suitable for colonization. After his return to Plymouth, England, on August 4, he confided to his "honourable friende Sir Ferdinando Gorge, and some others" his plan to start a colony there (1:352). Though Smith's *Description of New England* (1616) promoted fishing expeditions to New England, he wrote that if the merchant adventurers thought he dreamed of nothing more than fishing, "they mistake mee. I know a ring of golde from a graine of barley, aswell as a goldesmith." Fishing was merely the grain of barley. A New England colony would be the ring of gold. He wanted, Smith told the adventurers, "to plant there a Colony, and make further search, and discovery in those parts there yet unknowne" (1:311–12).

Despite Smith's enthusiasm for New England, the Pilgrims decided to sail for a part of Virginia (now New York) explored by Henry Hudson. But when they found themselves north of Cape Cod and considered the possibility of settling there, they recalled Smith's praise for that part of the world. Circumstances had changed the site of their intended settlement, but Smith's writings had prepared them to think that New England was a possible site for a successful colony.

Before the Pilgrims sailed for America in 1620, I assume the leaders eagerly read all the available literature concerning colonization. They had agents in England from 1616 on, trying to secure a patent for an American colony. They contacted Dr. Matthew Sutcliffe (1550?–1629), dean of Exeter, who had backed Smith's abortive 1615 effort to return to New England (1:353, 2:427). They also sounded out Sir Ferdinando Gorges (1566?–1647), military governor of Plymouth, England, Smith's friend and associate.[14] Smith could hardly have been ignorant of their efforts. Later, Smith knew that John Pierce of the Council for New England had supplied them with a patent (1:440; cf. 2:468 n.1) and that James Sherley ("Cherley") was the treasurer of the Plymouth colony "adventurers" (2:468). Just as he knew their plans and projectors, so the Pilgrims and their backers knew Smith and his writings. Smith was the greatest living expert on America. The Plymouth colonists read Smith and talked over the project with him. In 1619 he was eager to return to America and offered to accompany them. They rejected him, perhaps because of his anti-Puritan attitudes,[15] perhaps because of his strong personality and indomitable will, or perhaps because he wanted too great a role in the plantation. Smith reported in *The True Travels* that they said "my books and maps were much better cheape to teach them, than my selfe." According to Smith's marginal heading, "The effect of [the Puritans'] niggardlinesse" was that they endured "a wonderfull deale of misery, with an infinite patience" (3:221). He discussed their finances and the history of the 1620 expedition knowledgeably in *New Englands Trials* (1622) and in *The Generall Historie* (1:429–31, 2:472–73).

In *Advertisements* Smith added that the Pilgrims "at the first landing at Cape Cod . . . thinking to finde all things better than I advised them, spent six or seven weekes in wandring up and downe in frost and snow, wind and raine, among the woods, cricks, and swamps [so that] forty of them died" (3:283). Smith knew that they were complete greenhorns both as sailors and as colonists. Had Smith, an expert navigator as well as experienced planter, been on the *Mayflower* in 1620, the Pilgrims no doubt would have reached the Hudson River, their intended place of settlement, and the whole history of early America would have been dramatically different.[16]

The Pilgrims carefully read Smith, asked him for his advice, and took his maps and writings about Virginia and New England with them. To think that they did not do so is to believe that they sailed without reasonable preparations for an extremely hazardous and highly expensive voyage. The New England map proved of more value than they had originally intended when they found themselves at the location that Prince Charles had named Plymouth, rather than at what is now called New York. Darrett B. Rutman has argued that since the Pilgrims fumbled around searching for a good harbor in New England, they could not have had Smith's New England map with them. But with much better maps, I have been confused in a boat on unfamiliar coasts, and the fact that their captain missed the Hudson River and landed north of Cape Cod testifies that the guide of those landlubbers was inexpert.[17] Like Worthington Chauncey Ford and all other authorities (except Rutman), Samuel Eliot Morison stated that the Pilgrims "doubtless had a copy" of Smith's map of New England, "since they took from it the name Plymouth."[18] The Pilgrims continued to read Smith's publications. William Bradford later cited the eighth state of Smith's map of New England, which first appeared in his last publication, *Advertisements for the Unexperienced Planters of New England, or Any Where* (1631; 1:319 n.1).

Smith may have been partly responsible for the Puritans' famous friendship with the Indian Squanto, who, according to Bradford, "was a spetiall instrument sent of God for their good beyond their expectation." Squanto was probably captured by Captain George Waymouth in Maine in 1605. Smith found him in England and returned him to New England in 1614.[19] After Smith left, his subordinate captain, Thomas Hunt, kidnapped twenty-four Indians, including Squanto, and sold them in Spain. Squanto somehow managed to get to England again where, Bradford reported, he was "imployed to New-found-land and other parts, and lastly brought hither into these parts by one Mr. Dermer, a gentle-man imployed by Sir Ferdinando Gorges and others, for discovery, and other designes in these parts."[20] Thomas Dermer had sailed with Smith in 1614 and commanded the second ship on Smith's ill-fated 1615 expedition. In 1619 Dermer explored the New England coast and returned Squanto.[21]

The organizers, sponsors, and Plymouth colonists themselves were all comparatively ill-prepared greenhorns, but the Massachusetts Bay colonists were well organized and thoroughly prepared. They too read Smith and consulted him. The editors of the *Winthrop Papers* have noted the similarity between John Winthrop's "The Grounds of Settling a Plantation in New England" and Smith's *Description of New England*.[22] At the end of Francis Higginson's *New Englands Plantation* (third edition, 1630), the first Massachusetts Bay promotion tract actually written in the colony, the London editor appended the following note: "But whoever disereth to know as much as yet can be discouered, I aduise them to buy Captain Iohn Smiths booke of the description of *New-England* in Folio; and reade from Fol. 203 to the end; and there let the Reader expect to haue full content."[23] The reference is to the sixth and last book of Smith's *Generall Historie* (1624). Later, Smith added at the end of his *True Travels* (1630) a number of chapters to bring *The Generall Historie* up to date. He told of the "great company of people of good ranke, zeale, meanes, and quality" who set sail from the Thames in April and May in "this yeare 1629" (3:222). And in his *Advertisements* (1631), Smith spoke familiarly of John Winthrop, "their now Governour, a worthy Gentleman both in estate and esteeme" (3:292). It seems certain that Winthrop, like other Massachusetts Bay colony leaders, consulted Smith. William Wood, writing *New England's Prospect* (1634), a Massachusetts Bay promotion tract, cited "the Thrice memorable discoverer of those parts, Captain Smith, who hath likewise fully described the southern and northeast part of New England, with the noted headlands, capes, harbors, rivers, ponds, and lakes, with the nature of the soil, and commodities both by the sea and land, etc."[24]

Smith had connections with more than a dozen leaders, consultants, and colonists of the Massachusetts Bay Company. Leaders included the Saltonstalls, the earl of Lincoln, and the Mildmays.[25] Smith, like the Massachusetts Bay Company's "Boston men," came from Lincolnshire and knew the families and many of the individual Massachusetts Bay emigrants. Smith said he was familiar with the Massachusetts Bay Company's common farmers and praised them. Winthrop and others had read and probably heard in person Smith's repeated complaints that decisions for the colonists were made in London by people who did not know the local situation. A memorable bit of prose in the *Generall Historie* was Smith's "rude Answer," written about December 1, 1608, to instructions from the London Company. He objected to the instructions but, though

president, was outvoted by Matthew Scrivener, Christopher Newport, and the two new members of the council, Peter Winne and
Richard Waldo. He therefore complied with the instructions to
crown Powhatan, to search for the lost colonists of 1587, and to
attempt to bring back gold—but he denounced the measures as
impractical, expensive, foolish, and stupid. His greatest scorn, however, was reserved for the Londoners' most expensive and, to Smith
(and all we latter-day experts), most ridiculous instruction. At enormous expense, the Virginia Company sent over a boat carefully cut
into five parts that could be, supposedly, easily carried and reassem-
bled. The colonists were instructed to assemble it, sail it up the
James River to the falls, take it apart, carry it around the falls, put
it back together, and float on down to the South Sea (1:234, 2:181–
82). Smith sarcastically said that if they burned the boat, one explorer might carry it in a bag, but "as she is, five hundred cannot"
(2:188).

Captain John Smith advised the Massachusetts Bay Company
leaders that the emigrants to America should control their own decisions. In one complaint about the London Company's system of
government, Smith had written: "as they can make no Lawes in
Virginia till they be ratified here [in England]; so they [the colo-
nists] thinke it but reason, none should bee inacted here without
their consents, because they onely feele them, and must live under
them" (2:292).[26] Smith repeatedly said that the experience of colonists on the spot, not the foolish ideas of governors in England,
should be the basis of the colonists' decisions:

> In these eight yeares which I have been conversant with
> these affairs, I have not learned there is a great difference,
> betwixt the directions and judgement of experimentall
> knowledge, and the superficiall conjecture of variable rela-
> tion: wherein rumor, humor, or misprision have such
> power, that oft times one is enough to beguile twentie, but
> twentie not sufficient to keep one from being deceived.
> Therefore I know no reason but to beleeve my own eies,
> before any mans imagination, that is but wrested from the
> conceits of my owne projects and indeavors. [1:351–52]

Much has been written about the transfer of the Massachusetts
Bay charter to Massachusetts.[27] Herbert Levi Osgood considered

the transfer "a fact of the greatest importance, not only in the history of New England, but in the development of modern social and governmental forms."[28] No one has pointed out Smith's probable influence. Surely some leaders of the Massachusetts Bay Company had appreciated Smith's repeated written complaints about the foolish instructions from the Virginia Company at home, and surely some of them talked with Smith and heard him declaim against the policy. Decisions regarding the colony should be made by the colonists on the spot. That was Smith's firm opinion. John Winthrop may have echoed it while talking (and writing) himself into going to New England. In "Reasons to be considered for . . . the intended Plantation in New England," Winthrop posed as one objection the "ill success of other Plantations." He had Virginia in mind and specified it in his first reply. Winthrop gave as a reply to another objection the argument that "they [other plantations] did not establish a right forme of gouerment."[29] Winthrop evidently believed that Virginia's experience proved that the colonists should govern themselves.

Though the Massachusetts Bay colonists at first kept their plan to remove the charter a secret, the decision involved so many people that it must have shortly become known to all interested in the colony. Smith surely found out about the removal. I suspect that he obliquely referred to the transfer in *Advertisements*. He stated that the Massachusetts Bay settlers "take not that course the Virginia Company did for the Planters there, their purses and lives were subject to some few here in London who were never there" (3:270). And in writing of "The differences betwixt the beginning of Virginia, and them of Salem," Smith complimented the Massachusetts Bay settlers for not being saddled with "a multitide of voluntary contributers, superfluity of officers, and unexperienced Commissioners." The New Englanders "will neither beleeve nor use such officers, in that they are overseers of their owne estates" (3:275). He celebrated the New Englanders' ability to make their own decisions, writing that "any reasonable man there may better advise himselfe, than one thousand of them here who were never there" (3:299). Smith found it especially promising that the Massachusetts Bay Company's settlers were not subject to laws made by a group of wealthy stay-at-home Englishmen. The ability to create their own laws meant that the New England settlers would be able to create their own destiny. In what may have been a last slap at the situation in Virginia, he wrote, "nor will any man, that hath any wit, throw himselfe into such a kinde of subjection, especially at his owne cost and charges" (3:299).

No doubt many common people who emigrated to Massachusetts hoped that the social situation in America would be wholly different from England's existing social order. But Smith's vision of freedom and liberty in America was too radical for the leaders of the Massachusetts Bay Company. They had read Smith's writings, talked with him, and knew that he, at least, envisioned a different kind of American social order. John Winthrop, Thomas Dudley, John Cotton, and other leaders of the Massachusetts Bay Company had no intention of creating a new secular society in the New World. Winthrop's most famous single writing, his "Modell of Christian Charity," delivered the official philosophy of the Massachusetts Bay Company in reply to the rumors and hopeful beliefs of some emigrants about a new social order in the New World. Since Captain John Smith was the person primarily (indeed, almost single-handedly) responsible for hopes of a new social order in America, Winthrop's text and lay sermon probably deliberately replied to Smith. Winthrop reaffirmed the traditional hierarchical social order. His text (the fundamental statement that was supposed, in any Puritan sermon, to state an uncontestable truth—almost always a biblical quotation) affirmed the old philosophy: "God Almightie in his most holy and wise providence hath soe disposed of the Condicion of mankinde, as in all times some must be rich some poore, some high and eminent in power and dignitie; others meane and in subieccion."[30]

The leaders of the Plymouth colony (1620) and Massachusetts Bay Colony (1630) emigrations intended to return to the "purity" and "simplicity" of biblical times in order to enjoy eternal life with God after death. As Theodore Dwight Bozeman has argued, the Puritans were essentially biblical primitivists.[31] Smith looked forward, not backward. He hoped to create a society where all people had the opportunity to fulfill their own personal ambitions in this world. Both dreams are an essential part of the American Dream, that most important single theme in American history, literature, and culture. But ultimately, Smith's secular American Dream became the dominant political philosophy of America, though its realization has never been completely fulfilled.

Available Land

In the Middle Ages and the Renaissance, wealth was synonymous with land. Social position traditionally accompanied ownership of large estates. And America was up for grabs! Hundreds of thousands of square miles of supposedly uninhabited land (almost all promoters ignored the Indian's presence) awaited the ambitious. Naturally the English expected the land to be parceled out in great baronies, as Ireland had been only a generation before. Although Sir Humphrey Gilbert's and Sir Walter Ralegh's projects for American colonies had failed in the sixteenth century, various schemes for new baronies continued on in America through the seventeenth century; and some of them, like Cecil Calvert's Maryland, succeeded. (After all, Calvert had been granted an Irish barony, Baltimore, before he attempted to establish American ones—first in Newfoundland and then in the upper Chesapeake.)[32]

It is important to realize that in his 1616 promotional passage from *A Description of New England*, Smith was offering the possibility of owning land and improving their situation to settlers in a future colony. In 1616 no colonies or colonists existed in New England. The attempted settlement at Sagadahoc (now Maine) had been abandoned in 1608.[33] Virginia had colonists, but the Virginia Company, despite Smith's repeated urging and criticisms (cf. 2:247), still held all land in reserve with only the vague promise of large land grants for the great investors at some future time.[34] In 1614 Sir Thomas Dale finally allotted every Virginian three acres of land upon which to plant and raise his own crops (2:247), although retaining ownership of the land for the company. The Virginia Company conceded that the new policy was a major improvement. Ralph Hamor, writing Virginia Company propaganda in 1615, said that before, the "most honest" colonists "would not take so much faithful and true paines, in a weeke, as now he will doe in a day." Under the old system, individuals did not care how well their crops grew, since all the supplies went into the general store and the colonists knew that whether their crops flourished or not, the general store must feed them. The result, said Hamor, was that "we reaped not so much corne" then "from the labours of 30 men, as three men have" now "done for themselves."[35] But the colonists were still only tenant farmers who had to work for the company one month a year and contribute annually two and a half barrels of corn to the common supply. Smith approved of the policy change and copied Hamor's account (with minor revisions) in his *Generall Historie* (2:247), but he said the company still offered settlers too little.

A Description of New England indirectly criticized the Virginia Company's policies. In New England, Smith promised, "every man may be master and owner of his owne labour and land." (What a contrast to Virginia!) Echoing the old proverb, Smith said that if the immigrant had "nothing but his hands," he could "by industrie quickly grow rich" (1:332, 2:410). Smith pointed out that in England, most farmers rented land at "20, 30, 40, 50 shillings yearely for an acre of ground, and meat drinke and wages to use it." Some English farmers nevertheless did "grow rich." But in New England, he claimed, "better, or at least as good ground, may be had and cost nothing but labour" (1:348, 2:425). On November 18, 1618, two years after Smith's proposals and promises for New England colonists appeared, the Virginia Company finally began offering fifty acres of land with an annual quitrent of one shilling to every emigrant who could pay his own passage to America. This policy began the headright system, and the headright system peopled America.[36]

Sigmund Diamond has pointed out that the Virginia Company was finally forced to take the crucial step by the impossibility of getting able farmers to emigrate under the former terms. He explained that the concessions the colonizers had to make to recruit and motivate a labor force that was adequate both quantitatively and qualitatively made it impossible to reproduce in America the rigidity of social structure characteristic of contemporary Europe or to maintain for any considerable time the harshness and rigor of the Virginia Company's initial efforts at society building. Diamond observed that "the result was a veritable social revolution in the early seventeenth-century colonies." Though the concessions were gradually forced upon the Virginia Company, Captain John Smith articulated the radical social ideals throughout his writings from 1608 to 1631. No one seems previously to have realized that the London Company was goaded into the headright system partially by competition with Smith's projected New England colony.[37]

Smith stressed that New England was not an island but part of a vast continent. An incredible amount of land was available in

America. The mapmaker Smith was among the first to realize that America contained far more land than all of Great Britain. When the Massachusetts Bay Company had "laid the foundations, and provided meanes beforehand," the new settlement would be able to "entertain all the poore artificers and laborers in England, and their families which are burthensome to their Parishes and Countries where they live upon almes and benevolence for want of worke." Smith guaranteed that America contained "vast land enough for all the people in England, Scotland and Ireland." If the parishes "would but pay for" the "transportation" of the poor, then England "should never be troubled with them more" (3:275).

Smith thought that the Virginia Company's granting fifty acres was a step in the right direction,[38] but he believed more land could and should be offered. He was the first American to argue that the social conditions in the New World should be not only different from but also better than those in England.[39] Smith thought it unfair and absurd that neither in Virginia nor in New England did he own "one foot of Land, nor the very house I builded, nor the ground I digged with my owne hands." Though he said that the lack of some reward did not "much trouble me" in comparison with his fear that the colonies might fail (2:326), he clearly thought that in America the persons who adventured their lives, who planted the ground and built the houses, should be given the land they tilled and the houses they built. But instead "I see ordinarily those two Countries shared before me by them that neither have them nor knowes them, but by my descriptions" (2:326).

In *Advertisements for the Unexperienced Planters* (1631), Smith offered his final thoughts on social structure in the New World. The North American continent contained more land than Great Britain and all of Europe together. "Here in Florida, Virginia, New-England, and Cannada, is more land than all the people in Christendome can" cultivate. "And shall we here keepe such a coyle for land, and at such great rents and rates, when there is so much of the world uninhabited, and as much more in other places, and as good, or rather better than any wee possesse, were it manured and used accordingly" (3:276). Smith condemned the mean terms of Sir William Alexander's patent of 1621 for present-day Nova Scotia (the name itself descends from Alexander's project), New Brunswick, and the land between New Brunswick and the St. Lawrence River. It created baronies and forbade prospective settlers to "plant without commission, leave and consent of the Lord of that division or Mannor." In consequence, predicted Smith, the divisions or manors "will be tenantlesse this thousand yeare" (3:287). Of course, Smith was right; the project failed.[40]

The Massachusetts Bay Company should, he said, establish plantations as close to one another and with as many people "as you can; for many hands make light worke." He urged John Winthrop and the other Massachusetts Bay Company leaders to create a new social scheme of relationships based upon the enormous land resources available in America.[41] The individual's reward should be proportional to his effort. "Let every man," Smith argued, "plant freely without limitation as much as hee can, bee it by the halfes or otherwayes." Settlers, he said, would work harder and accomplish more under these conditions; "and at the end of five or six yeares, or when you make a division, for every acre he hath planted, let him have twenty, thirty, forty, or an hundred . . . to him and his heires for ever" (3:287). Smith was the first person to appreciate the significance of the frontier for American civilization.[42]

Large amounts of land granted in outright ownership (fee simple) in return for actually working the land would be the greatest attraction for the prospective emigrants. And it would be just. Smith advocated a radical agrarianism. Why, with so much land available, should the Massachusetts Bay Company be miserly? The marginal heading promised that Smith's agrarian policy would be the greatest of "Incouragements for servants." If the company followed Smith's advice, a hardworking servant could, "within foure or five yeares . . . live as well" in America "as his master did" in England. Smith claimed that "where there is so much land lie waste, it were a madnesse in a man at the first to buy, or hire, or pay any thing more than an acknowledgement to whom it shall be due." In the nature of things, Smith said, the land was free. Besides, only greater social and economic opportunities than existed in England would attract colonists to America: "hee is double mad that will leave his friends, meanes, and freedome in England, to be worse there than here" (3:287). Smith's scheme of land distribution necessarily meant the end of the old hierarchical system. In Smith's vision, America, that fresh, green breast of a new world, existed as an alternative to the unjust and severely restrictive social systems of England and Europe.

Liberty

In Smith's American Dream, the condition of people should be as free as possible. When he celebrated what a farmer in Virginia could and would do when he was working for himself rather than the common store, Smith added a marginal heading, "The benefit of libertie in the planters" (2:247). In a single sentence in *A Description of New England*, he encapsulated his public American Dream. The availability of nearly limitless land, the abundance of fish, fowl, and game, the incredible supply of lumber, and the lack of an existing social order—all created the possibility of making a new society where personal achievement rather than one's inherited social position would determine one's standing. "Heer" in America, "nature and liberty affords us that freely, which in England we want, or it costeth us dearely" (1:347; 2:423–24). Those two factors—nature, by which Smith meant the total natural environment, and liberty, by which he meant the social, political and institutional forces— would free the common man from the remnants of his feudal condition and would allow him to create *ab origine* his own Adamic role in the New World.[43]

Smith's battle experiences in Europe and especially his escape from slavery in the Middle East had created a typology of transformation that served as a paradigm for his vision of American metamorphosis. When he reached the Russian outpost in 1602, had his slave's irons removed, and found himself "kindly used," "he thought himselfe new risen from death" (3:201). Applying his experiences in Europe and America to the colonist, Smith generalized that "those can the best distinguish content, that have escaped most honourable dangers, as if out of every extremity he found himselfe now borne to a new life" (3:299). For Smith, as for so many later American writers, the American was to be the new Adam.[44] The American Dream was transformation. Smith believed that America offered people the possibility of recreating themselves, and he constantly urged them to fulfill their own platonic self-conceptions.

America was "onely as God made it when hee created the world." Smith accepted a version of the Fortunate Fall. From the time of Adam onward, the Old World had been "cultured, planted, and manured by men of industry, judgement, and experience."

That accounted for the great flourishing kingdoms of the past in Europe, the Middle East, and Asia. When America became cultivated by Englishmen, it would "equalize any of these famous Kingdomes in all commodities, pleasures, and conditions" (2:411). The wilderness of America needed to be cultivated to fulfill its potential, but Smith also thought that as the planters transformed the countryside, a corresponding re-creation would go on within them. The result would be both a productive, fertile landscape (complete with stands of original forests) and a new kind of people.

Smith objected to the condition of servants in Virginia and condemned the Virginia Company's "Governors, Captaines, and Officers" both for permitting and for engaging in the practice of "buying and selling men and boies." He said that such treatment of indentured servants was "so odious, that the very report thereof brought a great scandall" to colonization (2:268). In *New England's Trials* (1622), he said that "no man will go from" England "to have lesse freedome there then here." He warned that the Dutch and French were already fishing off the New England coasts and that it was foolish to attempt to restrict the fishing through monopolies granted by the English crown. "God forbid," Smith exclaimed, that colonists "in Virginia or any of his Majesties subjects should not have as free libertie as" the Dutch and French (1:440). Answering the king's commissioners who were investigating the Virginia Company in May 1623, Smith recurred to the condition of the indentured servants. He conceded that the merchants and captains who shipped them should make "their charges againe with advantage" and granted that masters in Virginia "should . . . have the same privilege over their servants" as in England, but he found it outrageous "to sell him or her for forty, fifty, or threescore pounds, whom the Company hath sent over for eight or ten pounds at the most" and shocking that servants were sold "without regard how they shall be maintained with apparrel, meat, drinke and lodging." The situation was "odious" and its "fruits sutable." He sarcastically and angrily said that the merchants who engaged in that trade should be "made such merchandize themselves" (2:330).[45]

Smith claimed that in America not only common sense and human psychology but also God and nature called for an amelioration of the human condition. In *The Generall Historie* Smith subsumed his paean to the farmer under the heading of "the benefit of libertie in the planters" (2:247). The traditional social order, based not only upon deference but also upon subservience, offered little liberty. Liberty implied equality. Liberty, or the freedom of mankind, meant the end of the old social order.

Smith examined the social order of southeastern Europe in *The True Travels* (1630) and found the society weakened by the extraordinary disparity between the rich and the poor. Most people lived in log cabins, had only "Russe bowes and arrowes" as weapons, traveled on makeshift log roads, and dwelt in the sparsely populated mountainous countryside. And yet the "Lords, Governours, and Captaines" were "civilized, well attired and acoutred with Jewells, Sables, and Horses, and after their manner with curious furniture." Smith judged the contrast between the ordinary people and the lords striking and objectionable. He concluded that a social system of such disparity was necessarily unstable: "but they are all Lords or slaves, which makes them so subject to every invasion" (3:202–3). Obviously Smith thought a society of English yeomen (or in his private vision, American freemen) more stable and really superior.

Smith most fully and clearly expressed his hostility to the existing social hierarchy in his last work. Human psychology, he said, dictated that men should be free. People worked harder when they worked for themselves than for others, and they were discontented when they were not entirely free. He flatly contradicted the common Renaissance belief that social hierarchy was based upon the providential system of degree in all nature. Shakespeare classically formulated the Renaissance doctrine of degree or social hierarchy:

> The Heavens themselves, the planets, and this center,
> Observe degree, priority, and place,
> Insisture, course, proportion, season, form,
> Office and custom, in all line of order.
> . . . O, when Degree is shak'd,
> (Which is the ladder to all high designs)
> The enterprise is sicke! How could communities,
> Degrees in schools, and Brother-hoods in Cities,
> Peaceful Commerce from diuidable shores,
> The primogenitive and due of birth,
> Prerogative of Age, Crowns, Sceptres, Laurels,

(But by degree) stand in authentic place?
Take but degree away, vn-tune that string,
And, hark, what Discord follows! Each thing meets
In mere oppugnancy.
            [*Troilus and Cressida* 1.3.91–94, 107–41)][46]

Shakespeare verbalized the old attitudes fully and gloriously. Smith was no Shakespeare. He had not the incredible vocabulary or the incomparable literary genius of Shakespeare, and he downplayed the great ability he had. Smith deliberately presented himself as a mere soldier, without literary ability. But he was as independent and indomitable in his opinions as he was in a fight. Challenging the omnipresent belief in degree and hierarchy, Smith flatly said that the very idea of servitude was "odious to God." How that must have irritated his contemporaries! They could understand that the former yeoman could want to forget his past and could even (like other radicals before his time) find servitude to be less than desirable—but to say that servitude was odious to God! That opinion, so far as Tudor and Stuart social systems and philosophy were concerned, was quite simply mad.

Smith's most radical statement of his belief in what should be the new—the American—conditions of man appeared in his last tract, *Advertisements for the Unexperienced Planters* (1631). Smith's statement of egalitarianism and the freedom of humanity was extraordinary in its day. It was the earliest and the noblest seventeenth-century statement of belief in the possibilities of a new American order. In the New World, humanity would enjoy greater democracy, greater freedom, and greater liberty than ever existed before. Americans, Smith believed, should and would live in a different and better social system. "Let all men have as much freedome in reason as may be, and true dealing, for it is the greatest comfort you can give them, where the very name of servitude will breed much ill bloud, and become odious to God and man" (3:287).

Conclusion

Thus far I have travelled in this Wilderness of Virginia,
not being ignorant for all my paines this discourse will be
wrested, tossed and turned as many waies as there is
leaves; that I have writ too much of some, too little of
others, and many such like objections. . . . Ah! were these
my accusers but to change cases and places with me but
2. yeeres, or till they had done but so much as I, it may
be they would judge more charitably of my
imperfections.

—Smith's conclusion of the Virginia portion of
The Generall Historie (1624; 2:333–34)

From Smith's map of "Ould Virginia" (1624), lower right compartment

John Smith's American Dream

*T*HE *American Dream of Captain John Smith* has several minor and two major subjects. One minor theme attempts to refute a long-standing criticism of Smith—that he was a braggart. Though George Percy and Thomas Fuller made this charge, most of Smith's contemporaries, like William Strachey, Samuel Purchas, and Richard James, believed that Smith essentially told the truth. A number of the greatest authorities on Smith and on Renaissance literature, like Edward Arber, Philip Barbour, Bradford Smith, and Laura Polanyi Striker, have believed that Smith characteristically understated rather than overstated his own adventures. I have tried, to some degree, to reconcile these different viewpoints by arguing that most critics, past and present, who have called Smith a braggart do not really mean that he consistently or even frequently overstated his achievements; instead, they are really objecting to his assertive, forthright, and formidable personality. I also have tried to prove that these are the very qualities in Smith's personality that allowed him to rise from an obscure yeoman's son to become, according to William Wood, the "thrice famous Captain John Smith," the sometime "Governor of Virgnia and Admiral of New England" as the title pages of his later books say. These same character traits enabled Smith to criticize the Renaissance social system and to write the most engaging early seventeenth-century autobiography. These qualities herald Smith as a new kind of man—one especially to be identified, in the future, with America: a self-made man, a believer in individualism, and a pragmatist. These proto-American qualities in Smith's character are in great part responsible for the charge that he was a braggart. In fact, Smith never bragged about his incredible feats.

A second minor concern replies to the modern and ahistorical charge that he mistreated and causelessly killed American Indians. I have examined his actual attitude and behavior toward the American Indian. Smith believed that they were essentially the same human beings as the Europeans, only at a different stage of civilization. I particularly refute the notion that Smith's attitude toward the American Indian changed as a result of the 1622 massacre, showing that many of the additions concerning Indians in *The Generall Historie* (1624) are favorable, and that Smith took pride in never causelessly harming or killing any Indians. He would, however, do so in order to survive. Smith was, I maintain, the greatest early expert on the Virginia Indians and was at the same time their best friend among the whites. His relations with Powhatan were a constant nightmare, a ritualistic dance of death, with the subtle savage ever trying to get Smith and his men to give up their arms, so that the Indians could kill them with impunity, and with the wily white constantly trading for the stuff of life—food—to feed the largely incompetent gentlemen sent by the Londoners to Virginia. Conversely, the relationship of Smith and Pocahontas has many of the ingredients of the Romeo and Juliet story, the star-crossed lovers from warring families. But added to the Shakespeare story, there is an American Dream of love between the races, a version of the peaceable kingdom where the lion lies down with the lamb. But the Edenic dream was shattered by the hurricane, the tempest, that struck the Gates-Somers fleet, delivering only Smith's old enemies back to Virginia in August 1609, and shattered too by the explosion of the Smith's gunpowder bag, which mutilated his genitals and sent him, critically ill, back to England.

I have also attempted to write an appreciation of the little-known (or at least rarely remarked) characteristics of Smith. I have shown that in addition to the usual personality traits commonly singled out, he was learned and studious (as proved by his navigational skills, his excellent maps, and his books), he was an idealist (who learned to scorn the way of life of a pirate and even of a soldier), he was a kindly humanitarian (having compassion both for the passengers on board ship and for the seamen), he was benevolent (even to enemies captured in sea fights), and he was amazingly considerate (celebrating the good qualities of renegades like Kendall and withholding the name of the oaf who accidentally exploded his powder bag, mutilating him and ruining his life). Smith celebrated the memory of his dead friends and stood by the living ones, like Sir Robert Bruce Cotton, when they were in disgrace. Smith had, I maintain, a very noble character underlying his American frontiersman's gruffness and his nearly universal competence.

Finally, the book has two major theses. First, the one I had in mind when I began the book: Smith was a social visionary who thought that the American society should be less aristocratic and more egalitarian than the societies he knew in England, Europe, the Middle East, and Africa. He respected physical work and craft skills of all kinds and had contempt for the abstract idea of a gentleman. The very idea of a king, like the idea of a servant, disgusted him. He espoused an agrarianism and was more responsible for the emergence of a headright system and for allowing American emigrants the right to own their own land than any other single individual. His belief in the aspirations of the ordinary individual and his respect for farmers, fishermen, skilled craftsmen, and merchants who worked hard enabled him to write the greatest promotional literature of the seventeenth century. He believed that America promised the possibility of a rise in this world, not a reward in the next. He took pride in being elected president of the council by the general desire of the colonists as well as by the technical vote of the councillors. He was the only democratically elected governor of colonial Virginia. His vision of the transforming experience of America made him the first person to celebrate the American, for the American, Smith believed, should be a new and different kind of person.

It seems ironic that the "Citty upon a hill" passage from John Winthrop's speech, which asserts belief in the social stratification of the feudal order, has become the best-known single quotation of seventeenth-century political rhetoric, echoed by several American presidents in the nineteenth and twentieth centuries. It is Captain John Smith, not the believer in the old status quo John Winthrop, who founded the American belief in the common man and who devoted his life to the greatest American Dream—the secular, unselfish, idealistic faith in a better way of life for the ordinary person.

My second major thesis is that Captain John Smith was the greatest single founder of the English colonies in America. Though I knew his role was central before I began writing this book, the process of composing it has continually reimpressed me with Smith's prominence. The Virginia colony would have failed without him. His map of the Chesapeake Bay prepared the way for the settlement of Maryland. His exploration, map, and celebration of New England allowed the Plymouth colonists of 1620 to settle there. I believe that John Winthrop's *Arbella* sermon directly replied to Smith's conversations and writings expressing a hope for a new kind of society in America. I think that the Massachusetts Bay colonists took their charter with them to America because of Smith's repeated statements that the colonists were better able to judge what was necessary for themselves than a group of stay-at-home Englishmen. No one can prove these two hypotheses, but they fit and explain the circumstances beautifully. Smith was the first Englishman to view America not simply as an obstacle—an unwelcome extent of land lying between England and the riches of the Orient—but as the site of a future great empire, larger than all of Great Britain, where a new and better civilization would flourish.

As early as 1612, reviewing the course of his adventure- packed life, Smith said, "It is the best service I ever did to serve so good a worke" (1:133). By then he knew that America was to be his life. The knight-errant Smith, transformed into the American frontiersman, re-created himself into the celebrant of America and emerged as the greatest authority on America of his day. He devoted his life to "knowledge by discoveries for any future good" (1:326). His achievements were awesome, and his vision of the possibilities of America was greater. Who could have foreseen that all his extraordinary accomplishments would be overshadowed for posterity by the mythic dimensions of his chance encounter with a young Indian maiden named Pocahontas?

Notes
Bibliography
Index

Notes

Introduction

1. All quotations not otherwise identified are from Barbour, *Complete Works of Smith* (*CW*).

2. See Louis B. Wright, *Colonial Search for a Southern Eden*; Sanford, *Quest for Paradise*; Cunliffe, "European Images of America"; Baudet, *Paradise on Earth*; Eliade, "Paradise and Utopia"; Bausum, "Edenic Images of the Western World."

3. Howard Mumford Jones, "Colonial Impulse," 146–52; Campbell, "'Of People Either too Few or Too Many'"; Bridenbaugh, *Vexed and Troubled Englishmen*, 396–97.

4. Louis B. Wright, *Dream of Prosperity in Colonial America*. See also Quinn, "Why They Came."

5. Howard Mumford Jones, "Colonial Impulse," 139–46; Parker, *Books to Build an Empire*, esp. 192–216.

6. Besides Louis B. Wright, *Religion and Empire*, see Quinn, *England and the Discovery of America*; Pennington, "Amerindian in English Promotional Literature."

7. No separate study exists of the promotion writers' satire of English society, but many accounts touch upon the subject: see Campbell, "'Of People Either Too Few or Too Many'"; Bridenbaugh, *Vexed and Troubled Englishmen*; Howard Mumford Jones, "Colonial Impulse." For some remarks on this subject in a single promotion tract (George Alsop's *Character of the Province of Maryland*, 1666), see my *Men of Letters in Colonial Maryland*, 55–69.

8. Winthrop, "Modell of Christian Charity," *Winthrop Papers* 2:282. See also Gray, "Political Thought of John Winthrop," and chap. 9 below. Rozwenc wrote that Smith "attempted to make an imaginative reconstruction of the origins and meaning of the American experience" ("Captain John Smith's Image of America," 28).

9. Stone, "Social Mobility in England."

10. Three essays specifically address the general social and political English background and the Virginia transformations: Diamond, "From Organization to Society"; Bailyn, "Politics and Social Structure in Virginia"; and Canny, "Permissive Frontier."

11. Strachey, *Historie of Travell*, 49–50; Wood, *New England's Prospect*, 25; Wharton, *Life of Smith* (1685).

12. Barbour, "Captain John Smith and the London Theatre"; Lloyd, *Legend of Captaine Iones* (1631); Vaughan, "John Smith Satirized."

13. Beckwith has shown that Smith's father, though a yeoman, was comparatively wealthy and gave Smith the advantage of an extraordinary education, one suitable for advancement into the professions or the university ("Captain John Smith"). Evidently Smith's father intended for the boy to rise out of the yeoman class.

14. Barbour, *Three Worlds of Smith.*

15. Fuller, *History of the Worthies of England* (1662), 1:274–75.

16. In his historiographical survey "John Smith and His Critics" (1935), Morse revealed that he believed Smith lied about his adventures in eastern Europe. Morse even criticized Arber (whose edition appeared in 1884, six years before Kropf's series of notes): "Arber must also be held responsible for a misapprehension, still current, concerning the authenticity of Smith's adventures in southeastern Europe" (129).

17. Barbour, "Captain John Smith's Observations on Life in Tartary," "Captain John Smith's Route through Turkey and Russia," "Fact and Fiction in Captain John Smith's *True Travels,*" *Three Worlds of Smith,* 17–77 and notes, 402–16; and *CW* 3:123–251, 328–63.

18. Morse, following Arber, called the controversy a "petty detail," but he did rehearse the scholarly history of the dispute. Morse declared that "too much effort has been expended trying to prove whether the Pocahontas incident did or did not occur," before he briefly examined the evidence and concluded: "Whatever mental reservations one may have as to the probability of the incident, by no sound application of the laws of historical testimony can it be disproved, save by the appearance of contrary evidence yet undiscovered" ("Captain John Smith and His Critics," 123, 134).

19. Henry Adams, "Captain John Smith."

20. Adams to John Gorham Palfrey, March 20, 1862, Levenson et al., *Letters of Henry Adams* 1:287.

21. My forthcoming monograph *Captain John Smith and Pocahontas* surveys the past literature and critically examines Henry Adams's attack, William Wirt Henry's rebuttal, and Smith's writings. Henry's key essay is "The Rescue of Captain John Smith by Pocahontas."

22. Morse, "Captain John Smith and His Critics."

23. Glenn, "Captain John Smith and the Indians." Glenn, of course, assumed that Smith was a liar (the common attitude at the time because of the reputation of his eastern European adventures). Though the earlier essay by Randel, "Captain John Smith's Attitudes toward the Indians," praises Smith, it is simplistic and makes such elementary errors as confusing Opechancanough with Powhatan. See also the two articles by Gilliam in *Tyler's Quarterly Magazine* in the 1940s.

24. Kupperman, *Captain John Smith: A Select Edition,* 8; Francis Jennings, *Invasion of America,* 78; Nash, "Image of the Indian in the Southern Colonial Mind," 69, 70; Fausz, "'Barbarous Massacre' Reconsidered," 51.

25. *JV* refers to Barbour, *Jamestown Voyages.* Quinn, however, has argued that Powhatan had already killed the Chesapeake Indians and that "the Indi-

ans who attacked the settlers at the first landing were Powhatan's own men, recently—possibly very recently—placed there" ("Lost Colony in Myth and Reality," 454).

26. Hulme, *Colonial Encounters*, 163. Fausz maintained that Powhatan orchestrated both the attack and the dining and wining of the whites: it was "Opechancanough's duty to keep the more important English leaders distracted some miles upriver from the settlement while other *werowances* attacked James Fort" ("Opechancanough," 23–24).

27. In *Settling with the Indians*, Kupperman argued that the colonists and those who had first-hand experience with the Indians saw the Indians as they saw the whites, within the terms of a society founded upon class differences. She specifically denied that Smith changed his attitudes toward the Indians as a result of the 1622 massacre (177–78).

28. Kupperman, *Captain John Smith: A Select Edition*, 12.

29. Among the secondary works that Jennings ignored, the most important are Lee, "American Indian in Elizabethan England"; Lovejoy et al., *Documentary History of Primitivism and Related Ideas*; McCann, *English Discovery of America to 1585;* Bernheimer, *Wild Man in the Middle Ages*; Hodgen, *Early Anthropology in the Sixteenth and Seventeenth Centuries*, esp. chaps. 9 and 10, "The Problem of Savagery" and "The Place of the Savage in the Chain of Being"; and (though Jennings cited the work, he ignores its findings) W. R. Jones, "Image of the Barbarian in Medieval Europe."

30. Porter, *Inconstant Savage*, and especially Porter's "Tudors and the North American Indian." Also pertinent are Hayden White, "Forms of Wildness"; and Hahn, "Indians East and West."

31. Vaughan, "Expulsion of the 'Salvages,'" 65. Vaughan's accounts of these exploits in *American Genesis*, 47–48, are fairer to Smith.

32. Fausz typically misrepresented Smith's action: "In January 1609 he brazenly led a contingent of armed Englishmen into Opechancanough's Pamunkey enclave in search of food. When the warriors refused to supply corn to the English, an enraged Smith grabbed Opechancanough by the hair and held a loaded pistol to his chest" ("Opechancanough," 24–25). Fausz employed the same misrepresentation in "'Abundance of Blood Shed on Both Sides,'" 20. Here, however, he added a supposed reaction by Powhatan: "Wahunsonacock [Powhatan] reacted with some intimidating tactics of his own. Before he broke off relations with the dangerous captain, he showed Smith the twenty-four scalps his warriors had recently taken from the conquered Piankatanks, and he allegedly boasted of having killed the 'Lost Colonists' of Roanoke Island a few years before." But Smith went from Powhatan's village to Opechancanough's, not the reverse (1:243–54, 2:192–204).

33. Kupperman, *Captain John Smith: A Select Edition*, 50 n.6.

34. The Chesapeakes and the Payankatanks were Indian tribes whom Powhatan annihilated. Lurie pointed out that "long before any European arrived at Jamestown, the Indians had been fighting over matters of principle important to them, such as possession of land and tribal leadership." She sug-

gested that Powhatan's motivation in befriending the whites may have been to control and use them against his traditional enemies ("Indian Cultural Adjustment to European Civilization," 36, 44).

35. Taylor, *Original Writings and Correspondence of the Two Richard Hakluyts* 2:503, from the preface to Hakluyt's translation of *Virginia Richly Valued* (1609). Compare his dedication of Laudonniere (1587), ibid., 2:377–78.

36. Peckham, "True Reporte of the Late Discoveries of the Newfound Landes (1583)," in Quinn, *Voyages and Colonising Enterprises of Gilbert*, 2:451, 453.

37. This detail is from Strachey, *Historie of Travell*, 60.

38. The incident is told in *A True Relation* and in the *Generall Historie*, 1:45–47, 2:146–47. Fausz stated that Powhatan sent Opechancanough to capture Smith because he wanted to interview an English leader ("Opechancanough," 24). Had that been the case, Opechancanough would have taken Smith directly to Powhatan, rather than leading him in circles and off to other Indian tribes first.

39. Kupperman, *Captain John Smith: A Select Edition*, 60 n.12.

40. Fuller, *Histories of the Worthies of England*, 276; Kupperman, *Captain John Smith: A Select Edition*, 3; Morse, "John Smith and His Critics," 131.

41. See also the forthcoming article by Kevin J. Hayes, "Defining the Ideal Colonist."

42. I thought such social sneers had dropped permanently from the charges against Smith, but Fausz revived them in "'Abundance of Blood Shed on Both Sides,' 19 ("considering himself . . . wiser than his social betters") and 22 ("the haughty, low-born Smith").

43. "And any book, any essay, any note in *Notes and Queries*, which produces a fact even of the lowest order about a work of art is a better piece of work than nine-tenths of the most pretentious critical journalism, in journals or in books" (Eliot, "The Function of Criticism" in *Selected Prose of T. S. Eliot*, 75).

44. This is the primary thesis of Kupperman's first book, *Settling with the Indians*: "It is the argument of this book that neither savagery nor race was the important category for Englishmen looking at Indians. That is, English colonists assumed that Indians were racially similar to themselves and that savagery was a temporary condition which the Indians would quickly lose. The really important category was status" (2).

45. Especially Rozwenc, "Captain John Smith's Image of America"; Lankford, in his "Introduction" to *Captain John Smith's America*; and, most recently, Innes, "Fulfilling John Smith's Vision." More briefly, Eisinger, "Land and Loyalty," placed Smith within the radical traditions of his day.

Chapter 1

1. Ferguson, *Indian Summer of English Chivalry*; Jewkes, "Literature of Travel and the Mode of Romance in the Renaissance."

2. For the enormous popularity of the most famous single medieval romance, see Crane, "Vogue of Guy of Warwick." The scholarship about English medieval romances through 1970 is listed in the *New Cambridge Bibliography of English Literature* 1: cols. 429–36.

3. *Saint George's Commendation* (London: W. W., 1612), in Rollins, *Pepys Ballads* 2:62; cf. 1:39–46. Firth stressed the popularity of the poems, songs, and ballads on the Elizabethan seamen in *Naval Songs and Ballads*, xiv–xix; Louis B. Wright sketched the topic in *Middle-Class Culture in Elizabethan England*, 421–22.

4. For Bertie (1555–1601), see the *DNB*; Barbour, *Three Worlds of Smith*, 9–15, 419–21; and esp. C[ockayne], *Complete Peerage* 12:676–79.

5. Thomas Percy, *Reliques of Ancient English Poetry* 2:238–41; *Roxburghe Ballads* 4:1–11; Lord Crawford, *Bibliotheca Lindesiana*, no. 92; Sola Pinto and Rodway, *Common Muse*, 40–42. In editorial notes to the *Roxburghe Ballads*, J. W. Ebsworth argued that the surviving 1612 ballad entitled *Lord Willoughby* is an early seventeenth-century creation reflecting two late sixteenth-century ballads on Willoughby—*Lord Willobie's Welcome Home* and *Lord Willoughby's March* (neither extant). No listings for *Lord Willoughby* appear in Rollins, *Analytical Index*.

6. Lanham emphasized that patronage was all-important in creating Sidney's reputation ("Sidney"). In general, see Lytle and Orgel, *Patronage in the Renaissance*, and Marotti's somewhat overstated claim therein that all Renaissance literature is literature of patronage ("John Donne and the Rewards of Patronage," 207–34).

7. In "Captain John Smith and the London Theatre," Barbour proved that Smith's adventures were the subject of a play at the *Fortune* theater, managed by Smith's friend Richard Gunnell. Barbour speculated that Gunnell's play, *The Hungarian Lion*, which was licensed for performance on Dec. 4, 1623, may have been about Sigismundus Bathory, Smith's patron. Since Smith signed his name at least once as "Captain *John Smith*, Hungariensis" (3:370), and since he first acquired fame as a champion in the Hungarian army, it seems to me possible that Gunnell (who called Smith in 1616 "my verie good friend" [1:314]) made Smith himself *The Hungarian Lion*. Vaughan, "John Smith Satirized" pointed out that David Lloyd satirized Captain John Smith in *The Legend of Captaine Iones* ([London: R. Young] for I. M[arriott], 1631 [STC no. 16614]; see also editions of 1636 [STC no. 16615], 1648 [Wing no. L2630], 1656 [Wing no. L2631], 1659 [Wing no. L2632], 1670–71 [Wing no. L2633], and 1766 [copy at the Library of Congress]; the Wing entries are mistakenly listed under Martin Llewellyn). The above discussion expands a passage in my "Voice of Captain John Smith," 124–25.

8. For Pike, see *DNB*; Rowe, *Richard Pecke of Tavistocke*; Rollins, *Pepys Ballads* 2:55–56; and *Dick of Devonshire*. The commoner Pike fought on foot and won his battles with a pike, whereas Smith began on horseback and employed the usual weapons of the aristocratic knight in a tournament.

9. Goodman argued "the essential role of a chivalric ideal in Captain Smith's image of himself" ("Captain's Self-Portrait," 27). Goodman best dis-

cussed Smith as "knight-errant," his common epithet from the early nineteenth century to the present.

10. Brown, *Genesis* 1:252–53, 354–55, and Abbot E. Smith, *Colonists in Bondage*, 8–20. Though focusing on a later period, Ekirch, *Bound for America*, is valuable.

11. 11. Johnson, *New Life of Virginea*, sig. A3.

12. Brown, *Genesis* 2:738–40.

13. *OED*, s.v. "spirit," 5a; "kidnap"; and "kidnapper."

14. Hammond, *Leah and Rachel*, 16. Spirits had won their heinous reputation by 1620. See Konig, "'Dale's Laws' and the Non-Common Law Origins of Criminal Justice in Virginia," 366.

15. See also Abbot E. Smith, *Colonists in Bondage*, 67–74, 89–95.

16. Horace, *Satires, Epistles, and Ars Poetica*, 324–25 (*Epistles* 1.11.27).

17. Marlowe, *Tamburlaine the Great* (1590), pt. 2, 1.2.35: "Fraughted with gold of rich America"; Sebastian Brant, *Shyppe of Fooles*, 190; Taylor, *Original Writings and Correspondence of the Two Richard Hakluyts*, 1:142–43; Quinn, *Voyages and Colonising Enterprises of Gilbert* 2:245–78; Brigham, *British Royal Proclamations Relating to America*, 1–4, 7–8. The speech of "Seagull" in *Eastward Hoe!* 2.2 (quoted in chap. 4) beautifully demonstrates the dual image. For the idea of America in Elizabethan England, see Cawley, *Voyagers and Elizabethan Drama*, 296–97, 308–9, 337–38; Rowse, *Elizabethans and America*, 188–215; and Blanke, *Amerika im Englischen Schrifttum des 16. und 17. Jahrhunderts*.

18. Bacon, *Essayes or Counsels, Civill and Morall*, 106; *Winthrop Papers* 2:143.

19. Quoted from Cawley, *Voyagers and Elizabethan Drama*, 296–97.

20. Two seventeenth-century chapbooks illustrate the negative image of early Virginia. *The Poor Unhappy Transported Felon's Sorrowful Account of His Fourteen Years Transportation at Virginia in America*, by James Revel, probably originally appeared in London between 1665 and 1671, though it is only known from six eighteenth-century editions; see John Melville Jennings, "The Poor Unhappy. . . ." Revel's account may be fiction, though I agree with Jennings that it is probably true. An undoubtedly true pamphlet—one, however, that proves that truth is not only sometimes stranger but more poetic than fiction—is *The Vain Prodigal Life, and Tragical Penitent Death of Thomas Hellier . . . Executed . . . neer the Plantation Called* Hard Labour, *Where He Perpetrated the Said Murders* (London, 1680). See Breen, Lewis, and Schlesinger, "Motive for Murder" which partially reprints the tract.

21. Boswell, *Life of Johnson* 2:312. The best survey of eighteenth-century English attitudes toward America is still Heilman, *America in English Fiction*, esp. 16–26.

22. Smith may echo Rev. Jonas Stockham, who referred to the "many Italiannated and Spaniolized Englishmen [who] envies our prosperities" (2:285).

23. *OED*, s.v. "planter," 2 and 3; *English New England Voyages*, 137. The earliest listing in the *Dictionary of American English*, s.v. "planter," 1, is for 1618. See also the discussion in Lemay, "*New England's Annoyances*," 60–61.

24. For American identity in the first half of the seventeenth century, see chap. 3, "The Earliest American Identities," in Lemay, *"New England's Annoyances,"* 50–65. Bridenbaugh ignored Smith and the seventeenth-century South, and Eisinger concentrated on the pre-Revolutionary period (Bridenbaugh, *Spirit of '76*; Eisinger, "Land and Loyalty"). Zuckerman has written two essays on colonial American identity, but my interpretation disagrees with his; see Zuckerman, "Identity in British America" and "Fabrication of Identity in Early America."

25. Franklin, *Benjamin Franklin: Writings*, 979. The Virginia aristocrat, planter, lawyer, and businessman John Mercer (1704–1768) apprenticed his son James Mercer (1736–1793) to a carpenter so that he would learn a trade, but James Mercer nevertheless became a lawyer and burgess. For the most recent account of Mercer, see Lemay, "John Mercer and the Stamp Act in Virginia." In *Advice to the Privileged Orders* (1792), Barlow wrote: "useful industry gives a title to respect. The men that were formerly dukes and marquises are now exalted to farmers, manufactures, and merchants" (*Works of Barlow* 1:128).

26. Barbour, "Note on the Discovery of the Original Will of Captain John Smith."

27. Cumming, "Early Maps of the Chesapeake Bay Area," 270; Taylor, *Original Writings and Correspondence of the Two Richard Hakluyts* 2:492 n.3; cf. Barbour, *JV*, 49 n.3.

28. Strachey, *Historie of Travell*, 31.

29. Purchas had written: "Geographie without Historie seemeth a carkasse without life and motion: Historie with Geographie moveth, but in moving wandreth as a vagrant, without certaine habitation" (2:339 n.4).

30. Cumming, "Early Maps of the Chesapeake Bay Area," 281–82.

31. Thus James Rosier in *A True Relation* (1605) explained that he neither wrote "of the latitude or variation most exactly obserued by our Captaine with sundrie instruments" nor published Captain George Waymouth's map "because some forrein Nation (being fully assured of the fruitfulnesse of the countrie) haue hoped hereby to gaine some knowledge of the place" (*English New England Voyages*, 252–53).

32. Waterhouse, *Declaration of the State of the Colony in Virginia*, STC no. 25104.

33. Verner, *Smith's "Virginia" and Its Derivatives*, 39–40; Cumming, "Early Maps of the Chesapeake Bay Area," 281–83.

34. Leary, "Adventures of Captain John Smith as Heroic Legend," 18–19.

35. Barbour suggested that the title was only a promise in 1616 (*CW* 1:306), but I cannot believe that Smith would use it on the title page and on his portrait if it had not already been awarded him.

36. See Beckwith, "Captain John Smith."

37. Quoted in Lemay and Zall, *Benjamin Franklin's Autobiography*, 277, from "Editor's Easy Chair," *Harper's* 119 (1905): 795–96.

38. Delany, *British Autobiography in the Seventeenth Century*, 17. On the other hand, Rowse said, "It is true that Smith's was an assertive personality—

in that, truly Elizabethan—with himself well in the centre of action and no doubt making himself out to be more important than he was. But what is the point of an autobiographer suppressing himself? It makes for bad autobiography" (*Elizabethans and America*, 207).

39. "Among which Fooles (Marke Baldwyn) I am one / That would not stay my selfe in mine estate. / I thought to rule, but to obey to none, / And therefore fel I with my Kyng at bate," (*Mirror for Magistrates*, 172).

40. "An Anatomie of the World. The First Anniversary," ll. 213–18, in Donne, *Epithalamions, Anniversaries, and Epicedes*, 28.

41. *Roxburghe Ballads* 7:578–86; Weiss, "American Editions of 'Sir Richard Whittington and His Cat'"; Piper, "Dick Whittington and the Middle Class Dream of Success." On the early English ballads and the American tradition, see Lemay, "Franklin's *Autobiography* and the American Dream," 349–51.

42. *DNB*, s.v. "Whittington, Richard."

43. On its mythic appeal, see Lemay, "Franklin's *Autobiography* and the American Dream," 352.

44. Cochrane, "Francis Bacon and the Architect of Fortune"; quotations given under "Fortune: Architects of Fortune" in Stevenson, *Home Book of Quotations*, 715–16.

45. Cochrane, "Bacon, Pepys, and the *Faber Fortunae*."

46. *Sallust*, 444–45; *Plautus* 5:132–33; and *Livy* 11:348–39.

Chapter 2

1. Sabin nos. 82844–82847, STC nos. 22795 +.3, +.5, and +.7, Church no. 333, EA 608/158–61. Note that Sabin no. 82845, example no. 4, Sabin no. 82845, example no. 2, and Sabin no. 82847, example nos. 1 and 2, all lack the prefatory address to the reader by I. H. (John Healey). The Smith entries in Sabin were masterfully done by Wilberforce Eames.

2. Barbour indicated by ellipses in the text of *A True Relation* those passages where he believed cuts have been made. Where he has a note by the ellipsis, I cite the page and the note; but where he has no note, I cite the page and line. For possible cuts of references to the Indians' hostility, see 1:33 n.46, 39 n.66, 47 nn.102, 103, 49 n.108, 49.25, 63.8, 71 n.177, and 93 n.236; for possible cuts of references to bickering among the leaders and criticism of the Virginia Company at home, see 1:27 n.22, 27.29, 33.19, 33 n.51, 83 n.207, and for possible cuts of references to Smith's supposed mutiny, see 1:27 nn.15, 16.

3. Since Smith sent Henry Hudson "letters and maps from Virginia" (evidently at the same time that he sent the manuscript of *A True Relation*), he probably kept some notes on the happenings in Virginia, and he must have kept a series of map sketches. His draft map of the lower part of the Chesapeake Bay includes the route of his captivity trail (*JV* 238–40, 274).

4. Sabin 82832, STC 22791, Church 359, EA 612/119.

5. Cumming, "Early Maps of the Chesapeake Bay Area."

6. Verner, *Smith's "Virginia" and Its Derivatives*, 9; Barbour, "Samuel Purchas." Barbour pointed out that since the *Pilgrimage* was dedicated on Nov. 5, 1612, it could be that Smith's two tracts were not published until after Nov. 5 (39). In his edition of the *Complete Works* (1:125), Barbour further noted that in the second edition of the *Pilgrimage* (1614, p. 760), Purchas added that the books have been "since printed at Oxford."

7. Brown, "Queries"; Ford, "Captain John Smith's Map of Virginia 1612."

8. Sabin 82832, STC 22791, Church 359, and EA 612/119 all consider *The Proceedings* to be the second part of *A Map of Virginia*.

9. See Barbour's discussion at *CW* 1:195. At 1:197 Barbour added evidence for additional minor contributions by Thomas Abbay, Jeffrey Abbot, Anthony Bagnall, Robert Fenton, Edward Harington, Thomas Hope, Thomas Momford, and William Tankard.

10. Howard Mumford Jones, *Literature of Virginia in the Seventeenth Century*, 27–30.

11. Louis B. Wright, *Voyage to Virginia*; Sanders, "William Strachey, the Virginia Company, and Shakespeare"; Shakespeare, *The Tempest*, ed. Kermode, introduction; Frey, "*The Tempest* and the New World."

12. Sabin 82819, STC 22788 + .3 + .5, Church 369, EA 616/107.

13. STC 22788.3 and 22788.5. See *CW* 1:306–7.

14. Sabin 82833, STC 22792, EA 620/156.

15. Taylor, *Late Tudor and Early Stuart Geography*, 163.

16. Sabin 82833, no. 3, and STC 22792; see *CW* 1:394. For Coke, see Morgan, *Inventing the People*, 48–49.

17. See the chapter "The Plain Style," in Miller, *New England Mind*, esp. pp. 332–46.

18. Sabin 82835, STC 22793, Church 395, EA 622/138.

19. The letter, known only from this pamphlet, testifies that Smith was continuously collecting materials from America. It also appears to be the earliest extant reference to the name of the place where the Pilgrims landed, "New Plimmoth in New England."

20. Sabin 82824 (see also 82823), STC 22790, Church 402, EA 624/152.

21. See the description and appreciation of the title page in Corbett and Lightbrown, *Comely Frontispiece*, 172–82.

22. Barbour disagreed with Arber's suggestion that Smith had written thus far in composing the book. Barbour's argument, however, that Smith "whipped his *Generall Historie* into shape during the period of receivership (May 9, 1623–May 24 1624)" (2:29) does not necessarily contradict either Arber's suggestion or the clear reference to Sept. 23, 1622.

23. A point made by Morse, "John Smith and His Critics," 124.

24. *A Relation or Journal* (1622), Sabin 51198, is often called "Mourt's Relation," from the name of the person "G. Mourt[on]" who wrote the preface. The first Plymouth colony promotion tract was Robert Cushman, *A Sermon Preached at Plimmoth in New England* (1622), Sabin 18132, STC 6149.

25. I examine Henry Adams's changing attacks on Smith and the replies of William Wirt Henry in my forthcoming monograph *Captain John Smith and Pocahontas*.

26. Tyler, *History of American Literature*, 25, 26.

27. Sabin 82812, STC 22784, EA 626/126. Though Smith may have been saying that Saltonstall paid for printing *An Accidence*, I believe that the booksellers would have gambled on the pamphlet's sale and that Saltonstall simply urged him to write it (3:11, 142).

28. Waters, *Art of Navigation in England*, 467–68.

29. Barbour noted that *The Souldier's Accidence* was entered for publication Jan. 3, 1625/26 (3:10); it therefore appeared about two months before Smith's *An Accidence* (3:37).

30. Sabin 82839, STC 22794, Church 412, EA 627/108.

31. Waters, *Art of Navigation in England*, xxxiv, 474.

32. Sabin 82851, STC 22796, Church 417, EA 630/162.

33. Sabin 82815, STC 22787, Church 419, EA 631/101.

34. George Watson Cole in Church, no. 419; Howard Mumford Jones, *Literature of Virginia in the Seventeenth Century*, 45–47; Emerson, *Captain John Smith*, 113–18.

35. Howard Mumford Jones, *Literature of Virginia in the Seventeenth Century*, 45.

36. Barbour, "Note on the Discovery of the Original Will of Captain John Smith."

Chapter 3

1. *Journal of Henry D. Thoreau* 3:117.

2. I use the epithet "American" deliberately. See my essay "Captain John Smith: American(?)."

3. Bush, *English Literature in the Earlier Seventeenth Century*, 177–79.

4. Smith first explained the ritual for Purchas, *Purchase His Pilgrimage* (1613), 638: "This they pretended to doe, to know if any more of his countrymen would arriue, and what hee there intended."

5. Mossiker suggested that the clause "Love you not me" represents Smith's decorous version of English coarse words "taught the Indian Nymphes by English seamen and adventurers" (*Pocahontas*, 110).

6. Lawson, *New Voyage to Carolina*, 45.

7. Bartram, *Travels*, 225–26.

8. Mossiker has a good discussion (*Pochantas*, 109–14).

9. In the top right of Smith's map of Virginia.

10. Cf. the description of the Algonquian targets at 2:117.

Chapter 4

1. Lefler, "Promotional Literature of the Southern Colonies," 10; Pennington, "Amerindian in English Promotional Literature," 192 n.8.

2. Peckham, "True Reporte of the Late Discoveries of the Newfound Landes" (1583), in Quinn, *Voyages and Colonising Enterprises of Gilbert* 2:450.

3. Hereford, Simpson, and Simpson, *Works of Ben Jonson* 4:569–70, and see the sources cited at 9:663–64.

4. Earle, "Environment, Disease, and Mortality in Early Virginia," 108 n.35. Bradley conveniently gathered together nearly all of Smith's references to population in Virginia from 1607 to 1609; see Arber and Bradley, *Travels and Works of Captain John Smith (AB)*, cxxix.

5. Brown, *Genesis* 648; Craven, *Dissolution of the Virginia Company*, 301–2, cf. 148–75; Morgan, "First American Boom," 170 n.2.

6. Firth, *American Garland*, collected most of the sixteenth and seventeenth-century ballads concerning America. For a few additions and a survey of the anti-American propaganda emphasizing New England, see Lemay, *"New England's Annoyances,"* 21–35.

7. *English New England Voyages*, 454.

8. For a summary of these various impressions, see Sir Fernando Gorges to Robert Cecil, earl of Salisbury, Dec. 1, 1607, ibid., 447–48.

9. Edward Winslow admitted in 1624 that he and others had praised New England too highly in their early reports. Captain Christopher Levett in 1628 and Thomas Dudley in 1630 complained about the exaggerations of earlier writers. For a survey of the promotion writers' excesses, see Lemay, *"New England's Annoyances,"* 21–35, 63, 68, 80.

10. *English New England Voyages*, 152–53.

11. Emerson, *Captain John Smith*, 105.

12. Morison, *Builders of the Bay Colony*, 12; French, *Charles I and the Puritan Upheaval*, 328.

13. The most recent and most thorough study, David Cressy, *Coming Over*, 74–106, provides a good survey of twentieth-century scholarship, investigates the historiography of the question from the beginnings to Cotton Mather, and concludes that the religious reason for emigration, though important, has been consistently overemphasized.

14. Banks, "Religious 'Persecution' as a Factor in Emigration to New England," 151.

15. Captain John Underhill (c.1597–1672) came to Boston in 1630, organized the colonial militia, and was disenfranchised and discharged by the Massachusetts authorities in 1637, banished in 1638, and reinstated in 1640. Underhill wrote that he received grace while smoking a pipe of tobacco. (*DAB*, s.v. "Underhill, John").

16. Quinn, "Why They Came."

17. Even Barbour mistook Smith's meaning (1:415). For the general background, see Louis B. Wright, *Religion and Empire*.

18. Louis B. Wright, *Religion and Empire*, 84–114.

19. Such observations on the success of Holland were not uncommon in Smith's day. See Ralegh's "Observations on Trade and Commerce," in *Works of Ralegh* 8:370. Masselman said: "Marliana, the physician of Emperor Charles V, wrote, 'the Hollanders fish more gold and silver out of the sea than other

countries dig out of the ground'" (*Cradle of Colonialism*, 12). Masselman's entire book 3, chap. 4, "The English versus the Dutch," 266–75, is pertinent. Barbour suggested that Smith "seems to have drawn here on some such source as John Keymour's *Observations made upon the Dutch fishing, about the year 1601*" (1:331 n.3), but I see no necessity to attribute Smith's observations to a particular printed source.

20. Innes, "Fulfilling John Smith's Vision," 3–15.

21. Freneau, *Poems Written and Published during the American Revolutionary War*, 72, ll. 230–35.

22. Franklin's note: "'. . . born / Merely to eat up the corn.'—Watts." The Latin is from Horace, *Epistles* 1.2.27; and the Isaac Watts quotation was taken from his *Miscellaneous Thoughts*, 61.

23. *Benjamin Franklin: Writings*, 977.

24. On the saying "God Almighty is himself a Mechanic," see my discussion of the reasons for attributing "Obadiah Plainman defends the Meaner Sort" to Franklin, particularly the anecdote that Franklin told his grandson, William Temple Franklin, concerning God as the greatest mechanic in the universe (Lemay, *Canon of Benjamin Franklin*, 96–101, esp. 100). Franklin's saying of a Negro bears resemblance to a Barbadan seventeenth-century slave saying: "*The Devel was in the English-man, that he makes every thing work; he makes the Negro work, the Horse work, the Ass work, the Wood work, the Water work, and the Winde work*" (Greene, "Changing Identity in the British Caribbean," 222).

25. As Beard said of Franklin at the Constitutional Convention, he "held a more hopeful view of democracy than any other member of that famous group" (*Economic Interpretation of the Constitution*, 107). And Irving Brant, though naturally devoted to James Madison, agreed: "Madison and Franklin contributed more than any others to the trend of the Convention toward popular self-government" (*James Madison, Father of the Constitution*, 159).

26. Bridenbaugh, *Fat Mutton and Liberty of Conscience*, 14, 17, 50–57; Walcott, "Husbandry in Colonial New England," 246.

27. Although Tichi uses some southern materials from my *Men of Letters in Colonial Maryland* and from Seelye's *Prophetic Waters* in her *New World, New Earth*, she generally ignores the South and barely mentions Captain John Smith.

28. See Lemay, "*New England's Annoyances*," 36–37, 47.

29. The usual attitude of the time was that American nature was smaller and inferior. See Gerbi, *Nature in the New World*.

30. Commenting on Smith's *Map of Virginia*, George W. White wrote that his "description of soil is probably the first one in English." He continued, "Smith clearly recognizes the variation of vegetation with soil types" ("Geological Observations of Captain John Smith in 1607–1614," 126).

31. Compare the occasional idyllic passages in George Percy's "Discourse" with Smith's (*JV* 133–34, 139).

32. All whisks shown in Strong, *National Portrait Gallery*, are more elaborate.

33. See Cunnington and Cunnington, *Handbook of English Costume in the Seventeenth Century*, 13, 37, 41, 71; see also La Mar, *English Dress in the Age of Shakespeare*.

34. Vaughan described Smith as "a short, muscular man with bristling moustache and a full, round beard (not the aristocratic pointed style)" (*American Genesis*, 20). And Goodman thanked William M. E. Rachal "for drawing to my attention the contemporary portrait of Smith in armor; this visual evidence reinforces the chivalric effect of the captain's autobiographical writings" ("The Captain's Self-Portrait," 38n.).

35. The gorget reinforces the impression that the doublet was also of chain mail, but gorgets were often worn without any other armor.

36. The painting of Sir Richard Bingham (1528–99) by an unknown artist, executed in 1564, is closer in its general posture and apparel to the engraving of Smith than any other portrait illustrated in Strong, *National Portrait Gallery* (1:22–23, 2: nos. 44 and 45). Bingham has his right hand on his hip (a dagger hilt may be seen behind his hand) and his left hand resting across his sword hilt. He is wearing a plain white tasseled collar over a steel gorget; his doublet and sleeves are of chain mail. A doublet as plain as Smith's appears in the engraving of Michael Drayton by William Hole in Drayton's *Poems* (1619) (ibid., 2: no. 131).

37. For comparable poses, see Strong, *English Icon*, nos. 40, 150, 152, 156, 179, 203, 221, 230, 269, 273, 301, 316–17, 323–24, 341. All the standing collars in the dozens of portraits reproduced are lace.

38. Lemay and Zall, *Benjamin Franklin's Autobiography*, 78–79.

39. See the remarkable tribute to him, signed by Richard Pots and W[illiam] P[hettiplace], in *The Proceedings* (1:273). And, since Smith obviously revised the whole *Proceedings* (1612), where this account is found, see also the commendatory verses by Ensign Thomas Carlton and Sergeant Edward Robinson, two Englishmen who escaped from the battle in Transylvania where Smith was left for dead on the field (1:363, 362, 2:393). Though one must allow for the normal exaggerations of commendatory verses, these poems, as well as the ones by the colonists who served with him in Virginia (1:313, 316–18, 2:51), all express extraordinary loyalty and praise.

Chapter 5

1. *American Heritage Dictionary of the English Language*, ed. Morris (1978).

2. Two other colonists, William Bentley and Francis Perkins, change from laborers to gentlemen (1:223, 2:161), but nothing is known about them.

3. Rolfe seems to have confused Spence with Ensign William Spence[r] who was elected a burgess in 1619. The burgess Ensign William Spence[r] is generally thought to have been killed in the 1622 massacre (2:302), but the enumeration of the five persons who died "at Ensigne Spence his house" does not list him or any member of his family (Kingsbury, *Records* 3:570). And in May 1625 Ensign William Spence[r] possessed 300 acres in Archer's Hope

(ibid., 4:556). For the best and most recent attempt to compile information on Spencer and to discriminate him from Spence, see Jester and Hiden, *Adventurers of Purse and Person*, 580–85. Whether William Spence and William Spencer were two persons is moot; Smith believed that William Spence was a laborer who came over with him in 1607 and was in 1624 a successful farmer and gentleman.

4. The chief carpenter, William Laxon, one of the original colonists, was evidently also gradually changing status in Virginia. In the spring of 1609 Smith sent "Ensigne Laxon" down the James River with "60 or 80" men to live upon oysters (1:208, 263; cf. 2:142, 212).

5. For an appreciation of the roles of several interpreters, see Fausz, "Middlemen in Peace and War."

6. The greenhorn narrator of Ebenezer Cook's burlesque *Sot-Weed Factor* (London, 1708), ll. 216–35, has similar experiences and reactions.

7. See chapter 1, "Promotion Tracts and Satirical Ballads," in Lemay, *"New England's Annoyances,"* 21–35.

8. Kupperman noted: "It is revealing that, despite Smith's bravado, his party had not brought along any equipment to catch fish; this meant that they would be dependent on the Indians they met for fresh food" (*Captain John Smith: A Select Edition*, 94n). I am not sure what the passage has to do with Smith's supposed "bravado," but one may reasonably assume that Smith had hooks and lines to catch fish; as the text says, he lacked nets suitable for scooping fish found in schools.

9. I agree with Arner that Smith added the passage (Arner, "John Smith, the 'Starving Time,' and the Genesis of Southern Humor"). See also Lemay, "Southern Colonial Grotesque."

10. George Percy, "Treue Relacyon," 266–67.

Chapter 6

1. Morgan conceded that "we do not read of any atrocities committed upon them [the Indians] under his [Smith's] direction, nor did he feel obliged to hang, break, or burn any Englishman who went off to live with them" (*American Slavery / American Freedom*, 79). Though in one place Fausz judged Smith to have been "a talented, experienced culture-broker who intimidated *selectively* and more to avoid, than to provoke, wholesale slaughter," in the same sentence he echoed Nash and said that Smith "purchased short-term survival at an extravagant price in long-term enmity" (Fausz, "Patterns of Anglo-Indian Aggression and Accommodation along the Mid-Atlantic Coast," 239; Nash, "Image of the Indian in the Southern Colonial Mind," 214). I can hardly believe that Smith regarded his survival and that of the Virginia colony as a "short-term" matter. Canny agreed with Morgan ("'To Establish a Common Wealthe,'" 217–18).

2. For definitions of the comparative method and the stage theory and

a survey of the background of the ideas, see Lemay, "Frontiersman from Lout to Hero," esp. 194–203.

3. STC 12785, Sabin 30377, Church 135, EA 588/40. The introduction by Randolph G. Adams to the facsimile reprint of Harriot's *Briefe and True Report* (1951) suggests that only a small number of the 1588 quarto edition was published. The 1590 folio edition, though more expensive, was common.

4. Feest, "Virginia Indian in Pictures."

5. Cf. Sabin 8784, STC 12786, cf. Church 203, EA 590/32. The 1590 folio of Harriot's *Briefe and True Report* is conveniently available in a facsimile (1972), with a valuable introduction by Paul Hulton.

6. Sabin 131, STC 94, Church 328, EA 604/1. John H. Rowe observed: "The Renaissance rediscovery of the Classical theory that the earliest men were naked forest dwellers provided a basis for the development of a theory of progress. This development took place in the sixteenth century, about a hundred years earlier than Bury suggested ("Ethnography and Ethnology in the Sixteenth Century," 7). Rowe found that Jose de Acosta developed a full-scale theory of the stages of civilization in the 1570s and 1580s.

7. Bock pointed out that "with Thucydides the comparative method was already complete" (*Acceptance of Histories*, 48). Arthur Barlow's account of Virginia used the comparative method (Quinn, *Roanoke Voyages* 1:108). Fenton, introducing Lafitau's *Customs of the American Indians Compared with the Customs of Primitive Times* (xliii–lxxxiii), gives other sixteenth-century precursors of Lafitau who used the comparative method.

8. For a thorough scholarly survey, see Smits, "'Abominable Mixture.'"

9. Quinn has written: "Later, they were made out to be members of the Chesapeake tribe but there are very serious doubts if they could have been ("A Colony Is Lost and Found," 362–63).

10. Smith, who was not present, reported that "400. Indians" attacked the fort (1:31). Edward Maria Wingfield said that "above. 200" Indians attacked (*JV* 95). Smith did not give a number in *The Proceedings* (1:206) or in *The Generall Historie* (2:138).

11. The likely villain seems to have been Samuel Mace (Quinn, "'Virginians' on the Thames in 1603," 428, and "A Colony Is Lost and Found?" 356).

12. *Dictionary of Canadian Biography*, s.v. "Tisquantum." Salisbury, however, remarked that "Smith visited Squanto's home village of Patuxet *before* reaching Cape Cod on that voyage, and Smith did not mention 'Tantum' in accounts of New England he published in 1616, 1620, and 1622, only inserting him in a 1624 edition" (*Manitou and Providence*, 265–66). Salisbury's latter point seems irrelevant, and the former one may be explained in various ways.

13. Waterhouse, *Declaration of the State of the Colony in Virginia*, 16.

14. Kupperman first called attention to Smith's omission (*Settling with the Indians*, 87).

15. Fausz, "Fighting 'Fire' with Firearms," 34.

16. Bradford described the Pilgrims' first encounter: "a lustie man, and

no less valiante, stood behind a tree within halfe a musket shot, and let his arrows flie at them. He was seen shoot 3 arrowes, which were all avoyded. He stood 3 shot of a musket, till one taking full aime at him, and made the barke or splinters of the tree fly about his ears, after which he gave an extraordinary shrike, and away they wente all of them" (*History of Plymouth Plantation* 1:171).

17. Fausz, "'Abundance of Blood Shed on Both Sides,'" 22. Earlier, however, Fausz credited Smith with establishing and preserving a detente with the Indians throughout his years in Virginia ("Patterns of Anglo-American Aggression and Accommodation Along the Mid-Atlantic Coast," 239).

18. Earle applauded Smith's decision, arguing that Smith appreciated and analyzed the reasons behind the Indians' seminomadic economy: "Smith's genius was in placing the puzzling Indian behavior and subsistence strategies into a coherent ecological whole. He realized the colony's survival, no less than the Indians,' depended upon seminomadism, at least during the deadly summer season" ("Environment, Disease, and Mortality in Early Virginia," 107).

19. Purchas, *Purchas His Pilgrimage*, 641.

20. Lurie, "Indian Cultural Adjustment to European Civilization," 45.

21. For a historiographical survey of the literature concerning the 1622 massacre, see Fausz, "'Barbarous Massacre' Reconsidered."

22. Washburn, "Moral and Legal Justifications for Dispossessing the Indians," 23; Eisinger, "Puritans' Justification for Taking the Land."

23. Earle, "Environment, Disease, and Mortality in Early Virginia," 106, n.30.

Chapter 7

1. Craven, "Indian Policy in Early Virginia," 68.

2. Lurie noted that Powhatan at first probably considered the whites "useful allies" ("Indian Cultural Adjustment to European Civilization," 36–38).

3. Surprisingly, when Ralph Hamor took Thomas Savage to be his interpreter to visit Powhatan in the spring of 1614, Powhatan told Savage: "My child, I gave you leave, being my boy, to goe see your friends, and these foure yeeres I have not seene you, nor heard of my own man Namontack whom I sent to England" (2:248). Did Powhatan forget that Namontack had returned? Or had Namontack sailed for England again?

4. In 1614 Powhatan told Ralph Hamor that he had "resolved upon no termes to put himselfe into our hands, or come amongst us" (2:249).

5. Strachey, *Historie of Travell*, 60–61. Not all Indian chiefs were impressive. Smith comments on few others. Captain Gabriel Archer thought the queen of Appomattoc possessed "more majesty" than Powhatan but found Opechancanough foolish: he "set his Countenance stryving to be stately, as to our seeming he became foole" (*JV* 92). George Percy was especially impressed with "the Werowance of Rapahanna" and devoted an extended description to

his dress and actions, concluding, "he entertained vs in so modest a proud fashion, as though he had beene a Prince of ciuil gouernmnet, holding his countenance without laughter or any such ill behauiour" (*JV* 137).

6. Quinn, "Lost Colony in Myth and Reality," 466–68, and "A Colony Is Lost and Found?" 357–66. See also Barbour, "Ocanahowan and Recently Discovered Linguistic Fragments from Southern Virginia."

7. Kingsbury, *Records* 3:17–18.

8. Quinn, "Lost Colony in Myth and Reality," 467.

9. Purchas, *Hakluytus Posthumus* (1625), 4:1813, 1728; reprint edition (1906), 19:227–28, 18:527.

10. Strachey, *Historie of Travell*, 64.

11. George Percy, "Trewe Relacyon," 266.

12. Kingsbury, *Records* 3:12 (paragraph no. 2), 16 (paragraph no. 14).

13. Brown, *Genesis* 1:346; Clayton-Torrence, no. 13.

14. Brown, *Genesis* 1:503.

15. Culliford, *William Strachey*, 178.

16. Strachey, *Historie of Travell*, 174. Strachey also gave the same explanation for the two names in the text on p. 41 ("we call the *Kings River*, they call *Powhatan*"), but the marginal heading simply says: "*Powhaton or the Kings Riuer.*"

17. Brown, *Genesis* 2:778; Sabin 99873, STC 24834, EA 616/55.

18. Also printed in Brown, *Genesis* 1:84.

19. Also printed in ibid., 1:484.

20. Ibid., 2:583.

21. Kingsbury, *Records* 3:228.

22. The whites often called rivers by the names of the major tribes living by them. Thus Edward Maria Wingfield wrote that Smith "went vp the Ryuer of the Chechohomynaies to trade for Corne" (*JV* 226). Tooker pointed out that though the early colonists commonly called the river the Chickahominy, "it will be observed from Wingfield's statement that he was aware that the appellation properly belonged to the people and not to the stream" ("The Name Chickahominy," 259).

23. Kingsbury, *Records* 3:465, 481, 499, 553, 591, 595, 4:529, 551.

24. Verner, *Smith's "Virginia" and Its Derivatives*.

25. Brown, *Genesis* 1: facing p. 150, gives a poor engraving of the map. It is studied in detail and well reproduced in Mook, "Ethnological Significance of Tindall's Map of Virginia." The legend identifying the river reads: "King James his River." The map is reproduced in color in Cumming, Skelton, and Quinn, *Discovery of North America*, 237.

26. Don Alonso de Velasco succeeded Zuniga as Spanish ambassador to England. He sent this map to King Philip II in 1611. Cumming, Skelton, and Quinn, *Discovery of North America*, 266–67 (in color).

27. Reproduced in ibid., 262.

28. Ibid., 268, 269.

29. Verner, *Smith's "Virginia" and Its Derivatives*, 38.

30. See n. 22 above.

31. For some observations on the drift away from honoring the monarch on English maps during the Renaissance, see Helgerson, "The Land Speaks." Smith, an expert mapmaker, probably knew the major English mapmakers. Two connections between Smith and the celebrants of England are George Wither, who wrote commendatory verses for both Smith and Michael Drayton's *Poly-Olbion* (1612), and the antiquarian circle including Robert Cotton and John Speed, though Smith's epitaph (3:390) in Speed's *Survey of London* (London, 1633) was added after Speed's death.

Chapter 8

1. Porter, *Inconstant Savage*, 299.

2. Kelso, *Doctrine of the English Gentleman in the Sixteenth Century*, 18–30, 42–69, esp. 19, 26; Stone, *Crisis of the Aristocracy*, 331; Rabb, "Expansion of Europe and the Spirit of Capitalism," 683.

3. Strachey, *Historie of Travell*, 47.

4. Kupperman, "Apathy and Death in Early Jamestown," 40.

5. George Percy, "Treue Relacyon," 264.

6. Rozwenc, "Captain John Smith's Image of America," 33.

7. Perhaps Rev. William Symonds or the printer supplied the marginal headings (*AB* 42; *CW* 1:122).

8. Strachey, "True Reportory," 69, in Louis B. Wright, *Voyage to Virginia*.

9. Brief biographical sketches and bibliographical references for the councillors may be found in *CW* 1:xxvii–liv. My reasons for assigning Wingfield an earlier date of birth than that given by Barbour are presented below.

10. Smith said in *A True Relation* that Kendall "was by a Jury condemned and shot to death" (1:41). But in *The Generall Historie*, he carelessly reported that Kendall was fleeing in the pinnace for England and was killed in a battle (2:145). Wingfield, however, confirmed the first account and added a few details (*JV* 225).

11. Kingsbury, *Records* 3:89.

12. Ibid., 3:87, 88.

13. Strachey, "True Reportory," in Louis B. Wright, *Voyage to Virginia*, 98; cf. *CW* 1:275.

14. Hamor, *True Discourse*, 7.

15. Kingsbury, *Records* 3:86.

16. Barbour, "The Honorable George Percy," 12.

17. Bemiss, *Three Charters*, 158, 65. See also Diamond, "From Organization to Society," 467–68, and "Values as an Obstacle to Economic Growth," 564.

18. Strachey, *For the Colony in Virginia*, 2. Strachey may have been echoing passages from Donne and Shakespeare quoted below.

19. Bemiss, *Three Charters*, 58.

20. Hamor, *True Discourse*. The most recent examination proves that even after Dale's reign, law in early Virginia continued to be more severe than in England, though Konig has pointed out that "children, servants, convicts, or rebels" would also have been unlikely to claim the protection of common law in England ("'Dale's Laws' and the Non-Common Law Origins of Criminal Justice in Virginia," 365).

21. See, for example, *Hamlet* 3.1.73: "the insolence of Office"; *Measure for Measure* 2.4.12: "O place, O form, / How often dost thou with thy case, thy habit, / Wrench awe from fools"; and *King Lear* 4.6.159: "a dog's obeyed in office." Cf. the contexts of the proverb "Jack in an office," *Oxford Dictionary of English Proverbs*, 408.

22. Shirley, "George Percy at Jamestown," 239.

23. *DNB*, s.v. "Percy, George."

24. Hill paraphrased Bruno Ryves's account of the "lower classes of Chelmsford at the beginning of the civil war" as saying that "gentlemen should be made to work for their living, or else should not eat" (*World Turned Upside Down*, 31). Hill believed this radical attitude existed continuously from at least the Middle Ages ("From Lollards to Levellers," in Hill, *Collected Essays* 2:89–116).

25. Compare such medieval moralists as Boethius (*On the Consolation of Philosophy*) and John Gower (*Confessio Amantis*), as well as the medieval and Renaissance preachers (see Owst, *Literature and Pulpit in Medieval England*, 287–374; Helen C. White, *Social Criticism in Popular Religious Literature of the Sixteenth Century*, 1–81; T. Wilson Hayes, "John Everard and the Familist Tradition," 60–69).

26. Diamond, "From Organization to Society," 466.

27. Tilley, *Dictionary of the Proverbs in England*, no. H116. The context of the proverb in *The Troublesome Raigne of King John* (1591) is especially telling: "Madame, I am bold to make my selfe your nephew, / The poorest kinsman that your Highnes hath: / And with this Proverb gin the world anew, / Help hands, I have no lands, honour is my desire" (Bullough, *Narrative and Dramatic Sources of Shakespeare* 4:80, ll. 288–91).

28. *Gentleness and Nobility*, in Axton, *Three Rastell Plays*, 105, 116, ll. 295, 793–95. For sources and parallels to the play, see Cameron, *Authorship and Sources of* Gentleness and Nobility. Another play expressing popular dissatisfaction with the social order is William Wager's *Enough Is as Good as a Feast* (1565?). Bevington discussed the radical social themes in these plays and others in *Tudor Drama and Politics*, esp. 75–85, 212–29. Heinemann found connections between the drama of Smith's day and the levellers of the interregnum (*Puritanism and Theatre*, esp. "From Popular Drama to Leveller Style: A Postscript," 237–57).

29. *Oxford Dictionary of English Proverbs*, 3; also Tilley, *Dictionary of the Proverbs in England*, no. A30. For the proverb's social and literary contexts, see Resnikow, "Cultural History of a Democratic Proverb," and esp. Friedman, "'When Adam Delved . . . .'"

30. "Song of the Husbandman," *Historical Poems of the XIVth and XVth Centuries*, 7–9.

31. Reprinted in *Roxburghe Ballads* 2:334–38, and in Sola Pinto and Rodway, *Common Muse*, 102–5. Rollins pointed out that the ballad was registered on March 12, 1629/30, by Francis Grove (*Analytical Index*, 185, no. 2135). It twice used another radical proverb of the Renaissance: "The weakest go to the wall," lines 78 and 110 (*Oxford Dictionary of English Proverbs*, 873; Tilley, *Dictionary of Proverbs in England*, no. W185).

32. Lomax, *Folk Songs of North America*, 132.

33. Holstun, *Rational Millennium*, 72.

34. Child, *English and Scottish Popular Ballads* 3:56.

35. Holt, *Robin Hood*, 171; cf. 166, 183–84.

36. For the topos of *mundus inversus*, see Curtius, *European Literature and the Latin Middle Ages*, 94–98; A. W. Smith, "Some Folklore Elements in Movements of Social Protest"; Donaldson, *World Upside-Down*; Torrance, *Comic Hero*; Caputi, *Buffo*.

37. Compare Smith's paragraph on malcontents in *A Map of Virginia* (1:175–76) with Harriot's words (Quinn, *Roanoke Voyages* 2:323).

38. Indeed, his maps are so good that some scholars doubted that Smith made them: see Brown, "Queries," and Ford, "Captain John Smith's Map of Virginia 1612."

39. Barbour briefly traced Purchas's use of Virginia materials in "Samuel Purchas."

40. Sharpe, *Sir Robert Cotton*, 119, 241–45.

41. See also Barbour, *Three Worlds of Smith*, 14–15, 27, and notes, 401–2, 407.

42. For the background, see Sekora, *Luxury,*, 23–62.

Chapter 9

1. Sir George Yeardley's Southhampton Hundred contained 80,000 acres, though he had a number of partners (*DAB*, s.v. "Yeardley, Sir George"). The Virginia Company's continued unwillingness to give out land to the colonists is the best evidence of its intentions (Craven, *Dissolution of the Virginia Company*, 57–66; Hatch, *First Seventeen Years*, 34–40; Robinson, *Mother Earth*, 19–21). For Humphrey Gilbert's plans for a "gigantic fiefdom in the New World," see McManis, *European Impressions of the New England Coast*, 61.

2. Kenneth R. Andrews, *Trade, Plunder, and Settlement*, 219, and other scholars have written that the first president of the council was appointed by the instructions. Smith, however, wrote that Wingfield was "elected" (1:27). In his more detailed account in *The Proceedings*, after listing the members of the council who were "to choose a President amongst them for a yeare, who with the Councell should governe," Smith added: "Matters of moment were to be examined by a Jurie, but determined by the major part of the Councell in

which the Precedent had 2 voices. Untill the 13 of May they sought a place to plant in, then the Councell was sworne, Master Wingfield was chosen President, and an Oration made, whie Captaine Smith was not admitted of the Councell as the rest" (1:205, 2:138). Kupperman mistakenly said the sealed box containing the names of the council was "opened at sea" (*Captain John Smith: A Select Edition*, 6; cf. *CW* 1:27, 205, 2:138).

3. Although Barbour estimated Wingfield's dates as "c. 1565–1613," Wesley Frank Craven in his *DAB* sketch of Wingfield said that "the known facts regarding his parentage prove that he was past middle age when he sailed for Virginia in 1606." I do not know what Craven meant by "middle age" (my own definition is ages forty to sixty, but Wingfield could not have been sixty or older in 1606). The key facts are: Thomas Maria Wingfield's first wife died in 1546, Edward Maria was his eldest son and heir by his second wife, and in 1586 Edward Maria Wingfield sought in return for his services in Ireland and the Netherlands "a grant of 3,000 acres in Limerick and 4,000 in Munster" (*DAB*). I suspect he was at least thirty in 1586. He could not have been born before 1548, and his military service in Ireland makes it unlikely that he was born after 1556. I therefore assign his date of birth as c. 1553.

4. References to Smith's supposed mutiny, his exclusion from the council, and his petition and reconciliation all evidently were cut (see 1:27, 33, 98–99 nn. 15, 16, 22, 46). References to dissension within the council, to the foolish gold fever of John Martin and others, and to Ratcliffe's "palace" may also have been cut (see 1:33, and 87, 100nn. 50, 51, 107 n.214).

5. Kingsbury, *Records* 3:22, 28.

6. Arber's speculation (*AB* 42) was followed by Brown, who pointed out that the "Stationers' Company of London was a member of the Virginia Company and it was evidently against their interest to license the publication of such tracts and maps as these" (*Genesis* 2:597), and by Madan, *Oxford Books* 1:83–85; Emerson, *Captain John Smith*, 52; Barbour, *JV*, 322–23; Davis, *Intellectual Life* 1:19; and Kupperman, *Captain John Smith: A Select Edition*, 25. But Barbour later suggested that the fact that William Symonds was an Oxford man (though then preaching in London) itself could account for the place of publication (*CW* 1:121–22). George Watson Cole said: "That this work was printed at Oxford instead of London is accounted for by the fact that many members of the Stationers' Company of London were also members of the Virginia Company. It was not, therefore, in the interest of the Company to publish such books and maps; and, as it could not be published in London without a license, Smith was compelled to look elsewhere for a publisher. It is well known that Crashaw, Symonds, and Purchas were in sympathy with Smith, and it was doubtless through their influence that this tract was printed by the single hand-press at Oxford, which usually produced only sermons, theology, and other learned works" (Church 359).

7. Diamond explained that the concession the English and French colonizers had to make "to recruit and motivate a labor force that was adequate

both quantitatively and qualitatively made it impossible here [in America] to reproduce the rigidity of social structure characteristic of contemporary Europe or to maintain for any considerable time the harshness and rigor characteristic of their initial efforts at society building." He observed, "the result was a veritable social revolution in the early seventeenth-century colonies" (Diamond, "Values as an Obstacle to Economic Growth," 565). Although the changing social order was forced upon the Virginia Company and the following colonizers, the social ideals that gradually emerged had been articulated throughout the earliest period of colonization by Smith. In this case, as in several details of the London Company's later instructions to the governor and council of Virginia, the company abandoned its earlier positions and adopted Smith's.

8. Wingfield wrote that he could not be overthrown as governor unless it were "eyther by Captaine Gosnold, or Master Archer; for the one was strong with freinds and followers, and could if he would; and the other was troubled with an ambitious spirit, and would if he could" (*JV* 214).

9. When Newport returned to England on April 10, 1608 (after having brought over the first supply), he took back Wingfield and Archer (1:219, 2:158; *JV* 229). Archer had been elected to the council while Smith was a captive in December 1607; he thus had not been a councillor at the 1607 election and was not present for the 1608 election. When Captain Francis Nelson returned for England on June 2, 1608, he took back Captain John Martin (2:160).

10. Charles M. Andrews, *Colonial Period of American History* 1:142n. French wrote: "More than anyone else, Captain John Smith encouraged settling in New England, giving to the enterprise much more time and effort than ever he did to Virginia" (*Charles I and the Puritan Upheaval*, 325). Andrews and French followed Morison, who included Smith "among the builders of the Massachusetts Bay" (*Builders of the Bay Colony*, 9). Though Smith publicized New England more than Virginia after 1612, he did not devote the remainder of his life entirely to New England. The sequence of colonies in his greatest work, *The Generall Historie of Virginia, New-England, and the Summer Isles*, was deliberate.

11. Craven, *Southern Colonies in the Seventeenth Century*, 72.

12. *English New England Voyages*, 466.

13. Gorges, *Briefe Narration*, 11.

14. See the numerous entries for Gorges in the indexes of both *CW* and Bradford, *History of Plymouth Plantation*, ed. Ford.

15. Because Smith did not gamble, smoke, or drink to excess, many scholars have thought him a Puritan. But Smith showed none of that scrupulosity regarding conscience and religious matters that characterized Puritanism, and he spoke with scorn of the Plymouth colony group as "Brownists" (3:221, 281–82, 285–86). He praised the leaders of the Massachusetts Bay colony in part because they supposedly would not, contrary to rumor, admit "discontented Brownists, Anabaptists, Papists, Puritans, Separatists, and such

factious Humorists [fanatics]" to their company (3:270). Later, he automatically castigated the remigrants among the Massachusetts Bay Company—a group for whom Smith had absolute contempt—as Puritans: "some could not endure the name of a Bishop, others not the sight of a Crosse nor Surplesse, others by no meanes the booke of common Prayer. This absolute crue, only of the Elect, holding all (but such as themselves) reprobates and cast-awaies, now make more haste to returne to Babel, as they tearmed England, than stay to enjoy the land they called Canaan" (3:292–93).

16. The Pilgrims intended to settle in what is now New York (Morison, "Plymouth Colony and Virginia").

17. Rutman argued that the Pilgrims did not adopt the name Plymouth (the name that Prince Charles gave Smith's Accomack [1:319]) until some later time. He asserted that they adopted the name because Plymouth "was the last town they left in their native country" and because "they received many kindnesses from some Christians there" ("Pilgrims and Their Harbor," 178). Rutman's reasoning is unconvincing. They must have had all the printed maps of the Eastern seaboard available and no doubt had as many manuscript maps as they could secure. They called their settlement "New Plimmoth" at least as early as 1621 (1:430).

18. Morison, "*Mayflower's* Destination," 393.

19. *Dictionary of Canadian Biography*, s.v. "Tisquantum," or Squanto.

20. Bradford, *History of Plymouth Plantation*, ed. Ford, 1:204.

21. *Dictionary of Canadian Biography*, s.v. "Dermer, Thomas."

22. *Winthrop Papers* 2:145n.

23. Reprinted in Mitchell, "Founding of Massachusetts," 321.

24. Wood, *New England's Prospect*, 25–26.

25. Besides Sir Humphrey Mildmay and his family; Henry Clinton, earl of Lincoln, and his family; Richard, Samuel, and Wye Saltonstall; Sir Ferdinando Gorges; and Dr. Matthew Sutcliffe; it seems likely that Smith knew Isaac and Mary Allerton, Sir Thomas Coventry, Sir Edward Harwood, John Peirce, Sir Nathaniel and Sir Robert Rich, James Shirley, Miles Standish, Thomas Weston, Captain Richard Whitbourne, and John Winthrop. These persons are all indexed in *CW*; Bradford's *History of Plymouth Plantation*, ed. Ford; and Rose-Troup, *Massachusetts Bay Company and Its Predecessors*.

26. Smith here anticipated a complaint about the colonial laws and legal system that continued until the Revolution (cf. Franklin to Governor William Shirley, Dec. 4, 1754, *Benjamin Franklin: Writings*, 399).

27. Mitchell surveyed and summarized the older scholarship ("Founding of Massachusetts," 243–46).

28. Osgood, *American Colonies in the Seventeenth Century* 1:142.

29. *Winthrop Papers* 2:143.

30. Winthrop, "A Modell of Christian Charity," *Winthrop Papers* 2:282. Winthrop's most famous phrase, "wee shall be as a Citty upon a hill," more memorably expressed a sentiment of Smith's, which, though written at the same time as Winthrop's sermon, surely repeated advice he had given to Win-

throp and other leaders of the company: "In this your infancy, imagine you have many eyes attending your actions, some for one end, and some onely to find fault" (3:298). For John Cotton's conservative views on democracy, see *Abstract on the Laws of New England* (popularly called "Moses His Judicials," 1636; pub. 1641), his code of law founded on Scripture. Cotton said: "Democracy, I do not conceive that ever God did ordain as a fit government either for church or commonwealth. If the people be governors, who shall be governed?" (Miller and Johnson, *Puritans*, 209–10). New England leaders generally remained conservative into the eighteenth century. Ebenezer Pemberton advised his parishioners to aspire to "those things that are proper, and pertinent to you; which belong to that order, place, vocation, and those Relations Divine Providence has disposed you in, whether of a Superior or Inferiour nature" (*Christian Fixed at His Post*, 3). For a survey of the Massachusetts Bay Puritans' ideas on order and love (the basic themes of Winthrop's speech), see Foster, *Their Solitary Way*, 11–64. Morgan has compared Winthrop's "Modell" to other appeals for brotherly love delivered on shipboard or in the early colonization period ("John Winthrop's 'Modell of Christian Charity' in a Wider Context").

31. Bozeman, *To Live Ancient Lives*.

32. Quinn surveyed the conflicting reasons for emigration and pointed out the desire of the London Company's leaders for baronial holdings in America ("Introduction: Prelude to Maryland" and "Why They Came," *Early Maryland in a Wider World*, 11–29, 119–48).

33. Charles M. Andrews, *Colonial Period of American History* 1:78–97.

34. Hamor, *True Discourse*, 17; Charles M. Andrews, *Colonial Period of American History* 1:124–26; Craven, *Dissolution of the Virginia Company*; Robinson, *Mother Earth*, 15–16; Harris, *Origin of the Land Tenure System in the United States*, 82–88; Morgan, "First American Boom."

35. Hamor, *True Discourse*, 17.

36. In the "Instructions to George Yeardley" (Kingsbury, *Records* 3:101). See also Craven, *Dissolution of the Virginia Company*, 55–57; Charles M. Andrews, *Colonial Period of American History* 1:124–26; Harris, *Origin of the Land Tenure System in the United States*, 82–91, 194–204.

37. Diamond, "Values as an Obstacle to Economic Growth," 565. See also Diamond, "From Organization to Society," 465–66, 469–71; *AB* 42; *JV* 328.

38. By the "Instructions to George Yeardley," Nov. 18, 1618, the Virginia Company gave the "old planters" (i.e., those who had emigrated before 1616 and paid their own way) one hundred acres in fee simple. Later settlers received fifty acres and another fifty for every person whose transportation costs they paid (Kingsbury, *Records* 3:100–101; Craven, *Dissolution of the Virginia Company*, 47–80).

39. Later, Benjamin Franklin did so in three letters to William Shirley in late 1754. The last, written Dec. 22, 1754, concluded, "In fine, why should the countenance of a state be *partially* afforded to its people, unless it be most in favour of those, who have most merit? and if there be any difference [between

the people in England and in the colonies], those, who have most contributed to enlarge Britain's empire and commerce, encrease her strength, her wealth, and the numbers of her people, at the risque of their own lives and private fortunes in new and strange countries, methinks ought rather to expect some preference" (*Benjamin Franklin: Writings*, 409–10).

40. Charles M. Andrews agreed: "the charter conferred upon the proprietor powers that in their range and archaic peculiarities are a witness to the entire disregard by the contemporary legal mind in Scotland of the element of time and to its solemn ignorance of the conditions in America" (*Colonial Period of American History* 1:315). For a sketch of Alexander, *Dictionary of Canadian Biography*, s.v. "Alexander, Sir William."

41. For an evaluation of Smith's radical agrarian position, see Eisinger, "Freehold Concept in Eighteenth-Century American Letters," and esp. "Land and Loyalty," where he wrote, "Smith exhibits an insight into the implications of freehold tenure that was rare in his time" (164).

42. As I have elsewhere shown, however, Crèvecoeur (amplifying Franklin) formulated a full-scale theory of the frontier's significance based upon the comparative method and stage theory of civilization (Lemay, "Frontiersman from Lout to Hero").

43. Smith proves the exception to Kammen's observation that "the colonists gradually 'discovered' liberty during the seventeenth century, and then became obsessed by it during the course of the eighteenth" (*Spheres of Liberty*, 17). The first three definitions of "liberty" in the *OED* are especially pertinent: "1. Exemption or release from captivity, bondage, or slavery. . . . 2. Exemption or freedom from arbitrary, despotic, or autocratic rule or control. . . . 3. The condition of being able to act in any desired way without hindrance or restraint; faculty or power to do as one likes."

44. The classic exposition of the Adamic theme in American literature, R. W. B. Lewis, *American Adam*, ignored the colonial period.

45. Morgan explained the Virginians' abuse of servants as "a simple outgrowth of the extreme demand for labor in combination with the long terms of service that were enacted for transportation to Virginia" ("First American Boom," 197).

46. Hillebrand and Baldwin, eds., Shakespeare, *Troilus and Cressida*, New Variorum Edition, 389–410, cite numerous analogues.

Bibliography

AB. *See* Arber and Bradley, eds.

Acosta, José de. *The Naturall and Morall Historie of the East and West Indies*. Tr. E. Grimstone. London: V. Simms for E. Blount & W. Aspley, 1604.

Adams, Henry. "Captain John Smith." *North American Review* 104 (1867): 1–30.

Adams, Percy G. *Travel Literature and the Evolution of the Novel*. Lexington: Univ. Press of Kentucky, 1983.

Allen, John William. *English Political Thought, 1603–1660*. London: Methuen, 1938.

The American Heritage Dictionary of the English Language. Ed. William Morris. Boston: Houghton Mifflin, 1978.

Andrews, Charles M. *The Colonial Period of American History*. 4 vols. New Haven: Yale Univ. Press, 1934.

Andrews, Kenneth R. *Trade, Plunder, and Settlement: Maritime Enterprise and the Genesis of the British Empire, 1480–1630*. Cambridge: Cambridge Univ. Press, 1984.

Arber, Edward, and A. G. Bradley, eds. *Travels and Works of Captain John Smith*. 2 vols. Edinburgh: John Grant, 1910.

Arner, Robert D. "John Smith, the 'Starving Time,' and the Genesis of Southern Humor: Variations on a Theme." *Louisiana Studies* 12 (1973): 383–90.

Axton, Richard, ed. *Three Rastell Plays: Four Elements, Calisto and Melebea, Gentleness and Nobility*. Cambridge, Eng.: D. S. Brewer, 1979.

Bacon, Francis. *The Essayes or Counsels, Civill and Morall*. Ed. Michael Kiernan. Cambridge: Harvard Univ. Press, 1985.

———. *The Philosophical Works of Francis Bacon*. Ed. John M. Robertson. London: Routledge and Sons, 1905.

Bailyn, Bernard. "Politics and Social Structure in Virginia." In *Seventeenth-Century America: Essays in Colonial History*. Ed. James Morton Smith. 1959; rpt. New York: W. W. Norton, 1972, 90–115.

Banks, Charles E. "Religious 'Persecution' as a Factor in Emigration to New England." *Proceedings of the Massachusetts Historical Society* 63 (1931): 136–54.

Barbour, Philip L. "Captain John Smith and the London Theatre." *Virginia Magazine of History and Biography* 83 (1975): 277–79.

———. "Captain John Smith's Observations on Life in Tartary." *Virginia Magazine of History and Biography* 68 (1960): 271–83.

———. "Captain John Smith's Route through Turkey and Russia." *William and Mary Quarterly*, 3d ser., 14 (1957): 358–69.

———. "Fact and Fiction in Captain John Smith's *True Travels*." *Bulletin of the New York Public Library* 67 (1963): 517–28.

———. "A French Account of Captain John Smith's Adventures in the Azores, 1615." *Virginia Magazine of History and Biography* 72 (1964): 293–303.

———. "The Honorable George Percy: Premier Chronicler of the First Virginia Voyage." *Early American Literature* 6 (1971): 7–17.

———. "A Note on the Discovery of the Original Will of Captain John Smith, with a Verbatim Transcription." *William and Mary Quarterly*, 3d ser., 25 (1968): 625–28.

———. "Ocanahowan and Recently Discovered Linguistic Fragments from Southern Virginia, *c.* 1650." *Papers of the Seventh Algonquian Conference, 1975.* Ed. William Cowan. Ottawa: Carleton Univ., 1976.

———. "Samuel Purchas: The Indefatigable Encyclopedist Who Lacked Good Judgment." In *Essays in Early Virginia Literature Honoring Richard Beale Davis.* Ed. J. A. Leo Lemay. New York: Burt Franklin, 1977, 35–52.

———. *The Three Worlds of Captain John Smith.* Boston: Houghton Mifflin, 1964.

———. "Two 'Unknown' Poems by Captain John Smith." *Virginia Magazine of History and Biography* 75 (1967): 157–58.

———, ed. *The Complete Works of Captain John Smith.* 3 vols. Chapel Hill: Univ. of North Carolina Press, 1986.

———, ed. *The Jamestown Voyages under the First Charter, 1606–1609.* 2 vols. Hakluyt Society, 2d ser., vols. 136 and 137. Cambridge: Cambridge Univ. Press, 1969.

Barlow, Joel. *Advice to the Privileged Orders,* 1792. In *The Works of Joel Barlow.* Ed. William K. Bottorrff and Arthur L. Ford. 2 vols. Gainesville, Fla.: Scholars' Facsimiles and Reprints, 1970.

Bartram, William. *Travels through North and South Carolina, Georgia, East and West Florida . . . .* Ed. Francis Harper. New Haven: Yale Univ. Press, 1958.

Baudet, Henri. *Paradise on Earth.* Tr. Elizabeth Wentholt. New Haven: Yale Univ. Press, 1965.

Bausum, Henry S. "Edenic Images of the Western World: A Reappraisal." *South Atlantic Quarterly* 67 (1968): 672–87.

Beard, Charles A. *An Economic Interpretation of the Constitution.* New York: Macmillan, 1935.

Beckwith, Ian. "Captain John Smith: The Yeoman Background." *History Today* 26 (1976): 444–51.

Bemiss, Samuel M., ed. *The Three Charters of the Virginia Company of London with Seven Related Documents.* Williamsburg: Virginia 350th Anniversary Celebration Corporation, 1957.

Bercovitch, Sacvan. "'Delightful Examples of Surprising Prosperity': Cotton Mather and the American Success Story." *English Studies* 56 (1970): 40–43.

Bernheimer, Richard. *The Wild Man in the Middle Ages: A Study in Art, Sentiment, and Demonology*. Cambridge: Harvard Univ. Press, 1952.

Bevington, David. *Tudor Drama and Politics*. Cambridge: Harvard Univ. Press, 1968.

Bible. See *Geneva Bible*.

Blackstock, Walter. "Captain John Smith: His Role in American Colonial History." *Florida State Univ. Studies*, no. 6 (1952): 23–45.

Blanke, Gustav H. *Amerika im Englishchen Schrifttum des 16. und 17. Jahrhunderts*. Bochum-Langendreer: Verlag Heinrich Poppinghaus, 1962.

Boas, George. *Essays on Primitivism and Related Ideas in the Middle Ages*. Baltimore: Johns Hopkins Univ. Press, 1948.

Bock, Kenneth E. *The Acceptance of Histories: Towards a Perspective for Social Science*. Univ. of California Publications in Sociology and Social Institutions, vol. 3, no. 1. Berkeley, 1956.

Boethius. *The Consolation of Philosophy* [with *The Theological Tractates*]. Tr. S. J. Tester. Loeb Classical Library. Cambridge: Harvard Univ. Press, 1973.

Boswell, James. *Life of Johnson*. Ed. G. Birkbeck Hill; rev. L. F. Powell. 6 vols. 1934; rpt. Oxford: Clarendon Press, 1979.

Bozeman, Theodore Dwight. *To Live Ancient Lives: The Primitivist Dimension in Puritanism*. Chapel Hill: Univ. of North Carolina Press, 1988.

Bradford, William. *History of Plymouth Plantation*. Ed. Worthington C. Ford. 2 vols. Boston: Massachusetts Historical Society, 1912.

[———, Edward Winslow, et al.] *A Relation or Journal of the Beginning and Proceedings of the English Plantation Settled at Plimoth in New England*. London: for J. Bellamy, 1622.

Brant, Irving. *James Madison, Father of the Constitution, 1787–1800*. New York: Bobbs-Merrill, 1950.

Brant, Sebastian. *The Shyppe of Fooles*. 1509; rpt. Amsterdam: Theatrum Orbis Terrarum, 1970.

Breen, T. H., James H. Lewis, and Keith Schlesinger, "Motive for Murder: A Servant's Life in Virginia, 1678." *William and Mary Quarterly*, 3d ser., 40 (1983): 106–20.

Bridenbaugh, Carl. *Fat Mutton and Liberty of Conscience: Society in Rhode Island, 1636–1690*. Providence: Brown Univ. Press, 1974.

———. *The Spirit of '76: The Growth of American Patriotism before Independence*. New York: Oxford Univ. Press, 1975.

———. *Vexed and Troubled Englishmen, 1590–1642*. New York: Oxford Univ. Press, 1968.

Brigham, Clarence S. *British Royal Proclamations Relating to America, 1603–1783*. Worcester, Mass.: American Antiquarian Society, 1911.

Brown, Alexander. *The Genesis of the United States*. 2 vols. Boston: Houghton, Mifflin, 1890.

———. "Queries: The Map of Virginia." *Magazine of American History* 8 (1882): 576.

Bullough, Geoffrey, ed. *Narrative and Dramatic Sources of Shakespeare*. 4 vols. London: Routledge & Kegan Paul, 1962.

Bush, Douglas. *English Literature in the Earlier Seventeenth Century*. Oxford: Clarendon Press, 1945.

Cameron, Kenneth Walter. *The Authorship and Sources of* Gentleness and Nobility. Raleigh: Thistle Press, 1941.

Campbell, Mildred. "'Of People Either Too Few or Too Many': The Conflict of Opinion on Population and Its Relation to Emigration." In *Conflict in Stuart England: Essays in Honour of Wallace Notestein*. Ed. William A. Aitken and Basil Dike Henning. London: Jonathan Cape, 1960, 169–201.

———. "Social Origins of Some Early Americans." In *Seventeenth-Century America: Essay in Colonial History*. Ed. James Morton Smith. 1959; rpt. New York: W. W. Norton, 1972, 63–89.

Canny, Nicholas P. "The Permissive Frontier: The Problem of Social Control in English Settlements in Ireland and Virginia." In *The Westward Enterprise*. Ed. K. R. Andrews et al. Detroit: Wayne State Univ. Press, 1979, 17–44.

———. "'To Establish a Common Wealthe': Captain John Smith as New World Colonist." *Virginia Magazine of History and Biography* 96 (1988): 213–22.

Caputi, Anthony. *Buffo: The Genius of Vulgar Comedy*. Detroit: Wayne State Univ. Press, 1978.

Carson, Jane. "The Will of John Rolfe." *Virginia Magazine of History and Biography* 58 (1950): 58–65.

Cawley, Robert Ralston. *The Voyagers and Elizabethan Drama*. 1938; rpt. New York: Kraus Reprint, 1966.

Child, Francis James. *The English and Scottish Popular Ballads*. 5 vols. 1882–98; rpt. New York: Dover Publications, 1965.

Church. *See* George Watson Cole.

Clayton-Torrence, William. *A Trial Bibliography of Colonial Virginia*. 2 vols. Richmond: Virginia State Library, 1908–10.

Cochrane, Rexmond C. "Bacon, Pepys, and the *Faber Fortunae*." *Notes and Queries*, n.s., 3 (1956): 525–28.

———. "Francis Bacon and the Architect of Fortune." *Studies in the Renaissance* 5 (1958): 176–95.

C[okayne], G. E. *The Complete Peerage of England, Scotland, Ireland, Great Britain, and the United Kingdom, Extant, Extinct, or Dormant*.

Ed. Geoffrey H. White et al. 14 vols. London: St. Catherine Press, 1910–59.

Cole, George Watson, comp. *A Catalogue of Books Relating to the Discovery and Early History of North and South America, Forming a Part of the Library of E. D. Church*. 5 vols. New York: Dodd, Mead, 1907.

Cole, Richard D. "Sixteenth-Century Travel Books as a Source of European Attitudes toward Non-White and Non-Western Culture." *Proceedings of the American Philosophical Society* 116 (1972): 59–67.

Cook, Ebenezer. *The Sot-Weed Factor*. London: B. Bragg, 1708.

Corbett, Margery, and Ronald Lightbrown. *The Comely Frontispiece: The Emblematic Title Page in England, 1550–1660*. London: Routledge & Kegan Paul, 1979.

Cotton, John. *An Abstract of the Laws of New England* ["Moses His Judicials"; STC 6408]. London: Printed for F. Coules and W. Ley, 1641.

Council for Virginia. *A Briefe Declaration of the Present State of Things in Virginia*. [London: T. Snodham, 1616.]

Crane, R. S. "The Vogue of Guy of Warwick." *PMLA* 30 (1915): 125–94.

Craven, Wesley Frank. *The Dissolution of the Virginia Company: The Failure of a Colonial Experiment*. 1932; rpt. Gloucester: Peter Smith, 1964.

———. "Indian Policy in Early Virginia," *William and Mary Quarterly*, 3d ser., 1 (1944): 65–82.

———. *The Southern Colonies in the Seventeenth Century, 1607–1689*. Baton Rouge: Louisiana State Univ. Press, 1949.

Crawford, Lord. *Bibliotheca Lindesiana: Catalogue of a Collection of the XVIIth and XVIIIth Centuries*. 2 vols. 1890; rpt. New York: Burt Franklin, 1962.

Cressy, David. *Coming Over: Migration and Communication between England and New England in the Seventeenth Century*. Cambridge: Cambridge Univ. Press, 1987.

Crouse, Nellis M. "Causes of the Great Migration, 1630–1640." *New England Quarterly* 5 (1932): 3–36.

Culliford, S. G. *William Strachey, 1572–1621*. Charlottesville: Univ. Press of Virginia, 1965.

Cumming, William P. "Early Maps of the Chesapeake Bay Area: Their Relation to Settlement and Society." In *Early Maryland in a Wider World*. Ed. David B. Quinn. Detroit: Wayne State Univ. Press, 1982, 267–310.

———, R. A. Skelton, and D. B. Quinn. *The Discovery of North America*. New York: American Heritage Press, 1971.

Cunliffe, Marcus. "European Images of America." In *Paths of American Thought*. Ed. Arthur M. Schlesinger, Jr., and Morton White. Boston: Houghton Mifflin, 1963, 492–514 and notes, 586–88.

Cunnington, C. Willett, and E. Grace Cunnington. *Handbook of English Costume in the Seventeenth Century*. London: Faber and Faber, 1955.

Curtius, Ernest Robert. *European Literature and the Latin Middle Ages*. Tr. Willard R. Trask. 1948; rpt. Princeton, N.J.: Princeton Univ. Press, 1973.

Cushman, Robert. *A Sermon Preached at Plimmoth in New England, December 9 1721*. London: J. D[awson], 1622.

CW. *See* Barbour, ed. *The Complete Works of Captain John Smith*.

Davies, G. "English Political Sermons." *Huntington Library Quarterly* 3 (1939): 1–22.

Davis, Richard Beale. *Intellectual Life in the Colonial South, 1585–1763*. 3 vols. Knoxville: Univ. of Tennessee Press, 1978.

Delany, Paul. *British Autobiography in the Seventeenth Century*. London: Routledge & Kegan Paul, 1969.

Diamond, Sigmund. "From Organization to Society: Virginia in the Seventeenth Century." *American Journal of Sociology* 63 (1958):457–75.

———. "Values as an Obstacle to Economic Growth: The American Colonies." *Journal of Economic History* 27 (1967): 561–75.

Dick of Devonshire. Ed. James G. McManaway and Mary R. McManaway. Oxford, Eng.: Malone Society Reprints, 1955.

Dictionary of American English. Ed. William Craigie and James R. Hulbert. 4 vols. Chicago: Univ. of Chicago Press, 1933–44.

Dictionary of Canadian Biography / Dictionnaire biographique du Canada. Ed. George W. Brown and Marcel Trudel. Vol. 1. Toronto: Toronto Univ. Press, 1965.

Donaldson, Ian. *The World Upside-Down: Comedy from Jonson to Fielding*. Oxford: Clarendon Press, 1970.

Donne, John. *The Epithalamions, Anniversaries, and Epicedes*. Ed. W. Milgate. Oxford: Clarendon Press, 1978.

EA. *See European Americana*.

Earle, Carville V. "Environment, Disease, and Mortality in Early Virginia." In *The Chesapeake in the Seventeenth Century: Essays on Anglo-American Society*. Ed. Thad W. Tate and David L. Ammerman. Chapel Hill: Univ. of North Carolina Press, 1979, 96–125.

Eisinger, Chester E. "The Freehold Concept in Eighteenth-Century American Letters." *William and Mary Quarterly*, 3d ser., 4 (1947): 42–59.

———. "Land and Loyalty: Literary Expressions of Agrarian Nationalism in the Seventeenth and Eighteenth Centuries." *American Literature* 21 (1949–50): 160–78.

———. "The Puritans' Justification for Taking the Land." *Essex Institute Historical Collections* 84 (1948): 131–43.

Ekirch, A. Roger. *Bound for America: The Transportation of British Convicts to the Colonies, 1718–1775*. Oxford: Clarendon Press, 1987.

Eliade, Mircea. "Paradise and Utopia: Mythical Geography and Eschatology." In *Utopia and Utopian Thought*. Ed. Frank E. Manuel. Boston: Houghton Mifflin, 1966, 260–80.

Eliot, T. S. *Selected Prose of T. S. Eliot*. Ed. Frank Kermode. New York: Harcourt, Brace, Jovanovich, 1975.

Emerson, Everett. *Captain John Smith*. New York: Twayne, 1971.

The English New England Voyages, 1602–1608. Ed. David B. Quinn and Alison M. Quinn. Hakluyt Society, 2d ser., no. 161. London, 1983.

European Americana: A Chronological Guide to Works Printed in Europe Relating to the Americas. Ed. John Alden and Dennis C. Landis. 2 vols. (to 1650). New York: Readex Books, 1980–82.

Fausz, Frederick J. "An 'Abundance of Blood Shed on Both Sides': England's First Indian War, 1609–1614." *Virginia Magazine of History and Biography* 98 (1990): 3–56.

———. "The 'Barbarous Massacre' Reconsidered: The Powhatan Uprising of 1622 and the Historians." *Explorations in Ethnic Studies* 1 (1978): 37–51.

———. "Fighting 'Fire' with Firearms: The Anglo-Powhatan Arms Race in Early Virginia." *American Indian Culture and Research Journal* 3, no. 4 (1979): 33–50.

———. "The Invasion of Virginia: Indians, Colonialism, and the Conquest of Cant: A Review Essay on Anglo-Indian Relations in the Chesapeake." *Virginia Magazine of History and Biography* 95 (1987): 133–56.

———. "Middlemen in Peace and War: Virginia's Earliest Indian Interpreters, 1608–1632." *Virginia Magazine of History and Biography* 95 (1987): 41–64.

———. "Opechancanough: Indian Resistance Leader." In *Struggle and Survival in Colonial America*. Ed. David G. Sweet and Gary B. Nash. Berkeley: Univ. of California Press, 1981, 21–37.

———. "Patterns of Anglo-Indian Aggression and Accommodation along the Mid-Atlantic Coast, 1584–1634." In *Cultures in Contact: The Impact of European Contacts on Native American Cultural Institutions, A.D.1000–1800*. Ed. William W. Fitzhugh. Washington, D.C.: Smithsonian Institution Press, 1985, 225–68.

Feest, Christian F. "The Virginia Indian in Pictures, 1612–1624." *Smithsonian Journal of History* 2, no. 1 (1967): 1–30.

Fenton, William N., and Elizabeth L. Moore. "Introduction" to Joseph François Lafitau. *Customs of the American Indians Compared with the Customs of Primitive Times*. 2 vols. Toronto: Champlain Society, 1977.

Ferguson, Arthur B. *The Indian Summer of English Chivalry: Studies in the Decline and Transformation of Chivalric Idealism.* Durham: Duke Univ. Press, 1960.

Fiedler, Leslie. *The Return of the Vanishing American.* New York: Stein and Day, 1968.

Fink, Zera S. *The Classical Republicans: An Essay in the Recovery of a Pattern of Thought in Seventeenth-Century England.* Evanston: Northwestern Univ. Press, 1945.

Firth, C. H., ed. *An American Garland.* Oxford: Blackwell, 1915.

————, ed. *Naval Songs and Ballads.* Navy Records Society Publications, vol. 33. London, 1908.

Fishwick, Marshall W. "Was John Smith a Liar?" *American Heritage* 9, no. 6 (1958): 28–33, 110–11.

Ford, Worthington C. "Captain John Smith's Map of Virginia 1612." *Geographical Review* 14 (1924–25): 433–43.

Foster, Stephen. *Their Solitary Way: The Puritan Social Ethic in the First Century of Settlement in New England.* New Haven: Yale Univ. Press, 1971.

Franklin, Benjamin. *Benjamin Franklin: Writings.* Ed. J. A. Leo Lemay. New York: Library of America, 1987.

French, Allen. *Charles I and the Puritan Upheaval: A Study of the Causes of the Great Migration.* Boston: Houghton Mifflin, 1955.

Freneau, Philip. *Poems Written and Published during the American Revolutionary War.* 3d ed. 2 vols. Philadelphia: Lydia Bailey, 1809.

Frey, Charles. "*The Tempest* and the New World." *Shakespeare Quarterly* 30 (1979): 29–41.

Friedman, Albert B. "'When Adam Delved . . .': Contexts of an Historical Proverb." In *The Learned and the Lewed: Studies in Chaucer and Medieval Literature.* Ed. Larry D. Benson. Cambridge: Harvard Univ. Press, 1974, 213–30.

Fuller, Thomas. *The History of the Worthies of England.* 1662. Ed. P. Austin Nuttall. 3 vols. London: Thomas Tegg, 1840.

The Geneva Bible: A Facsimile of the 1560 Edition. Madison: Univ. of Wisconsin Press, 1969.

Gerbi, Antonello. *Nature in the New World: From Christopher Columbus to Gonzala Fernandez de Oviedo.* Tr. Jeremy Moyle. Pittsburgh: Univ. of Pittsburgh Press, 1982.

Gilliam, Charles Edgar. "Ethno-Historical Demurrers to General English Indictments of the Great Powhatan Confederacy of Virginia Algonkians." *Tyler's Quarterly Magazine* 28 (1946): 139–62.

————. "Queen Oppussoquionuske." *Tyler's Quarterly Magazine* 23 (1941): 148–54.

Glenn, Keith. "Captain John Smith and the Indians." *Virginia Magazine of History and Biography* 52 (1944): 228–48.

Gooch, George Peabody. *English Democratic Ideas in the Seventeenth Century.* 2d ed. Cambridge: Univ. Press, 1927.

Goodman, Jennifer Robin. "The Captain's Self-Portrait: John Smith as Chivalric Biographer." *Virginia Magazine of History and Biography* 89 (1981), 27–38.

Gookin, Warner F. "The First Leaders at Jamestown." *Virginia Magazine of History and Biography* 58 (1950): 181–93.

Gorges, Ferdinando. *A Briefe Narration of the Original Undertakings of the Advancement of Plantations into the Parts of America. Especially Showing the Beginning, Progress, and Continuance of That of New England.* London: N. Brook, 1658.

Gower, John. *Confessio Amantis.* Ed. Russell A. Peck. New York: Holt, Rinehart and Winston, 1968.

Gray, Stanley. "The Political Thought of John Winthrop." *New England Quarterly* 3 (1930): 681–705.

Greenblatt, Stephen J. "Learning to Curse." In *First Images of America: The Impact of the New World on the Old.* Ed. Fredi Chiapelli. 2 vols. Berkeley: Univ. of California Press, 1976, 561–80.

Greene, Jack P. "Changing Identity in the British Caribbean: Barbados as a Case Study." In *Colonial Identity in the Atlantic World, 1500–1800.* Ed. Nicholas Canny and Anthony Pagden. Princeton, N.J.: Princeton Univ. Press, 1987.

Hahn, Thomas. "Indians East and West: Primitivism and Savagery in English Discovery Narratives of the Sixteenth Century." *Journal of Medieval and Renaissance Studies* 8 (1978): 77–114.

Hakluyt, Richard. *The Principal Navigations, Voyages, Traffiques, and Discoveries of the English Nation.* 3 vols. London: G. Bishop, R. Newberie, and R. E. Barker, 1598–1600. Rpt. 12 vols. London: Hakluyt Society, 1903–5.

———, ed. and tr. *Virginia Richly Valued, by the Description of the Main Land of Florida, Her Next Neighbour.* London: F. Kingston for M. Lownes, 1609.

Hammond, John. *Leah and Rachel, or The Two Fruitful Sisters Virginia and Mary-land.* London: T. Mabb, 1656.

Hamor, Ralph. *A True Discourse of the Present Estate of Virginia.* 1615. Ed. A. L. Rowse. Richmond: Virginia State Library, 1957.

Harriot, Thomas. *A Briefe and True Report of the New Found Land of Virginia.* London: [R. Robinson], 1588.

———. *A Briefe and True Report of the New Found Land of Virginia.* 1588. Ed. Randolph G. Adams. New York: History Book Club, 1951.

———. *A Briefe and True Report of the New Found Land of Virginia.* Frankfort: De Bry, 1590.

———. *A Briefe and True Report of the New Found Land of Virginia.* 1590. Ed. Paul Hulton. New York: Dover, 1972.

Harris, Marshall. *Origin of the Land Tenure System in the United States.*
1953; rpt. Westport, Conn.: Greenwood Press, 1970.

Hatch, Charles E., Jr. *The First Seventeen Years: Virginia, 1607–1624.*
Williamsburg: Virginia 350th Anniversary Celebration Corporation, 1957.

Hawke, David Freeman. Introduction. *Captain John Smith's History of
Virginia.* Indianapolis: Bobbs-Merrill, 1970.

Hawthorne, Nathaniel. *Tales and Sketches.* Ed. Roy Harvey Pearce.
New York: Library of America, 1982.

Hayes, Kevin J. *Captain John Smith: A Reference Guide.* Boston: G. K.
Hall, 1991.

———. "Defining the Ideal Colonist: Captain John Smith's Revisions
from the *Proceedings* to the Third Booke of the *Generall Historie.*"
Virginia Magazine of History and Biography, forthcoming.

Hayes, T. Wilson. "John Everard and the Familist Tradition." In *The
Origins of Anglo-American Radicalism.* Ed. Margaret and James Ja-
cob. London: Allen & Unwin, 1984, 60–69.

Heilbronner, Walter Leo. "The Earliest Printed Account of the Death
of Pocahontas." *Virginia Magazine of History and Biography* 66
(1958): 272–77.

Heilman, Robert B. *America in English Fiction, 1760–1800.* Baton
Rouge: Louisiana State Univ. Press, 1937.

Heinemann, Margot. *Puritanism and Theatre: Thomas Middleton and
Opposition Drama under the Early Stuarts.* Cambridge: Cambridge
Univ. Press, 1980.

Helgerson, Richard. "The Land Speaks: Cartography, Chorography,
and Subversion in Renaissance England." *Representations* 16
(1986): 51–85.

Hellier, Thomas. *The Vain Prodigal Life, and Tragical Penitent Death of
. . . .* London: for Sam. Crouch, 1680.

———. *See also* T. H. Breen, James H. Lewis, and Keith Schlesinger.

Henry, William Wirt. "A Defence of Captain John Smith." *Magazine of
American History* 25 (1891): 300–313.

———. "Did Percy Denounce Smith's History of Virginia?" *Virginia
Magazine of History and Biography* 1 (1893–94): 473–76.

———. "The Rescue of Captain John Smith by Pocahontas." *Potters
American Monthly* 4–5 (1875): 523–28, 591–97.

Hereford, C. H., Percy Simpson, and Evelyn M. Simpson, eds. *The
Works of Ben Jonson.* 11 vols. Oxford: Clarendon Press, 1925–52.

Hill, Christopher. *Collected Essays.* 3 vols. Amherst: Univ. of Massachusetts Press, 1986.

———. "From Lollards to Levellers." In *Rebels and Their Causes: Essays
in Honor of A. L. Morton.* Ed. Maurice Cornforth. Atlantic High-
lands, N.J.: Humanities Press, 1979, 49–67. Rpt. in Hill, *Collected
Essays* 2:89–116.

———. "The Many Headed Monster in Late Tudor and Early Stuart Political Thinking." In *From the Renaissance to the Counter-Reformation: Essays in Honor of Garret Mattingly*. Ed. Charles Howard Carter. New York: Random House, 1965, 296–324.

———. *The World Turned Upside Down: Radical Ideas during the English Revolution*. London: Temple Smith, 1972.

Historical Poems of the XIVth and XVth Centuries. Ed. Rossell Hope Robbins. New York: Columbia Univ. Press, 1959.

Hogden, Margaret T. *Early Anthropology in the Sixteenth and Seventeenth Centuries*. Philadelphia: Univ. of Pennsylvania Press, 1964.

Holstun, James. *A Rational Millennium: Puritan Utopias of Seventeenth-Century England and America*. New York: Oxford Univ. Press, 1987.

Holt, J. C. *Robin Hood*. Rev. and enlarged ed. London: Thames and Hudson, 1989.

Horace. *Satires, Epistles, and Ars Poetica*. Tr. H. Rushton Fairclough. Loeb Classical Library. Cambridge: Harvard Univ. Press, 1966.

Hulme, Peter. "John Smith and Pocahontas." In Hulme, *Colonial Encounters*. New York: Methuen, 1986, 136–73.

Hulton, Paul. "Images of the New World: Jacques Le Moyne de Morgues and John White." In *The Westward Enterprise: English Activities in Ireland, the Atlantic, and America, 1480–1650*. Ed. K. R. Andrews, N. P. Canny, and P. E. H. Hair. Detroit: Wayne State Univ. Press, 1979.

———. Introduction. *The Work of Jacques Le Moyne de Morgues, a Huguenot Artist in France, Florida, and England*. 2 vols. London: British Library, 1977.

———, and D. B. Quinn. *The American Drawings of John White, 1577–1590*. 2 vols. London: British Museum, 1964.

Innes, Stephen. "Fulfilling John Smith's Vision: Work and Labor in Early America." In *Work and Labor in Early America*. Ed. Innes. Chapel Hill: Univ. of North Carolina Press, 1988, 3–47.

Jantz, Harold S. "The Myths about America: Origins and Extensions." *Jahrbuch fur Amerikastudien* 7 (1962): 6–18.

Jennings, Francis. *The Invasion of America: Indians, Colonialism, and the Cant of Conquest*. Chapel Hill: Univ. of North Carolina Press, 1975.

Jennings, John Melville, ed. "The Poor Unhappy Transported Felon's Sorrowful Account of His Fourteen Years Transportation at Virginia in America." *Virginia Magazine of History and Biography* 56 (1948): 180–94.

Jester, Annie Lash, and Martha Woodroof Hiden, comp. *Adventurers of Purse and Person: Virginia, 1607–1624/5*. 3d ed., rev. Virginia M. Meyer and John Frederick Dorman. Richmond: Dietz Press for the Order of First Families of Virginia, 1987.

Jewkes, William T. "The Literature of Travel and the Mode of Romance in the Renaissance." In *Literature as a Mode of Travel*. New York: New York Public Library, 1963, 13–30.

Johnson, Robert. *The New Life of Virginea*. London: F. Kingston, 1612.

Jones, Howard Mumford. "The Colonial Impulse: An Analysis of the 'Promotion' Literature of Colonization." *Proceedings of the American Philosophical Society* 90 (1946): 131–61.

———. *The Literature of Virginia in the Seventeenth Century*. 2d ed. Charlottesville: Univ. Press of Virginia, 1968.

Jones, W. R. "The Image of the Barbarian in Medieval Europe." *Comparative Studies in Society and History* 13 (1971): 376–407.

JV. See Barbour, ed. *The Jamestown Voyages*.

Kammen, Michael. *Spheres of Liberty: Changing Perceptions of Liberty in American Culture*. Madison: Univ. of Wisconsin Press, 1986.

Kelso, Ruth. *The Doctrine of the English Gentleman in the Sixteenth Century*. Urbana: Univ. of Illinois Press, 1929.

Kingsbury, Susan M., ed. *The Records of the Virginia Company of London*. 4 vols. Washington, D.C.: GPO, 1906–35.

Konig, David Thomas. "'Dale's Laws' and the Non-Common Law Origins of Criminal Justice in Virginia." *American Journal of Legal History* 26 (1982): 354–75.

Kropf, Lewis L. "Captain John Smith of Virginia." *Notes and Queries*, 7th ser., 9 (1890): 1–2, 41–43, 102–4, 161–62, 223–24, 281–82.

Kupperman, Karen Ordahl. "Apathy and Death in Early Jamestown." *Journal of American History* 66 (1979): 24–40.

———. "English Perceptions of Treachery, 1583–1640: The Case of the American 'Savages.'" *Historical Journal* 20 (1977): 263–87.

———. *Settling with the Indians: The Meeting of English and Indian Cultures in America, 1580–1640*. Totowa, N.J.: Rowman and Littlefield, 1980.

———, ed. *Captain John Smith: A Select Edition of His Writings*. Chapel Hill: Univ. of North Carolina Press, 1988.

La Mar, Virginia. *English Dress in the Age of Shakespeare*. 1958; rpt. Charlottesville: Univ. Press of Virginia, 1973.

Lanham, Richard A. "Sidney: The Ornament of His Age." *Southern Review: An Australian Journal of Literary Studies* 2 (1968): 319–40.

Lankford, John. Introduction. In *Captain John Smith's America: Selections from His Writings*. New York: Harper & Row, 1967, vii–xxviii.

Lawson, John. *A New Voyage to Carolina*. Ed. Hugh Talmage Lefler. Chapel Hill: Univ. of North Carolina Press, 1967.

Leary, Lewis. "The Adventures of Captain John Smith as Heroic Legend." In *Essays in Early Virginia Literature Honoring Richard Beale Davis*. Ed. J. A. Leo Lemay. New York: Burt Franklin, 1977, 13–33.

Lee, Sidney. "The American Indian in Elizabethan England." In Lee, *Elizabethan and Other Essays*. Ed. Frederick S. Boas. Oxford: Clarendon Press, 1929, 263–301.

Lefler, Hugh T. "Promotional Literature of the Southern Colonies." *Journal of Southern History* 33 (1967): 3–25.

Lemay, J. A. Leo. *The Canon of Benjamin Franklin: New Attributions and Reconsiderations, 1722–1776*. Newark: Univ. of Delaware Press, 1986.

————. "Captain John Smith." In *The History of Southern Literature*. Ed. Louis D. Rubin, Jr., et al. Baton Rouge: Louisiana State Univ. Press, 1985, 26–33.

————. "Captain John Smith: American (?)." *Univ. of Mississippi Studies in English*, n.s., 5 (1984–87): 288–96.

————. "Franklin's Autobiography and the American Dream." In Lemay and Zall, eds., *Benjamin Franklin's Autobiography*, 349–60.

————. "The Frontiersman from Lout to Hero: Notes on the Significance of the Comparative Method and the Stage Theory in Early American Literature and Culture." *Proceedings of the American Antiquarian Society* 88 (1979): 187–223.

————. "John Mercer and the Stamp Act in Virginia." *Virginia Magazine of History and Biography* 91 (1983): 3–38.

————. *Men of Letters in Colonial Maryland*. Knoxville: Univ. of Tennessee Press, 1972.

————. *"New England's Annoyances": America's First Folk Song*. Newark: Univ. of Delaware Press, 1985.

————. "Southern Colonial Grotesque: Robert Bolling's 'Neanthe.'" *Mississippi Quarterly* 35 (1982): 97–126.

————. "The Voice of Captain John Smith." *Southern Literary Journal* 20, no. 1 (1987): 113–31.

————, and P. M. Zall, eds. *Benjamin Franklin's Autobiography: A Norton Critical Edition*. New York: W. W. Norton, 1986.

Levenson, J. C., et al., eds. *The Letters of Henry Adams*. 6 vols. Cambridge: Harvard Univ. Press, 1982–88.

Levin, Harry. *The Myth of the Golden Age in the Renaissance*. Bloomington: Indiana Univ. Press, 1969.

Lewis, Ewart. *Medieval Political Ideas*. 2 vols. New York: Knopf, 1954.

Lewis, R. W. B. *The American Adam: Innocence, Tragedy and Tradition in the Nineteenth Century*. Chicago: Univ. of Chicago Press, 1955.

Livy. Tr. Evan T. Sage. Loeb Classical Library. Cambridge: Harvard Univ. Press, 1936.

Lloyd, David. *The Legend of Captaine Iones*. London: I. M[arriott], 1631.

Lomax, Alan. *The Folk Songs of North America*. Garden City, N.Y.: Doubleday, 1960.

Lovejoy, Arthur O., Gilbert Chinard, George Boas, and Ronald S. Crane, eds. *A Documentary History of Primitivism and Related Ideas*. Baltimore: Johns Hopkins Univ. Press, 1935.

Lurie, Nancy Oestreich. "Indian Cultural Adjustment to European Civilization." In *Seventeenth-Century America: Essays in Colonial History*. Ed. James Morton Smith. 1959; rpt. New York: W. W. Norton, 1972, 33–60.

Lytle, Guy F., and Stephen Orgel, eds. *Patronage in the Renaissance*. Princeton, N.J.: Princeton Univ. Press, 1981.

McCann, Franklin T. *English Discovery of America to 1585*. New York: King's Crown Press, 1952.

McCary, Ben C., and Norman F. Barka. "The John Smith and Zuniga Maps in the Light of Recent Archaeological Investigations along the Chickahominy River." *Archaeology of Eastern North America* 5 (1977): 73–86.

McManaway, James G., and Mary R. McManaway, eds. *Dick of Devonshire*. Oxford, Eng.: Malone Society Reprints, 1955.

McManis, Douglas R. *European Impressions of the New England Coast*. Univ. of Chicago, Department of Geography, Research Paper no. 139. Chicago, 1972.

MacPherson, C. B. *Democratic Theory: Essays in Retrieval*. Oxford: Clarendon Press, 1973.

Madan, Falconer. *Oxford Books*. 3 vols. Oxford: Clarendon Press, 1895.

Mardis, Allen, Jr. "Visions of James Fort." *Virginia Magazine of History and Biography* 97 (1989): 463–98.

Markham, Gervase. *The Souldiers Accidence; or An Introduction into Military Discipline*. London: J. D[awson] for J. Bellamie, 1625.

Marlowe, Christopher. *Tamburlaine the Great*. In *The Revels Plays*. Ed. J. S. Cunningham. Baltimore: Johns Hopkins Univ. Press, 1981.

Marotti, Arthur F. "John Donne and the Rewards of Patronage." In *Patronage in the Renaissance*. Ed. Guy Fitch Lytle and Stephen Orgel. Princeton, N.J.: Princeton Univ. Press, 1981, 207–34.

Masselman, George. *The Cradle of Colonialism*. New Haven: Yale Univ. Press, 1963.

Mathews, Mitford M., ed. *A Dictionary of Americanisms on Historical Principles*. Chicago: Univ. of Chicago Press, 1951.

Miller, Perry. *The New England Mind: The Seventeenth Century*. 1939; rpt. Cambridge: Harvard Univ. Press, 1954.

———, and Thomas H. Johnson. *The Puritans*. New York: American Book Company, 1938.

The Mirror for Magistrates. Ed. Lilly B. Campbell. Cambridge: Cambridge Univ. Press, 1938.

Mitchell, Stewart, ed. "The Founding of Massachusetts: A Selection from the Sources." *Proceedings of the Massachusetts Historical Society* 62 (1930): 225–45.

Mook, Maurice A. "The Ethnological Significance of Tindall's Map of Virginia, 1608." *William and Mary Quarterly*, 2d ser., 23 (1943): 371–408.

Mooney, James. "The Powhatan Confederacy, Past and Present." *American Anthropologist* 9 (1907): 129–52.

Morgan, Edmund S. *American Slavery / American Freedom: The Ordeal of Colonial Virginia*. New York: W. W. Norton, 1975.

———. "The First American Boom: Virginia, 1618 to 1630." *William and Mary Quarterly*, 3d ser., 28 (1971): 169–98.

———. *Inventing the People: The Rise of Popular Sovereignty in England and America*. New York: W. W. Norton, 1988.

———. "John Winthrop's 'Modell of Christian Charity' in a Wider Context." *Huntington Library Quarterly* 50 (1987): 145–51.

———. "The Labor Problem at Jamestown, 1607–18." *American Historical Review* 76 (1971): 595–611.

Morison, Samuel Eliot. *Builders of the Bay Colony*. 1930; rpt. Boston: Houghton Mifflin, 1958.

———. "The *Mayflower*'s Destination and the Pilgrim Fathers' Patents." *Publications of the Colonial Society of Massachusetts* 38 (1959): 386–413.

———. "The Plymouth Colony and Virginia." *Virginia Magazine of History and Biography* 62 (1954): 147–65.

Morse, Jarvis M. "John Smith and His Critics: A Chapter in Colonial Historiography." *Journal of Southern History* 1 (1935): 123–37.

Mossiker, Frances. *Pocahontas: The Life and the Legend*. New York: Knopf, 1976.

Nash, Gary B. "The Image of the Indian in the Southern Colonial Mind." In *The Wild Man Within: An Image in Western Thought from the Renaissance to Romanticism*. Ed. Edward Dudley and Maximillian E. Novak. Pittsburgh: Univ. of Pittsburgh Press, 1972, 55–86.

———. *Red, White, and Black: The Peoples of Early America*. Englewood Cliffs, N.J.: Prentice-Hall, 1974.

New Cambridge Bibliography of English Literature. Ed. George Watson. 5 vols. Cambridge: Cambridge Univ. Press, 1969–77.

Osgood, Herbert Levi. *The American Colonies in the Seventeenth Century*. 3 vols. New York: Macmillan, 1904–7.

Owst, G. R. *Literature and Pulpit in Medieval England*. Cambridge: Cambridge Univ. Press, 1933.

Oxford Dictionary of English Proverbs. 3d ed. Comp. William George Smith. Ed. F. P. Wilson. Oxford: Clarendon Press, 1970.

Parker, John. *Books to Build an Empire: A Bibliographical History of English Overseas Interests to 1620*. Amsterdam: N. Israel, 1965.

Peckham, Sir George. "A True Reporte of the Late Discoveries of the Newfound Landes (1583)." In *The Voyages and Colonising Enterprises of Sir Humphrey Gilbert*. Ed. David B. Quinn. 2 vols. London: Hakluyt Society, 1940.

Pemberton, Ebenezer. *A Christian Fixed at His Post*. Boston: B. Green, 1704.

Pennington, Loren E. "The Amerindian in English Promotional Literature, 1575–1625." In *The Westward Enterprise: English Activities in Ireland, the Atlantic, and America, 1480–1650*. Ed. K. R. Andrews et al. Detroit: Wayne State Univ. Press, 1979, 175–94.

Percy, George. "A Treue Relacyon of the Procedeinges . . . in Virginia . . . 1609 until 1612." *Tyler's Quarterly* 3 (1922): 259–82.

Percy, Thomas. *Reliques of Ancient English Poetry*. Ed. Henry B. Wheatley. 3 vols. London: Bickers and Son, 1876–77.

Piper, Dan. "Dick Whittington and the Middle Class Dream of Success." In *Heroes of Popular Culture*. Ed. Ray B. Browne et al. Bowling Green, Ohio: Bowling Green Univ. Popular Press, 1972, 53–59.

Plautus. Tr. Paul Nixon. Loeb Classical Library. Cambridge: Harvard Univ. Press, 1968.

Porter, H. C. *The Inconstant Savage: England and the North American Indian, 1500–1660*. London: Duckworth, 1979.

———. "Reflections on the Ethnohistory of Early Colonial North America." *Journal of American Studies* 16 (1982): 243–54.

———. "The Tudors and the North American Indian." In Hakluyt Society. *Annual Report* for 1983. London, 1984, 3–23.

Purchas, Samuel. *Hakluytus Posthumus, or Purchas His Pilgrimes*. 4 vols. London: W. Stansby for H. Fetherstone, 1625.

———. *Hakluytus Posthumus, or Purchas His Pilgrimes*. 1625. Rpt. 20 vols. Glasgow: J. McLehose, 1905–7.

———. *Purchas His Pilgrimage*. London: W. Stansby for H. Fetherstone, 1613.

Quinn, David Beers. "A Colony Is Lost and Found?" In Quinn, *Set Fair for Roanoke, Voyages and Colonies, 1584–1606*. Chapel Hill: Univ. of North Carolina Press, 1985, 341–78.

———. "Introduction: Prelude to Maryland." In *Early Maryland in a Wider World*. Ed. Quinn. Detroit: Wayne State Univ. Press, 1982, 11–29.

———. "The Lost Colony in Myth and Reality, 1586–1625." In Quinn, *England and the Discovery of America, 1481–1620*. New York: Knopf, 1974, 432–81.

———. "'Virginians' on the Thames in 1603." In Quinn, *England and the Discovery of America, 1481–1620*. New York: Knopf, 1974, 419–31.

————. "Why They Came." In *Early Maryland in a Wider World*. Ed. Quinn. Detroit: Wayne State Univ. Press, 1982, 19–48.

————, ed. *The Hakluyt Handbook*. 2 vols. Hakluyt Society, 2d ser., nos. 194–95. London, 1974.

————, ed. *The Roanoke Voyages 1584–1590*. 2 vols. Hakluyt Society, 2d ser., nos. 104–5. London, 1955.

————, ed. *The Voyages and Colonising Enterprises of Sir Humphrey Gilbert*. 2 vols. Hakluyt Society, 2d ser., nos. 83–84. London, 1940.

————, and Alison M. Quinn, eds. See *The English New England Voyages, 1602–1608*.

————, Alison M. Quinn, and Susan Hillier, eds. *New American World*. 5 vols. New York: Arno Press and Hector Bye, 1979.

Rabb, Theodore K. "The Expansion of Europe and the Spirit of Capitalism." *Historical Journal* 17 (1974): 675–89.

Ralegh, Sir Walter. *The Works of Sir Walter Ralegh*. 8 vols. 1829; rpt. New York: Burt Franklin, n.d.

Randel, William. "Captain John Smith's Attitudes toward the Indians." *Virginia Magazine of History and Biography* 48 (1939): 218–29.

Resnikow, Sylvia. "The Cultural History of a Democratic Proverb." *Journal of English and Germanic Philology* 36 (1937): 391–405.

Robinson, W. Stitt, Jr. *Mother Earth: Land Grants in Virginia, 1607–1699*. Williamsburg: Virginia 350th Anniversary Celebration Corporation, 1957.

Rollins, Hyder E. *An Analytical Index to the Ballad-Entries (1557–1709) in the Registers of the Company of Stationers of London*. 1924; rpt. Hatboro, Pa.: Tradition Press, 1967.

————, ed. *The Pepys Ballads*, 8 vols. Cambridge: Harvard Univ. Press, 1929–32.

Rose-Troup, Frances. *The Massachusetts Bay Company and Its Predecessors*. New York: Grafton Press, 1930.

Rowe, J. Brooking. *Richard Pecke of Tavistocke*. Exeter, Eng.: J. G. Commin, 1905.

Rowe, John H. "Ethnography and Ethnology in the Sixteenth Century." *Kroeber Anthropological Society Papers*, no. 30 (1964): 1–20. Rpt. as "The Renaissance Foundation of Anthropology," *American Anthropologist* 67 (1965): 1–20.

Rowse, A[lfred] L. *The Elizabethans and America*. 1959; rpt. Westport, Conn.: Greenwood Press, 1978.

Roxburghe Ballads. Ed. William Chappell (vols. 1–3) and J[oseph] W. Ebsworth (vols. 4–9). 9 vols. Hartford: Printed for the Ballad Society, 1871–99.

Rozwenc, Edwin C. "Captain John Smith's Image of America." *William and Mary Quarterly*, 3d ser., 16 (1959): 27–36.

Rutman, Darrett B. "The Historian and the Marshal: A Note on the

Background of Sir Thomas Dale." *Virginia Magazine of History and Biography* 68 (1960): 284–94.

———. "The Pilgrims and Their Harbor." *William and Mary Quarterly*, 3d ser., 17 (1960): 164–82.

Sabin, Joseph; Wilberforce Eames; and R. W. G. Vail, *Bibliotheca Americana: A Dictionary of Books Relating to America, from Its Discovery to the Present Time*. 29 vols. New York: Sabin and the Bibliographical Society of America, 1868–1936.

Salisbury, Neal. *Manitou and Providence: Indians, Europeans, and the Making of New England, 1500–1643*. New York: Oxford Univ. Press, 1982.

———. "Squanto: Last of the Patuxets." In *Struggle and Survival in Colonial America*. Ed. David G. Sweet and Gary B. Nash. Berkeley: Univ. of California Press, 1981, 228–46.

Sallust. Tr. J. C. Rolfe. Loeb Classical Library. 1928; rpt. Cambridge: Harvard Univ. Press, 1980.

Sanders, Charles R. "William Strachey, the Virginia Company, and Shakespeare." *Virginia Magazine of History and Biography* 57 (1949): 115–32.

Sanford, Charles L. *The Quest for Paradise*. Urbana: Univ. of Illinois Press, 1961.

Schofield, William Henry. *Chivalry in English Literature*. Cambridge: Harvard Univ. Press, 1912.

Seelye, John. *Prophetic Waters: The River in Early American Life and Literature*. New York: Oxford Univ. Press, 1977.

Sekora, John. *Luxury: The Concept in Western Thought, Eden to Smollett*. Baltimore: Johns Hopkins Univ. Press, 1977.

Shakespeare, William. *The Tempest*. Ed. Frank Kermode. The Arden Shakespeare. Cambridge: Harvard Univ. Press, 1962.

———. *Troilus and Cressida*. Ed. Harold Newcomb Hillebrand and T. W. Baldwin. New Variorum Edition. Philadelphia: Lippincott, 1953.

Sharpe, Kevin. *Sir Robert Cotton*. Oxford: Univ. Press, 1979.

Sheehan, Bernard. *Savagism and Civility: Indians and Englishmen in Colonial Virginia*. Cambridge: Cambridge Univ. Press, 1980.

Shirley, John W. "George Percy at Jamestown, 1607–1612." *Virginia Magazine of History and Biography* 57 (1949): 227–43.

Skinner, Quentin. *The Foundations of Modern Political Thought*. 2 vols. New York: Cambridge Univ. Press, 1978.

Slavin, Arthur J. "The American Principle from More to Locke." In *First Images of America: The Impact of the New World on the Old*. Ed. Fredi Chiapelli. 2 vols. Berkeley: Univ. of California Press, 1976, 1:139–64.

Smith, A. W. "Some Folklore Elements in Movements of Social Protest." *Folklore* 77 (1967): 241–52.

Smith, Abbot E. *Colonists in Bondage: White Servitude and Convict Labor in America, 1607–1776*. Chapel Hill: Univ. of North Carolina Press, 1947.

Smith, Bradford. *Captain John Smith: His Life and Legend*. Philadelphia: Lippincott, 1953.

Smith, Captain John. *See* Arber and Bradley, eds.

————. *See* Barbour, ed., *Complete Works*.

————. *An Accidence or The Path-way to Experience. Necessary for All Young Sea-men*. London: For Jonas Man, and Benjamin Fisher, 1626.

————. *Advertisements for the Unexperienced Planters of New-England, or Any Where*. With the map, allowed by King Charles. London: John Haviland, sold by Robert Milbourne, 1631.

————. *A Description of New England: or The Observations, and Discoveries, of Captain John Smith*. London: Humfrey Lownes, for Robert Clerke, 1616.

————. *The Generall Historie of Virginia, New-England, and the Summer Isles*. London: Printed by J. D[awson] and J. H[aviland] for Michael Sparkes, 1624.

————. *The Generall History of Virginia, the Somer Isles, and New England*. Prospectus. London: [J. Dawson, 1623].

————. *A Map of Virginia*. Oxford: J[oseph] Barnes, 1612.

————. *New Englands Trials*. London: W[illiam] Jones, 1620. New ed., 1622.

————. *The Proceedings of the English Colonie in Virginia since Their First Beginning from England in . . . 1606, till This Present 1612*. Oxford: J[oseph] Barnes, 1612.

————. *A Sea Grammar, with the Plaine Exposition of Smiths Accidence for Young Sea-men, Enlarged*. London: J[ohn] Haviland, 1627.

————. *A True Relation of Such Occurrences and Accidents of Noate as Hath Hapned in Virginia*. London: [E. Allde] for J[ohn] Tappe, sold by W. W[elby], 1608.

————. *The True Travels, Adventures, and Observations of Captaine Iohn Smith, . . . from . . . 1593 to 1629. Together with a Continuation of His Generall History of Virginia*. London: J. H[aviland] for T[homas] Slater, sold [by M. Sparke], 1630.

Smits, David D. "'Abominable Mixture': Toward the Repudiation of Anglo-Indian Intermarriage in Seventeenth-Century Virginia." *Virginia Magazine of History and Biography* 95 (1987): 157–92.

Sola Pinto, Vivian de, and Allan Edwin Rodway, eds. *The Common Muse*. New York: Philosophical Library, 1957.

Southall, James P. C. "Captain John Smith (1580–1631) and Pocahontas (1595?–1617)." *Tyler's Quarterly* 28 (1946–47): 209–25.

STC. *A Short-Title Catalogue of Books . . . , 1475–1640*. Ed. A. W. Pollard and G. R. Redgrave. 2d ed., rev. by W. A. Jackson, F. S. Ferguson, and Katharine F. Pantzer. 2 vols. London: Bibliographical Society, 1976–86.

Stevenson, Burton. *The Home Book of Quotations: Classical and Modern*. New York: Dodd, Mead, 1945.

Stone, Lawrence. The *Crisis of the Aristocracy, 1558–1641*. Oxford: Clarendon Press, 1965.

———. "The English Revolution." *Preconditions of Revolution in Early Modern Europe*. Ed. Robert Forster and Jack P. Greene. Baltimore: Johns Hopkins Univ. Press, 1970, 55–108.

———. "Social Mobility in England, 1500–1700." *Past and Present*, no. 33 (1966): 16–55.

Strachey, William. *For the Colony in Virginia: Lawes, Divine, Morall, and Martiall, etc.* 1612. Ed. David H. Flaherty. Charlottesville: Univ. Press of Virginia, 1969.

———. *Historie of Travell into Virginia Britania*. 1612. Ed. Louis B. Wright and Virginia Freund. Hakluyt Society, 2d ser., vol. 103. London, 1953.

Striker, Laura Polanyi. "Captain John Smith's Hungary and Transylvania." In Bradford Smith, *Captain John Smith: His Life and Legend*. Philadelphia: Lippincott, 1953, 311–42.

———. "The Hungarian Historian, Lewis L. Kropf, on Captain John Smith's *True Travels*: A Reappraisal." *Virginia Magazine of History and Biography* 66 (1958): 22–43.

———, and Bradford Smith. "The Rehabilitation of Captain John Smith." *Journal of Southern History* 28 (1962): 474–81.

Strong, Roy. *The English Icon: Elizabethan and Jacobean Portraiture*. London: Routledge & Kegan Paul, 1969.

———. *National Portrait Gallery: Tudor and Jacobean Portraits*. 2 vols. London: Stationery Office, 1969.

Sturtevant, William C., gen. ed. *Handbook of North American Indians*. Vol. 15. Ed. Bruce G. Trigger. Washington, D.C.: GPO, 1978.

Swanton, John R. *The Indians of the Southeastern United States*. Bureau of American Ethnology, Bulletin no. 137. Washington, D.C., 1946.

Taylor, E. G. R. *Late Tudor and Early Stuart Geography, 1583–1650*. London: Metheun, 1934.

———, ed. *The Original Writings and Correspondence of the Two Richard Hakluyts*. 2 vols. Hakluyt Society, 2d ser., nos. 76–77. London, 1935.

Thoreau, Henry D. *The Journals of Henry D. Thoreau*. Ed. Bradford Torrey and Francis H. Allen. 14 vols. Boston: Houghton Mifflin, 1906.

Tichi, Cecelia. *New World, New Earth: Environmental Reform in American Literature from the Puritans through Whitman*. New Haven: Yale Univ. Press, 1979.

Tilley, Morris P. *A Dictionary of the Proverbs in England in the Sixteenth and Seventeenth Centuries*. Ann Arbor: Univ. of Michigan Press, 1950.

Tooker, William Wallace. "The Name *Chickahominy*: Its Origin and Etymology." *American Anthropologist* 8 (1895): 257–63.

Torrance, Robert M. *The Comic Hero*. Cambridge: Harvard Univ. Press, 1978.

Tyler, Moses Coit. *A History of American Literature, 1608–1765*. 1878; rpt. Ithaca, N.Y.: Cornell Univ. Press, 1949.

Vaughan, Alden T. *American Genesis: Captain John Smith and the Founding of Virginia*. Boston: Little, Brown, 1975.

———. "Expulsion of the 'Salvages': English Policy and the Virginia Massacre of 1622." *William and Mary Quarterly*, 3d ser., 35 (1978): 57–84.

———. "John Smith Satirized: The Legend of Captaine Iones." *William and Mary Quarterly*, 3d ser., 45 (1988): 712–32.

Verner, Coolie. *Smith's "Virginia" and Its Derivatives: A Carto-Bibliographical Study of the Diffusion of Geographical Knowledge*. Map Collectors' Series no. 45. London, 1968.

Walcott, Robert R. "Husbandry in Colonial New England." *New England Quarterly* 9 (1936): 218–52.

Washburn, Wilcomb E. "The Moral and Legal Justification for Dispossessing the Indians." In *Seventeenth-Century America: Essays in Colonial History*. Ed. James Morton Smith. 1959; rpt. New York: W. W. Norton, 1972, 15–32.

Waterhouse, Edward. *A Declaration of the State of the Colony in Virginia*. London: G. Elde for R. Mylbourne, 1622.

Waters, D. W. *The Art of Navigation in England in Elizabethan and Early Stuart Times*. New Haven: Yale Univ. Press, 1958.

Watts, Isaac. *Miscellaneous Thoughts*. London: R. Ford and R. Hett, 1734.

Wecter, Dixon. *The Hero in America: A Chronicle of Hero Worship*. New York: Scribner's, 1941.

Weiss, Harry B. "American Editions of 'Sir Richard Whittington and His Cat.'" *Bulletin of the New York Public Library* 42 (1938): 477–85.

Wharton, Henry. *The Life of John Smith, English Soldier*. Ed. and tr. Laura Polanyi Striker. Chapel Hill: Univ. of North Carolina Press, 1957.

White, George W. "Geological Observations of Captain John Smith in 1607–1614." *Transactions of the Illinois Academy of Science* 46 (1953): 124–32.

White, Hayden. "The Forms of Wildness: Archaeology of an Idea." In *The Wild Man Within: An Image in Western Thought from the Renaissance to Romanticism*. Ed. Edward Dudley and Maximillian E. Novak. Pittsburgh: Univ. of Pittsburgh Press, 1972, 3–38.

White, Helen C. *Social Criticism in Popular Religious Literature of the Six-teenth Century.* New York: Macmillan, 1944.

Wing, Donald. *Short Title Catalogue . . . 1641–1700.* 3 vols. 2d ed. New York: Modern Language Association, 1972–88.

Wingfield, Edward Maria. "A Discourse of Virginia." Ed. Charles Deane. *Transactions and Collections of the American Antiquarian Society* 4 (1860): 67–103.

Winthrop Papers. 5 vols. Ed. Stewart Mitchell, Allyn Bailey Forbes, et al. Boston: Massachusetts Historical Society, 1929–47.

Wood, William. *New England's Prospect.* Ed. Alden T. Vaughan. Amherst: Univ. of Massachusetts Press, 1977.

Woodhouse, A. S. P. "Religion and Some Foundations of English Democracy." *Philosophical Review* 61 (1952): 503–31.

Wright, Benjamin F., Jr. "The Early History of Written Constitutions in America." In *Essays in History and Political Theory in Honor of Charles H. McIlwain.* Ed. Carl Wittke. New York: Russell & Russell, 1936, 344–71.

Wright, Louis B. *The Colonial Search for a Southern Eden.* Birmingham: Univ. of Alabama Press, 1953.

———. *The Dream of Prosperity in Colonial America.* New York: New York Univ. Press, 1965.

———. *Middle-Class Culture in Elizabethan England.* Chapel Hill: Univ. of North Carolina Press, 1935.

———. *Religion and Empire: The Alliance between Piety and Commerce in English Expansion.* 1943; rpt. New York: Octagon Books, 1965.

———, ed. *A Voyage to Virginia in 1609: Two Narratives, Strachey's "True Reportory" and Jourdain's "Discovery of the Bermudas."* Charlottesville: Univ. Press of Virginia, 1964.

Zuckerman, Michael. "The Fabrication of Identity in Early America." *William and Mary Quarterly,* 3d ser., 34 (1977): 183–214.

———. "Identity in British America: Unease in Eden." In *Colonial Identity in the Atlantic World, 1500–1800.* Ed. Nicholas Canny and Anthony Pagden. Princeton, N.J.: Princeton Univ. Press, 1987, 115–57.

Index

Waldo, Richard, 103, 210
Walton, Isaac, 91
Warraskoyack, chief of, 157
Warwick, Guy of, 20
Waterhouse, Edward, 30, 129
Waters, D. W., 54, 57
Waters, Edward, 100, 104
Watkins, James, 103
Watson, Thomas, 40
Waymouth, George, 208
Waynman, Ferdinando, 174, 181
Wealth, 84; labor as, 85
Wecuttanow, 67
Werowocomoco, 46, 64, 72, 150, 154,
    155, 157, 161
West, Francis, 66, 135; castigated, 180;
    poisoned by Indians, 67; poor lead-
    ership of, 136–37; sent to Falls
    (Richmond), 136
West, Thomas, Baron De La Warr: and
    hierarchy, 183, 185; arrives in
    Jamestown, 162; made governor, 25,
    176, 181; regime imposed by, 174
Whitaker, Alexander, 164
White, Andrew, 165
White, John, 44, 117; drawings, 117
White, William, 156
Whittington Richard, 33, 34

Wiffin, Richard, 45, 48
Wighcocomoco, 118
Williams, Roger, 44, 84
Wingfield, Edward Maria, 108, 202; aris-
    tocratic attitude, 172; election of,
    201; president of council, 175–77;
    name of James River, 163; relations
    with Smith, 190–200; sails for En-
    gland, 45–46; satirized, 180; scorn
    for Martin, 179
Wingfield, Thomas Maria, 199
Winne, Peter, 103, 124, 210
Winslow, Edward, 51, 87, 203; *Relation or
    Journal,* 51
Winthrop, John, 16, 25, 84, 206, 209,
    211, 212, 216, 226; " A Modell of
    Christian Charity," 206, 212; " citty
    upon a hill," 226; " The Grounds of
    Settling a Plantation," 209
Wither, George, 48
Wood, William, 209, 224
Work. *See* Smith, respect for, labor
"World Turned Upside Down" motif, 189
Worseley, Edward, 32
Wright, John, 34

Yeardley, George, 109

V

MONACANS

MANN

POWHATAN
Held this state & fashion when Capt. Smith
was deliuered to him prisoner
1607

P

O

W

MAN-
GOAGS

CHI

WONS

H

A

T

James
Towne

Point comfort

Cape Henry

Cape Charles

Smyths Iles

KVSKA

THE

VIRGINIAN SEA